POLICIES AND ECONOMICS OF LATIN AMERICA

POLITICS AND ECONOMICS OF LATIN AMERICA VOLUME 6

POLICIES AND ECONOMICS OF LATIN AMERICA

Additional books in this series can be found on Nova's website under the Series tab.

Additional E-books in this series can be found on Nova's website under the E-books tab.

POLICIES AND ECONOMICS OF LATIN AMERICA

POLITICS AND ECONOMICS OF LATIN AMERICA VOLUME 6

SAMANTHA R. DAWES
EDITOR

Nova
Nova Science Publishers, Inc.
New York

For permission to use material from this book please contact us:
Telephone 631-231-7269; Fax 631-231-8175
Web Site: http://www.novapublishers.com

LIBRARY OF CONGRESS CATALOGING-IN-PUBLICATION DATA
Available upon request

ISBN: 978-1-61668-014-5

Published by Nova Science Publishers, Inc. ✦ New York

CONTENTS

PREFACE

Latin America comprises a diverse group of countries with extremely varied economies and political dynamics. Some are heavy in poverty and others are booming with petrodollars. They speak Spanish, Portuguese, and French. Topics include: Cuba and Issues for the 111th Congress; China's Foreign Aid Activities in Africa, Latin America, and Southeast Asia; Merida Initiative for Mexico and Central America-Funding and Policy Issues; Colombia-Issues for Congress; and Chile-Political and Economic Conditions and U.S. Relations. This book consists of public documents which have been located, gathered, combined, reformatted, and enhanced with a subject index, selectively edited and bound to provide easy access.

Chapter 1 - Cuba, which remains a hard-line communist state with a poor record on human rights, commemorated the 50th anniversary of its revolution on January 1, 2009. Cuba's political succession from the long-ruling Fidel Castro to his brother Raúl in 2006 was characterized by a remarkable degree of stability. Fidel stepped down from power temporarily in July 2006 because of health reasons, and Raúl assumed provisional control of the government until February 2008, when he officially became President. After Raúl Castro officially assumed the presidency, his government announced a series of economic changes that included lifting restrictions on the sale of some electronic consumer products and cell phones. A major reform effort has also focused on the agriculture sector in an effort to boost food production. While additional economic changes under Raúl Castro are likely, there was disappointment that further reforms were not forthcoming in the second half of 2008. The economy was hard hit by a series of hurricanes and storms from August to November 2008 that caused some $10 billion in damages, and the current global financial crisis is causing further strains on the economy. Few observers expect that there will be any change to the government's tight control over the political system, which is backed up by a strong security apparatus.

Since the early 1960s, U.S. policy toward Cuba has consisted largely of isolating the communist nation through economic sanctions. The Bush Administration tightened sanctions significantly in 2004 through increased restrictions on travel to Cuba, especially family travel. A second U.S. policy component over the years has consisted of support measures for the Cuban people, including private humanitarian donations, U.S.-sponsored radio and television broadcasting to Cuba (Radio and TV Marti), and support for human rights and democracy on the island. The Bush Administration significantly increased support for Cuba democracy funding in recent years.

As in past years, the main issue for U.S. policy toward Cuba in the 111th Congress will likely be how best to support political and economic change in Cuba. In light of Fidel Castro's departure as head of government, many observers have called for a re-examination of U.S. policy toward Cuba. In this new context, two broad policy approaches have been advanced: a status-quo or a stay the course approach that would maintain the U.S. dual-track policy of isolating the Cuban government while providing support to the Cuban people; and an approach aimed at changing attitudes within the Cuban government and Cuban society through increased contact and engagement. President Barack Obama vowed during the electoral campaign to change U.S. policy by allowing unlimited family travel and remittances to Cuba, although he also pledged to maintain the embargo as a source of leverage to bring about change in Cuba.

Over the past several years, various legislative initiatives have been introduced to ease U.S. economic sanctions on Cuba, but none of these have been enacted. In the 111th Congress, H.R. 1105, the FY2009 omnibus appropriations bill has three provisions that would ease U.S. sanctions on family travel, travel for the marketing of agricultural and medical goods, and payment terms for U.S. agricultural exports to Cuba. Other initiatives that would ease sanctions include H.R. 188 (overall embargo), H.R. 874/S. 428 (travel), and H.R. 332 (educational travel).

This chapter tracks developments in U.S. policy toward Cuba and legislative initiatives in the 111th Congress. Also see CRS Report RL3 1139, *Cuba: U.S. Restrictions on Travel and Remittances*, and CRS Report R40 139, *Closing the Guantanamo Detention Center: Legal Issues*.

Chapter 2 - In the past several years, the People's Republic of China (PRC) has bolstered its diplomatic presence and garnered international goodwill through its financing of infrastructure and natural resource development projects, assistance in the carrying out of such projects, and large economic investments in many developing countries. This chapter examines China's economic impact in three regions — Africa, Latin America (Western Hemisphere), and Southeast Asia — with an emphasis on bilateral foreign assistance.

China's foreign aid is difficult to quantify. The PRC government does not release or explain Chinese foreign aid statistics and much of PRC foreign aid does not appear to be accounted for in the scholarly literature on foreign aid. Some Chinese foreign assistance partially resembles *official development assistance* (ODA) as defined by the Organization for Economic Cooperation and Development (OECD), but in other aspects shares characteristics of foreign investment. In terms of development grants, the primary form of assistance provided by major OECD countries, China is a relatively small source of global aid. However, when China's concessional loans and state-sponsored or subsidized overseas investments are included, the PRC becomes a major source of foreign aid.

This chapter is based on research done by the New York University Robert F. Wagner Graduate School of Public Service in 2007-2008. The Wagner School study, while not comprehensive, suggests a dramatic increase in PRC foreign aid and related activity. According to the research, which is largely based upon news reports of Chinese foreign economic activity, PRC foreign assistance and government-supported economic projects in Africa, Latin America, and Southeast Asia grew from less than $1 billion in 2002 to $27.5 billion in 2006 and $25 billion in 2007. Aid and related investment to Africa showed the most significant increase. These totals, however, should be interpreted with caution. Some aggregate values may be inflated: Some PRC loans or aid pledges may not have been fulfilled and some aid pledges that include multiple projects or that span several years may have been counted more than once. Some PRC investment activities may more closely resemble FDI than aid. In other ways, totals may be undervalued, such as when economic projects or data have not been reported or when the values of Chinese materials and labor have not been included.

Overall, China's foreign assistance during the past several years has been driven primarily by Beijing's desire to secure and transport natural resources and secondarily for diplomatic reasons. According to the NYU Wagner School study, during the 2002-2007 period, Africa received the greatest amount of loans and development assistance, followed by Latin America and Southeast Asia. The study suggests that China's foreign aid activities in Africa and Latin America serve the PRC's immediate economic interests, while those in Southeast Asia relate to longer term diplomatic or strategic objectives. In Africa and Southeast Asia, Chinese infrastructure and public works projects constitute the most common form of aid, while in Latin America, where some countries are more developed, PRC-sponsored natural resource development activities are more prominent.

China is fast becoming a top trading partner to Africa and Southeast Asia, and it is second to the United States as a market for Latin American commodities and goods. Although the PRC's aid projects are a highly visible reminder of China's growing "soft power," other countries and regions, such as the European Union, the United States, and Japan, continue to dominate foreign direct investment in Africa, Latin America, and Southeast Asia.

Chapter 3 - Increasing violence perpetrated by drug trafficking organizations, gangs, and other criminal groups is threatening citizen security in Mexico and Central America. Drug-related violence claimed more than 5,300 lives in Mexico in 2008, and several Central American countries have some of the highest homicide rates in the world. Mexican drug cartels dominate the illicit drug market in most regions of the United States and are expanding their operations by forming partnerships with U.S. gangs. As a result, some of the drug-related violence in Mexico has begun to spillover into the United States.

On October 22, 2007, the United States and Mexico announced the Mérida Initiative, a multi-year proposal for $1.4 billion in U.S. assistance to Mexico and Central America aimed at combating drug trafficking and organized crime. The Administration requested $500 million for Mexico and $50 million for Central America in FY2008 supplemental appropriations, and another $450 million for Mexico and $100 million for Central America in the FY2009 budget request. While the Bush Administration did not request any additional funding for domestic programs to complement the Mérida Initiative, U.S. officials pledged to step up efforts to prevent arms, precursor chemicals, and bulk cash flows from the United States into Mexico, and to reduce U.S. drug demand.

In June 2008, the 110th Congress appropriated $465 million in FY2008 and FY2009 supplemental assistance for Mexico and Central America in the FY2008 Supplemental Appropriations Act, H.R. 2642 (P.L. 110-252). In the act, Mexico receives $352 million in FY2008 supplemental assistance and $48 million in FY2009 bridge fund supplemental assistance, while Central America, Haiti, and the Dominican Republic receive $65 million in FY2008 supplemental assistance. The 110th Congress did not include funding for Mérida in a continuing resolution (P.L. 110-329) providing FY2009 funding through March 6, 2009 at FY2008 levels.

The 111th Congress may examine the Mérida Initiative as it considers the Bush Administration's pending FY2009 foreign aid request, as well as the FY20 10 budget to be submitted by the Obama Administration. Policy debates that may emerge during congressional consideration of Mérida may include what levels and types of funding should be provided to Mexico and Central America; how well the interagency community, in coordination with its counterparts in partner countries, is implementing the Initiative; and the degree to which the nations involved, including the United States, are fulfilling their domestic obligations under Mérida. Congress may also maintain a keen interest in enforcement of Mérida's human rights conditions. This chapter provides an overview of the funding provided for the Mérida Initiative and a discussion of some policy issues that Congress may consider as it oversees implementation of the Initiative. For related information, see CRS Report RL32724, *Mexico-U.S. Relations: Issues for Congress*, by Mark P. Sullivan and June S. Beittel.

Chapter 4 - The 111th Congress will likely continue to review the progress of aid provided to Colombia through the Andean Counterdrug Program and continue oversight of human rights, alternative development, eradication efforts, the environmental consequences of aerial fumigation, and the paramilitary demobilization process.

Chapter 5 - Following a violent coup against democratically elected Marxist President Salvador Allende in 1973, Chile experienced 17 years of military rule under General Augusto Pinochet before reestablishing its elected civilian democracy in 1990. A center-left coalition of parties known as the Concertación has governed Chile for the nearly two decades since the end of the dictatorship. The coalition has enacted a number of constitutional changes to strengthen civilian control of the military and to undertake the prosecution of those alleged to be responsible for human rights violations during the Pinochet-era. Chile has made significant economic progress under the Concertación's free market economic policies and moderate social programs, which have produced notable economic growth and considerable reductions in poverty.

Current President Michele Bachelet has faced a number of challenges since her 2006 election. Widespread demonstrations over education, increased militancy by indigenous groups, and opposition control of the legislature have hindered President Bachelet's ability to govern. The international financial crisis is President Bachelet's latest challenge, though the government's timely decision to save recent fiscal surpluses will allow Chile to pursue counter-cyclical policies and minimize the effects of the economic downturn.

Chile has enjoyed close relations with the United States since its transition back to democracy. Both countries have emphasized similar priorities in the region, designed to strengthen democracy, improve human rights, and advance free trade. Chile and the United States have maintained strong commercial ties, which have become more extensive since the bilateral free trade agreement between them entered into force in 2004. U.S. officials have also expressed appreciation for Chile's leadership and moderating influence in a region increasingly characterized by political unrest and anti-American populism.

This chapter provides a brief historical background of Chile, summarizes recent political and economic developments, and addresses issues in U.S.- Chilean relations.

In: Politics and Economics of Latin America. Volume 6
Editor: Samantha R. Dawes ISBN: 978-1-61668-014-5

Chapter 1

CUBA: ISSUES FOR THE 111TH CONGRESS*

Mark P. Sullivan

SUMMARY

Cuba, which remains a hard-line communist state with a poor record on human rights, commemorated the 50th anniversary of its revolution on January 1, 2009. Cuba's political succession from the long-ruling Fidel Castro to his brother Raúl in 2006 was characterized by a remarkable degree of stability. Fidel stepped down from power temporarily in July 2006 because of health reasons, and Raúl assumed provisional control of the government until February 2008, when he officially became President. After Raúl Castro officially assumed the presidency, his government announced a series of economic changes that included lifting restrictions on the sale of some electronic consumer products and cell phones. A major reform effort has also focused on the agriculture sector in an effort to boost food production. While additional economic changes under Raúl Castro are likely, there was disappointment that further reforms were not forthcoming in the second half of 2008. The economy was hard hit by a series of hurricanes and storms from August to November 2008 that caused some $10 billion in damages, and the current global financial crisis is causing further strains on the economy. Few observers expect that there will be any change to the government's tight control over the political system, which is backed up by a strong security apparatus.

Since the early 1960s, U.S. policy toward Cuba has consisted largely of isolating the communist nation through economic sanctions. The Bush Administration tightened sanctions significantly in 2004 through increased restrictions on travel to Cuba, especially family travel. A second U.S. policy component over the years has consisted of support measures for the Cuban people, including private humanitarian donations, U.S.-sponsored radio and television broadcasting to Cuba (Radio and TV Marti), and support for human rights and democracy on the island. The Bush Administration significantly increased support for Cuba democracy funding in recent years.

* This is an edited, reformatted and augmented version of a CRS Report for Congress publication dated February 2009.

As in past years, the main issue for U.S. policy toward Cuba in the 111th Congress will likely be how best to support political and economic change in Cuba. In light of Fidel Castro's departure as head of government, many observers have called for a re-examination of U.S. policy toward Cuba. In this new context, two broad policy approaches have been advanced: a status-quo or a stay the course approach that would maintain the U.S. dual-track policy of isolating the Cuban government while providing support to the Cuban people; and an approach aimed at changing attitudes within the Cuban government and Cuban society through increased contact and engagement. President Barack Obama vowed during the electoral campaign to change U.S. policy by allowing unlimited family travel and remittances to Cuba, although he also pledged to maintain the embargo as a source of leverage to bring about change in Cuba.

Over the past several years, various legislative initiatives have been introduced to ease U.S. economic sanctions on Cuba, but none of these have been enacted. In the 111th Congress, H.R. 1105, the FY2009 omnibus appropriations bill has three provisions that would ease U.S. sanctions on family travel, travel for the marketing of agricultural and medical goods, and payment terms for U.S. agricultural exports to Cuba. Other initiatives that would ease sanctions include H.R. 188 (overall embargo), H.R. 874/S. 428 (travel), and H.R. 332 (educational travel).

This chapter tracks developments in U.S. policy toward Cuba and legislative initiatives in the 111th Congress. Also see CRS Report RL3 1139, *Cuba: U.S. Restrictions on Travel and Remittances*, and CRS Report R40 139, *Closing the Guantanamo Detention Center: Legal Issues*.

RECENT DEVELOPMENTS

On February 23, 2009, H.R. 1105, the Omnibus Appropriations Act, 2009, was introduced with three provisions that would ease U.S. sanctions on Cuba for family travel, travel related to the marketing and sale of agricultural and medical exports, and payment terms for U.S. agricultural exports to Cuba. (See "Legislative Initiatives in the 111th Congress" below.)

On February 2, 2009, the independent Cuban Commission on Human Rights and National Reconciliation (CCDHRN) documented at least 205 political prisoners in Cuba, down from 234 in January 2008. The Commission maintains that the government has resorted to short-term arbitrary detentions to target suspected dissidents, with more than 1,500 such detentions in 2008. (See "Human Rights" below.)

On January 22, 2009, the Government Accountability Office (GAO) issued a report citing concerns with Radio and TV Martí's adherence to relevant laws and standards, and maintaining that its audience is small despite its broadcasts to Cuba through multiple methods. (U.S. GAO, "Broadcasting to Cuba, Action Are Needed to Improve Strategy and Operations, GAO-09-127. January 22, 2009, available at: http://www.gao.gov/products/GAO-09-127)

On January 22, 2009, Fidel Castro stated that he had reduced the number of his published essays ("Reflections of the Commander") so as not to interfere with the authority of party or government officials, and insisted that they should not feel bound by his occasional essays or even his state of health or death. Castro also maintained that he does not expect to be in such a position to meditate and write about events when Obama's first term has ended. ("Text of Fidel Castro's Online Essay," *Associated Press Newswires*, January 22, 2009)

On January 15, 2009, during her Senate Foreign Relations Committee confirmation hearing for Secretary of State, Senator Hillary Clinton reiterated President-elect Obama's pledge to lift restrictions on family travel and remittances as well as his position that it is not time to lift the embargo since it provides an important source of leverage for further change in Cuba. Clinton also responded to written questions for the record that the new Administration expected to undertake a review of U.S. policy toward Cuba. (See "Obama Administration Policy" below.)

On January 15, 2009, Cuba released Varela Project activist Reynaldo Labrada Peña from prison following the completion of his six-year sentence. Peña was one of the "group of 75" political prisoners who have been incarcerated since 2003. With Peña's release, 54 of the "group of 75" remain in prison. Overall, there are more than 200 political prisoners in Cuba. (See "Human Rights" below.)

On January 1, 2009, Cuba celebrated the 50th anniversary of the Cuban Revolution.

On December 17, 2008, Cuban President Raúl Castro offered to exchange some imprisoned Cuban political dissidents for five Cubans imprisoned in the United States since 2001 for espionage. The State Department rejected the offer, insisting that the jailed dissidents in Cuba should be released immediately without any conditions.

On December 10, 2008, the House Appropriations Committee reported its version of the FY2009 Financial Services and General Government Appropriations bill, H.R. 7323, with several provisions that would have eased restrictions on the sale of U.S. agricultural exports and family travel to Cuba. No final action was taken on the measure.

On November 26, 2008, Cuban President Raúl Castro stated in an interview that he would be willing to meet with President-elect Barack Obama, and suggested the U.S. Naval Base at Guantanamo Bay, Cuba, as a location.

On November 24, 2008, the Government Accountability Office (GAO) issued a second report examining USAID's Cuba democracy program. While GAO lauded the efforts taken by USAID to improve oversight and address problems with the program, it also maintained that USAID needed to hire more staff to implement monitoring activities, and that it needed to periodically assess the program's efforts regarding grantees' adherence to internal controls, procurement practices, and compliance with laws and regulations. (U.S. GAO, *Foreign Assistance: Continued Efforts Needed to Strengthen USAID's Oversight of U.S. Democracy Assistance for Cuba*, GAO- 09-165, November 2008.)

On November 8, 2008, Hurricane Paloma struck Cuba devastating the town of Santa Cruz del Sur. Raúl Castro stated that overall damages from the series of hurricanes and tropical storm since August amounted to some $10 billion.

Source: Adapted by CRS from Magellan Geographix

Figure 1. Map of Cuba

Political Conditions

Raúl Castro officially became Cuba's President on February 24, 2008. On that day, Cuba's legislature selected him as President of the 31-member Council of State, a position that officially made him Cuba's head of government and state. Most observers expected this since he already had been heading the Cuban government on a provisional basis since July 2006 when his brother Fidel Castro, Cuba's long-ruling communist leader, stepped down as President because of poor health.[1]

For many years, Raúl, as First Vice President of the Council of State and the Council of Ministers, had been the officially designated successor and was slated to become chief of state with Fidel's departure. Raúl also had served as Minister of the Revolutionary Armed Forces (FAR) since the beginning of the Cuban Revolution. When Fidel stepped down from power in late July 2006 because of poor health, he signed a proclamation that ceded political power to Raúl on a provisional basis, including the positions of First Secretary of the Cuban Communist Party (PCC), Commander in Chief of the Revolutionary Armed Forces (FAR), and President of the Council of State. Despite the change in government in February 2008, Fidel still holds the official title of First Secretary of the PCC.

While it was not a surprise to observers for Raúl to succeed his brother Fidel as head of government, the selection of José Ramón Machado Ventura as the Council of State's First Vice President was a surprise. A physician by training, Machado is 77 years old, and is part of the older generation of so-called *históricos* of the 1959 Cuban revolution. He has been described as a hardline communist party ideologue, and reportedly has been a close friend and confident of Raul for many years.[2] Machado's position is significant because it makes him the official successor to Raúl, according to the Cuban Constitution. Many observers had expected that Carlos Lage, one of five other Vice Presidents on the Council of State, would have been chosen as First Vice President. He was responsible for Cuba's economic reforms in the 1990s, and at 56 years of age, represents a younger generation of Cuban leaders. While not rising to First Vice President, Lage nevertheless retained his position as a Vice President on the Council of State, and will continue to serve as the Council's Secretary.

Several key military officers and confidants of Raúl also became members of the Council, increasing the role of the military in the government. General Julio Casas Regueiro, 72 years of age, who already was on the Council, became one of its five vice presidents. Most significantly, Casas, who had been first vice minister in the FAR, was selected by Raúl as the country's new Minister of the FAR, officially replacing Raúl in that position. Casas also is chairman of GAESA (Grupo de Administracion Empresarial, S.A.), the Cuban military's holding company for its extensive business operations. Two other military appointments to the Council were Gen. Alvaro López Miera, the army's chief of staff, and Gen. Leopoldo Cintra Frías, who commanded the Western army, one of Cuba's three military regions.[3]

Since Fidel stepped down from power in 2006, Cuba's political succession from Fidel to Raúl Castro has been characterized by a remarkable degree of stability. Although initially there were not any significant economic changes under Raúl, there were signs that changes could be coming. In a July 2007 speech, Raúl maintained that structural changes were needed in the Cuban economy in order to increase efficiency and production. In his first speech as President in February 2008, Raúl promised to make the government smaller and more efficient, to review the potential revaluation of the Cuban peso, and to eliminate excessive bans and regulations that curb productivity.[4] Since March 2008, the government has implemented a number of economic changes that from the outside might not seem significant, but are noteworthy policy changes for a government that has heretofore followed a centralized communist economic model. (See "Economic Changes Under Raúl" below.)

While additional economic changes under Raúl Castro are likely, few expect there will be any change to the government's tight control over the political system, which is backed up by a strong security apparatus. Some observers point to the reduced number of political prisoners, from 283 at the end of 2006 to around 219 in mid-2008, as evidence of a lessening of repression, but dissidents maintain that the overall situation has not improved. Some observers contend that if the new government of Raúl Castro becomes more confident of ensuring social stability and does not feel threatened, it could move to soften its hard repression, but for now the government is continuing its harsh treatment of the opposition. The selection of José Ramón Machado as First Vice President also appears to be a clear indication that the Cuban government has no intention of easing tight control over the political system.

In early 2009, there were numerous press reports about a setback in Fidel Castro's health, but by late January 2009 new reports and photos of Castro with visiting Argentine President Cristina Fernández de Kirchner dispelled rumors that he was on his deathbed. Fidel did note in one of his published essays ("Reflections of the Commander") on January 22, 2009, that he had reduced the number of essays so as not to interfere with the authority of party or government officials, and insisted that they should not feel bound by his occasional writings or even his state of health or death. Castro also maintained that does not expect to be in such a position to meditate or write about events when Obama's first term has ended.[5]

In late April 2008, Raúl announced that the PCC's sixth congress would be held at the end of 2009 (the last was held in 1997). Some analysts believe that additional policy changes will become evident, with a more invigorated role for the party. Some observers speculate that Fidel Castro could officially be replaced as the head of the party at that time, and it is likely that some of the PCC's 25-member Political Bureau (Politburo) will also be replaced.

Some analysts maintain that once Fidel is gone, hardliners in Cuba's political system will have a more difficult time holding back the advance of needed economic reforms.[6] Some maintain that Raúl will be liberated to move more quickly to usher in needed economic reforms, although few observers believe that the Cuban leader will take any actions that could threaten the stability of the communist government. Some observers also do not expect Raúl Castro to serve another term as President, and believe that the government will pass to a younger generation after the next National Assembly election and selection of a new President in early 2013.

Background to the Succession

Until Fidel stepped down in 2006, he had ruled the island nation since the 1959 Cuban Revolution, which ousted the corrupt government of Fulgencio Batista. In April 1961, Castro stated that the Cuban Revolution was socialist, and in December 1961, he proclaimed himself to be a Marxist-Leninist. From 1959 until 1976, Castro ruled by decree. A Constitution was enacted in 1976 setting forth the PCC as the leading force in state and society, with power centered in a Political Bureau headed by Fidel Castro. In October 1997, the Cuban Communist Party held its 5th Congress (the prior one was held in 1991) in which the party reaffirmed its commitment to a single party state and reelected Fidel and Raúl Castro as the party's first and second secretaries.

Cuba's Constitution also outlines national, provincial, and local governmental structures. Legislative authority is vested in a National Assembly of People's Power that meets twice annually for brief periods. When the Assembly is not in session, a Council of State, elected by the Assembly, acts on its behalf. According to Cuba's Constitution, the President of the Council of State is the country's head of state and government. Executive power in Cuba is vested in a Council of Ministers, also headed by the country's head of state and government, i.e. the President of the Council of State. From the promulgation of the 1976 Constitution until February 24, 2008, Fidel served as served as head of state and government through his position as President of the Council of State.

Although National Assembly members were directly elected for the first time in February 1993, only a single slate of candidates was offered. Direct elections for the National Assembly were again held in January 1998 and January 2003, but voters again were not offered a choice of candidates. In contrast, municipal elections at the local level are competitive, with from two to eight candidates. To be elected, the candidate must receive more than half of the votes cast. As a result, runoff elections between the two top candidates are common.

National Assembly elections were held on January 20, 2008 (along with elections for 1,201 delegates to 14 provincial assemblies), and Fidel Castro was once again among the candidates elected to the now 614-member legislative body. As in the past, voters were only offered a single slate of candidates.

On February 24, 2008, the new Assembly was scheduled to select from among its ranks the members of the Council of State and its President. Many observers speculated that because of his poor health, Fidel would choose not be re-elected as President of the Council of State, which would officially confirm his departure from heading the Cuban government. Statements from Castro himself in December 2007 hinted at his potential retirement. That proved true on February 19, 2008, when Fidel announced that he would not accept the position as President of the Council of State, essentially confirming his departure as titular head of the Cuban government.

Before Fidel stepped down from power in July 2006 for health reasons, observers discerned several potential scenarios for Cuba's future after Fidel. These fit into three broad categories: the continuation of a communist government; a military government; or some type of democratic government, whether it be a democratic transition or fully democratic government. According to most observers, the most likely scenario, at least in the short term, was the continuation of the regime under the leadership of Raúl. This was likely for a variety of reasons, but especially because of Raúl's designation by Fidel as successor in the party and his position as leader of the FAR. The FAR has been in control of the government's security apparatus since 1989 and has played an increasing role in Cuba's economy through the ownership of numerous business enterprises. The scenario of a military-led government was viewed by some observers as a possibility only if a successor communist government failed because of divisiveness among leaders or political instability. For many observers, the least likely scenario upon Fidel's death or departure was a democratic transition government. With a strong totalitarian security apparatus, the Castro government successfully impeded the development of independent civil society, with only a small and tightly regulated private sector, no independent labor movement, and no unified political opposition.[7]

Human Rights

Overview

Cuba has a poor record on human rights, with the government sharply restricting freedoms of expression, association, assembly, movement, and other basic rights. It has cracked down on dissent, arrested human rights activists and independent journalists, and staged demonstrations against critics. Although some anticipated a relaxation of the government's oppressive tactics in the aftermath of the January 1998 visit of Pope John Paul II, government attacks against human rights activists and other dissidents have continued since that time. The Inter-American Commission on Human Rights maintains in its 2007 annual human rights report that the Cuban government's "restrictions on political rights, freedom of expression, and dissemination of ideas have created, over a period of decades, a situation of permanent and systematic violations of the fundamental rights of Cuban citizens."[8]

According to the State Department's human rights report for 2007, issued in March 2008, the Cuban government continued to commit numerous serious abuses during the year. Among the human rights problems cited in the State Department report were arbitrary arrest and detention of human rights advocates and members of independent professional organizations; harassment, beatings, and threats against political opponents by government-recruited mobs, police, and state security officials; beatings and abuse of detainees and prisoners (which led to the death of two prisoners in 2007); denial of fair trial; harsh and life-threatening prison conditions, including denial of medical care; and interference with privacy, including pervasive monitoring of private communications. As noted in the report, the government tightly controlled Internet access, with citizens only accessing it through government-approved institutions or through a few Internet facilities offered by foreign diplomatic offices. The government reviewed and censored e-mail, and forbade attachments. (See the full State Department human rights report on Cuba, available at http://www.state.gov/g/drl/rls/hrrpt/2007/100635.htm.)

In March 2003, the government conducted a severe crackdown and imprisoned 75 democracy activists, including independent journalists and librarians and leaders of independent labor unions and opposition parties. At present, 54 of the "group of 75" political prisoners remain incarcerated. On January 15, 2009, one of the detainees, Reynaldo Labrada Pena who had worked with the Varela Project, was released from prison after completing his sentence. In February 2008, Cuba released four political prisoners—union activist Pedro Pablo Alvarez Ramos, human rights activist Omar Pernet Hernández, and journalists Jose Gabriel Ramón Castillo and Alejandro González Raga—but sent them into forced exile to Spain. Prior to that, Hector Palacios was released for health reasons in December 2006.

For 2008, the independent Cuban Commission on Human Rights and National Reconciliation (CCDHRN) documented at least 205 political prisoners, down from 234 in January 2008. The number also reflected the continued decline from previous years when the Commission estimated at least 283 prisoners at the beginning of 2007 and 333 at the beginning of 2006. The Commission maintains, however, that the government has resorted to short-term arbitrary detentions to target suspected dissidents, with more than 1,500 such detentions in 2008.[9]

Despite the reduction in the number of prisoners, human rights activists maintain that the overall situation has not improved. Cuban human rights activist Elizardo Sánchez, the head of the CCDHRN, asserts that the government is still repressing dissidents, with threats, police searches of people's homes, interrogations, and short detentions. Sánchez asserts that the police state is still in force in Cuba, reflected in almost every aspect of national life.[10]

In late February 2008, Cuba signed two U.N. human rights treaties: the International Covenant on Civil and Political Rights and the International Covenant on Economic, Social, and Cultural Rights. Some considered this a positive step, but others stressed that it remains to be seen whether the Cuban government will take action to guarantee civil and political freedoms.[11] One significant step taken by the government in late March 2008 was the lifting of a ban on Cubans staying at tourist hotels. Although few Cubans will be able to afford the cost of staying in such hotels, the move is symbolically significant and ends the practices of what critics had dubbed "tourism apartheid." On the other hand, prior to the 60th anniversary of the signing of the Universal Declaration of Human Rights on December 10, 2008, up to a dozen Cuban human rights activists reportedly were detained in order to prevent them from attending planned events.[12]

In April 2003, a human rights group known as the Ladies in White (Damas de Blanco) was formed by the wives, mothers, daughters, sisters, and aunts of the members of the "group of 75" dissidents arrested a month earlier in Cuba's human rights crackdown.[13] The group conducts peaceful protests calling for the unconditional release of political prisoners. Dressed in white, its members attend Mass each Sunday at St. Rita's church in Havana and then walk silently through the streets to a nearby park. On April 21, 2008, ten members of the Ladies in White were physically removed from a park near the Plaza of the Revolution in Havana when they demanded the release of their husbands and the other members of the "group of 75" still imprisoned.

Although Cuban authorities continue to stifle dissent and repress freedoms, pro-democracy and human rights activists continue to call attention to Cuba's poor human rights record, and many have been recognized by the international community for their efforts. In October 2005, The Ladies in White group noted above received the Sakharov Prize for Freedom of Thought from the European Parliament.

In December 2006, independent Cuban journalist Guillermo Fariñas Hernández received the 2006 Cyber Dissident award from the Paris-based Reporters Without Borders. Fariñas went on a seven- month hunger strike in 2006, demanding broader Internet access for Cubans.

In November 2007, President Bush awarded Cuban dissident Dr. Oscar Elias Biscet with the Presidential Medal of Freedom. Biscet, who has spent most of the last eight years in jail, was sentenced in 2003 to 25 years in prison. Legislation was introduced in the 110th Congress in March 2008—H.R. 5627 (Diaz-Balart, Lincoln) and S. 2777 (Martinez)—to award the congressional gold medal to Biscet, although no action was taken on the measures.

Since late 2007, Cuban Internet blogger Yoaní Sánchez has received considerable international attention for her website, Generación Y, that includes commentary critical of the Cuban government. In May 2008, Sánchez was awarded Spain's Ortega y Gasset award for digital journalism, but the Cuban government did not provide her with an exit permit to accept the award. (Sánchez's website is available at http://www.desdecuba.com /generaciony/).

In late 2008, two international press rights groups gave awards to two Cuban independent journalists who have been imprisoned since 2003. In November 2008, the New York-based Committee for the Protection of Journalists selected Héctor Maseda Gutiérrez as a recipient of its international press freedom award, while in early December 2008, Reporters Without Borders awarded Ricardo González Alfonso its journalist of the year award. While in prison, Gutiérrez wrote a memoir that he managed to smuggle out of prison one page at a time. Before his imprisonment, González had started an association to improve independent journalism. As of December 2008, 23 journalists were imprisoned in Cuba.[14]

On December 17, 2008, Cuban President Raúl Castro offered to exchange some imprisoned Cuban political dissidents for five Cubans imprisoned in the United States since 2001 for espionage. The five Cubans are serving sentences ranging from 15 years to life. Cuba's National Assembly had dubbed the so-called Cuban Five as "Heroes of the Republic," and the Cuban government has called for their return to Cuba. In response to Raúl Castro's offer, the State Department rejected the offer, insisting that the jailed dissidents in Cuba should be released immediately without any conditions.[15]

Varela Project

Named for the 19th century priest, Felix Varela, who advocated independence from Spain and the abolition of slavery, the Varela Project has collected thousands of signatures supporting a national plebiscite for political reform in accordance with a provision of the Cuban Constitution. The referendum, if granted, would call for respect for human rights, an amnesty for political prisoners, private enterprise, and changes to the country's electoral law that would result in free and fair elections. The initiative is organized by Oswaldo Payá, who heads the Christian Liberation Movement.[16]

In May 2002, organizers of the Varela Project submitted 11,020 signatures to the National Assembly calling for a national referendum. This was more than the 10,000 required under Article 88 of the Cuban Constitution. Former President Jimmy Carter noted the significance of the Varela Project in his May 14, 2002 address in Havana that was broadcast in Cuba. Carter noted that "when Cubans exercise this freedom to change laws peacefully by a direct vote, the world will see that Cubans, and not foreigners, will decide the future of this country."[17] In response to the Varela Project, the Cuban government orchestrated its own referendum in late June 2002 that ultimately led to the National Assembly amending the Constitution to declare Cuba's socialist system irrevocable. The Varela Project has persevered despite the 2003 human rights crackdown, which included the arrest of 21 Project activists. In October 2003, Oswaldo Payá delivered more than 14,000 signatures to Cuba's National Assembly, again requesting a referendum on democratic reforms. More recently, in October 2008, Varela Project activists launched a third campaign to collect signatures.

ECONOMIC CONDITIONS

After the collapse of the former Soviet Union, Russian financial assistance to Cuba practically ended, and as a result, Cuba experienced severe economic deterioration from

1989-1993, with estimates of economic decline ranging from 35-50%. Since then, however, there has been considerable improvement. From 1994-2000, as Cuba moved forward with some limited market- oriented economic reforms, economic growth averaged 3.7% annually.

Economic growth was strong in the 2005-2007 period, registering an impressive 11.2% in 2005 (despite widespread damage caused by Hurricanes Dennis and Wilma), 12.1% in 2006, and 7.3% in 2007.[18] The economy benefitted from the growth of the tourism, nickel, and oil sectors, and support from Venezuela and China in terms of investment commitments and credit lines. Cuba benefits from a preferential oil agreement with Venezuela, which provides Cuba with more than 90,000 barrels of oil a day. Some observers maintain that Venezuela's oil subsidies amounted to more than $3 billion a year in 2006.[19] Venezuela also helped Cuba upgrade an oil refinery in Cienfuegos, which was inaugurated in 2007.

In 2008, economic growth slowed to an estimated 4.3%. This was prompted by several problems, including the declining price of nickel, which accounts for a major share of Cuba's exports, the rising cost of food imports, and the devastation wrought by Hurricanes Gustav and Ike, particularly in the agricultural sectors. The current global financial crisis is likely to have an effect on the Cuban economy because of lower world prices for nickel and a reduction in tourism from Canada and Europe. Cuba's reliance on Venezuela for oil could also be threatened as Venezuela faces a difficult domestic fiscal situation due to the rapid decline in the price of oil. The forecast for 2009 is for a slower economic growth rate of 3.9%.[20]

Over the years, Cuba has expressed pride for the nation's accomplishments in health and education. According to the U.N. Development Program's 2007/2008 *Human Development Report,* life expectancy in Cuba in 2005 was 77.7 years, adult literacy was estimated at almost 100%, and the infant mortality rate was 6 per 1,000 live births, the lowest rate in Latin America. For 2006 and 2007, Cuba has boasted an infant mortality rate of 5.3.[21]

When Cuba's economic slide began in 1989, the government showed little willingness to adopt any significant market-oriented economic reforms, but in 1993, faced with unprecedented economic decline, Cuba began to change policy direction. Beginning in 1993, Cubans were allowed to own and use U.S. dollars and to shop at dollar-only shops previously limited to tourists and diplomats. Self-employment was authorized in more than 100 occupations in 1993, most in the service sector, and by 1996 that figure had grown to more than 150 occupations. Also in 1993, the government divided large state farms into smaller, more autonomous, agricultural cooperatives (Basic Units of Cooperative Production, UBPCs). It opened agricultural markets in 1994, where farmers could sell part of their produce on the open market, and it also permitted artisan markets for the sale of handicrafts. In 1995, the government allowed private food catering, including home restaurants *(paladares),* in effect legalizing activities that were already taking place), and approved a new foreign investment law that allows fully owned investments by foreigners in all sectors of the economy with the exception of defense, health, and education. In 1996, it authorized the establishment of free trade zones with tariff reductions typical of such zones. In 1997, the government enacted legislation to reform the banking system and established a new Central Bank (BCC) to operate as an autonomous and independent entity.

After Cuba began to recover from its economic decline, the government began to backtrack on some of its reform efforts. Regulations and new taxes made it extremely difficult for many of the nation's self-employed. Some home restaurants were forced to close because of the new regulations. In 2004, the Cuban government limited the use of dollars by state companies for any services or products not considered part of their core business. Some analysts viewed the measure as an effort to turn back the clock on economic reform measures.[22] Also in 2004, Fidel Castro announced that U.S. dollars no longer would be used in entities that at the time accepted dollars (such as stores, restaurants, and hotels). Instead, dollars had to be exchanged for "convertible pesos," with a 10% surcharge for the exchange. Dollar bank accounts are still allowed, but Cubans are not able to deposit new dollars into the accounts. Beginning in April 2005, convertible pesos were no longer on par with the U.S. dollar, but instead were linked to a basket of foreign currencies. This reduces the value of dollar remittances sent to Cuba and provides more hard currency to the Cuban government.[23]

Economic Changes under Raúl

When Raúl Castro assumed provisional power in July 2006, there was some expectation that the government would be more open to economic policy changes, and a debate about potential economic reforms re-emerged in Cuba. On July 26, 2007, in a speech commemorating Cuba's revolutionary anniversary, Raúl Castro acknowledged that Cuban salaries were insufficient to satisfy needs, and maintained that structural changes were necessary in order to increase efficiency and production. He also maintained that the government was considering increasing foreign investment in the country. Some observers maintain that the speech was a forecast for economic reforms under Raúl, while others stress that only small marginal changes occurred in Raúl's first year in power.[24]

In the aftermath of Raúl's July 2007 speech, Cuban public expectations for economic reform increased. Thousands of officially sanctioned meetings were held in workplaces and local PCC branches around the country where Cubans were encouraged to air their views and discuss the future direction of the country. Complaints focused on low salaries and housing and transportation problems, and some participants advocated legalization of more private businesses.[25] Raised expectations for economic change in Cuba increased the chance that the government actually would adopt some policy changes. Doing nothing would run the risk of increased public frustration and a potential for social unrest. Increased public frustration was evident in a clandestine video, widely circulated on the Internet in early February 2008, of a meeting between Ricardo Alarcón, the head of Cuba's legislature, and university students in which a student was questioning why Cuban wages are so low and why Cubans are prohibited from visiting tourist hotels (a policy subsequently changed in late March 2008) or traveling abroad. The video demonstrated the disillusionment of many Cuban youth with the poor economic situation and repressive environment in Cuba.

Since Raúl Castro officially assumed the presidency in 2008, his government has announced a series of economic changes. In his first speech as President in February 2008, Raúl promised to make the government smaller and more efficient, to review the potential revaluation of the Cuban peso, and to eliminate excessive bans and regulations that curb productivity.[26] In mid-March, the government announced that restrictions on the sales of consumer products such as computers, microwaves, and DVD and video players would be lifted. In late March, it announced that it would lift restrictions on the use of cell phones. This officially occurred in mid-April.

One of Cuba's major reform efforts under Raúl Castro in 2008 was focused on the agriculture sector, a vital issue because Cuba reportedly imports some 80% of its food needs and is paying an increasing amount for such imports due to rising food prices. In an effort to boost food production, the government began giving farmers more discretion over how to use their land and what supplies to buy. Decision-making on agriculture reportedly has shifted from the national government to the local municipal level, with government bureaucracy cut significantly.[27]

In April 2008, the government announced that it would begin revamping the state's wage system by removing the limit that a state worker can earn. This is an effort to boost productivity and to deal with one of Cuba's major economic problems: how to raise wages to a level where basic human needs can be satisfied. The problem of low wages in Cuba is closely related to another major economic problem: how to unify the two official currencies circulating in the country—the Cuban convertible peso (CUC) and the Cuban peso, which traded at about 24 to 1 CUC in 2008. Most people are paid in Cuban pesos, and the minimum monthly wage in Cuba is about 225 pesos (about $9 U.S. dollars[28]), but for increasing amounts of consumer goods, convertible pesos are used. Cubans with access to foreign remittances or who work in jobs that give them access to convertible pesos are far better off than those Cubans who do not have such access.

Looking ahead, several factors could restrain the magnitude of economic policy change in Cuba. A number of observers believe that as long as Fidel Castro is around, it will be difficult for the government to move forward with any major initiatives that are viewed as deviating from Fidel's orthodox policies. Other observers point to the significant oil subsidies and investment that Cuba now receives from Venezuela that have helped spur Cuba's high economic growth levels over the past several years and maintain that such support lessens the government's impetus for economic reforms. Another factor that bodes against rapid economic policy reform is the fear that it could spur momentum for political change. Given that one of the highest priorities for Cuba's government has been maintaining social and political stability, any economic policy changes are likely to be smaller changes introduced over time that do not threaten the state's control.

There was some expectation that Raúl Castro would announce additional economic reforms in his July 26, 2008 speech on Cuba's revolutionary anniversary, but there were no such announcements. Instead, Castro acknowledged the "large number of problems that still need to be resolved, the majority of which directly affect the population."[29] Nevertheless, in an address earlier in the month to the National Assembly, Raúl pointed to the goal of increasing salaries based on job performance. According to Castro: "Socialism means social justice and equality, but equality of rights and opportunities, not salaries. Equality does not mean egalitarianism."[30]

CUBA'S FOREIGN POLICY

During the Cold War, Cuba had extensive relations with and support from the Soviet Union, with billions in annual subsidies to sustain the Cuban economy that helped fund an activist foreign policy and support for guerrilla movements and revolutionary governments abroad in Latin America and Africa. With the dissolution of the Soviet Union, an end to the

Cold War, and the loss of Soviet financial support, Cuba was forced to abandon its revolutionary exploits abroad. As its economy reeled from the loss of Soviet support, Cuba was forced to open up its economy and economic relations with countries worldwide, and developed significant economic linkages with Canada, Spain, other European countries, and China. In recent years, Venezuela -- under populist President Hugo Chávez -- has become a significant source of support for subsidized oil imports and investment. Relations with Russia have also intensified recently, with the visit of Russian President Dmitry Medvedev to Havana in November, the visit of several Russian warships to Cuba in December 2008, and Raúl Castro's visit to Moscow in late January 2009. Chinese President Hu Jintao also visited Cuba in November signing a dozen agreements.

In Latin America, Cuba has diplomatic relations with all nations with the exception of El Salvador, and has increasingly become more engaged in Latin America beyond the already close relations with Venezuela. Brazilian President Luiz Inácio Lula da Silva visited Cuba twice in 2008, and Cuba seems especially interested in expanding relations with Brazil. Cuba became a full member of the 23 member Rio Group of Latin American and Caribbean nations in November 2008; some observers see the group, which excludes the United States, as an alternative to the Organization of American States (OAS). (Cuba's participation in the OAS has been suspended since 1962.) Raúl Castro made his first foreign trip as President in December 2008, when he traveled to Venezuela, and then to Bahia, Brazil, where he attended the Latin American and Caribbean Integration and Development Summit, a regional initiative of President Lula.[31]

Cuba is an active participant in international forums, including the United Nations and the controversial United Nations Human Rights Council. Cuba hosted the 14th summit of the Nonaligned Movement (NAM) in 2006, and holds the Secretary Generalship of the NAM until its next summit in 2009. It is a member of the Bolivarian Alternative for the Americas, (ALBA), a Venezuelan-led integration and cooperation scheme founded as an alternative to U.S. efforts to negotiate a region-wide Free Trade Area of the Americas (FTAA).

U.S. Policy toward Cuba

Policy Overview

In the early 1960s, U.S.-Cuban relations deteriorated sharply when Fidel Castro began to build a repressive communist dictatorship and moved his country toward close relations with the Soviet Union. The often tense and hostile nature of the U.S.-Cuban relationship is illustrated by such events and actions as U.S. covert operations to overthrow the Castro government culminating in the ill-fated April 1961 Bay of Pigs invasion; the October 1962 missile crisis in which the United States confronted the Soviet Union over its attempt to place offensive nuclear missiles in Cuba; Cuban support for guerrilla insurgencies and military support for revolutionary governments in Africa and the Western Hemisphere; the 1980 exodus of around 125,000 Cubans to the United States in the so-called Mariel boatlift; the 1994 exodus of more than 30,000 Cubans who were interdicted and housed at U.S. facilities in Guantanamo and Panama; and the February 1996 shootdown by Cuban fighter jets of two

U.S. civilian planes operated by the Cuban American group, Brothers to the Rescue, which resulted in the death of four U.S. crew members.

Since the early 1960s, U.S. policy toward Cuba has consisted largely of isolating the island nation through comprehensive economic sanctions, including an embargo on trade and financial transactions. The Cuban Assets Control Regulations (CACR), first issued by the Treasury Department in July 1963, lay out a comprehensive set of economic sanctions against Cuba, including a prohibition on most financial transactions with Cuba and a freeze of Cuban government assets in the United States. The CACR have been amended many times over the years to reflect changes in policy, and remain in force today.

These sanctions were made stronger with the Cuban Democracy Act (CDA) of 1992 (P.L. 102- 484, Title XVII) and with the Cuban Liberty and Democratic Solidarity Act of 1996 (P.L. 104- 114), the latter often referred to as the Helms/Burton legislation. The CDA prohibits U.S. subsidiaries from engaging in trade with Cuba and prohibits entry into the United States for any sea-borne vessel to load or unload freight if it has been involved in trade with Cuba within the previous 180 days. The Cuban Liberty and Democratic Solidarity Act, enacted in the aftermath of Cuba's shooting down of two U.S. civilian planes in February 1996, combines a variety of measures to increase pressure on Cuba and provides for a plan to assist Cuba once it begins the transition to democracy. Most significantly, the law codified the Cuban embargo, including all restrictions under the CACR. This provision is especially noteworthy because of its long-lasting effect on U.S. policy options toward Cuba. The executive branch is circumscribed in lifting or substantially loosening the economic embargo without congressional concurrence until certain democratic conditions are met, although the CACR includes licensing authority that provides the executive branch with some administrative flexibility (e.g. travel-related restrictions in the CACR have been eased and tightened on numerous occasions). Another significant sanction in the law is a provision in Title III that holds any person or government that traffics in U.S. property confiscated by the Cuban government liable for monetary damages in U.S. federal court. Acting under provisions of the law, however, both President Clinton and President Bush have suspended the implementation of Title III at six-month intervals.

In addition to sanctions, another component of U.S. policy, a so-called second track, consists of support measures for the Cuban people. This includes U.S. private humanitarian donations, medical exports to Cuba under the terms of the Cuban Democracy Act of 1992, U.S. government support for democracy-building efforts, and U.S.-sponsored radio and television broadcasting to Cuba. In addition, the 106th Congress approved the Trade Sanctions Reform and Export Enhancement Act of 2000 (P.L. 106-387, Title IX) that allows for agricultural exports to Cuba, albeit with restrictions on financing such exports. This led to the United States becoming Cuba's largest supplier of food and agricultural products since 2002.

Debate on the Direction of U.S. Policy

Over the years, although U.S. policymakers have agreed on the overall objectives of U.S. policy toward Cuba—to help bring democracy and respect for human rights to the island—there have been several schools of thought about how to achieve those objectives. Some have advocated a policy of keeping maximum pressure on the Cuban government until reforms are enacted, while continuing efforts to support the Cuban people. Others argue for an approach, sometimes referred to as constructive engagement, that would lift some U.S. sanctions that they believe are hurting the Cuban people, and move toward engaging Cuba in dialogue. Still others call for a swift normalization of U.S.-Cuban relations by lifting the U.S. embargo. Legislative initiatives introduced over the past decade have reflected these three policy approaches.

Dating back to 2000, there have been significant efforts in Congress to ease U.S. sanctions, with, one or both houses at times approving amendments to appropriations measures that would have eased U.S. sanctions on Cuba. Ultimately, these provisions were stripped out of final enacted measures, in part because of presidential veto threats.

In light of Fidel Castro's departure as head of government, many observers have called for a re-examination of U.S. policy toward Cuba. In this new context, there are two broad policy approaches to contend with political change in Cuba: a status-quo approach that would maintain the U.S. dual-track policy of isolating the Cuban government while providing support to the Cuban people; and an approach aimed at influencing the attitudes of the Cuban government and Cuban society through increased contact and engagement.

In general, those who advocate easing U.S. sanctions on Cuba make several policy arguments. They assert that if the United States moderated its policy toward Cuba—through increased travel, trade, and diplomatic dialogue—then the seeds of reform would be planted, which would stimulate and strengthen forces for peaceful change on the island. They stress the importance to the United States of avoiding violent change in Cuba, with the prospect of a mass exodus to the United States and the potential of involving the United States in a civil war scenario. They argue that since the demise of Cuba's communist government does not appear imminent, even without Fidel Castro at the helm, the United States should espouse a more pragmatic approach in trying to induce change in Cuba. Supporters of changing policy also point to broad international support for lifting the U.S. embargo, to the missed opportunities for U.S. businesses because of the unilateral nature of the embargo, and to the increased suffering of the Cuban people because of the embargo. Proponents of change also argue that the United States should be consistent in its policies with the world's few remaining communist governments, including China and Vietnam, and also maintain that moderating policy will help advance human rights.

On the other side, opponents of changing U.S. policy maintain that the current two-track policy of isolating Cuba, but reaching out to the Cuban people through measures of support, is the best means for realizing political change in Cuba. They point out that the Cuban Liberty and Democratic Solidarity Act of 1996 sets forth the steps that Cuba needs to take in order for the United States to normalize relations. They argue that softening U.S. policy at this time without concrete Cuban reforms would boost the Castro government, politically and economically, and facilitate the survival of the communist regime. Opponents of softening U.S. policy argue that the United States should stay the course in its commitment to democracy and human rights in Cuba, and that sustained sanctions can work. Opponents of loosening U.S. sanctions further argue that Cuba's failed economic policies, not the U.S. embargo, are the causes of Cuba's difficult living conditions.

Clinton Administration's Easing of Sanctions

The Clinton Administration made several changes to U.S. policy in the aftermath of Pope John Paul II's 1998 visit to Cuba, which were intended to bolster U.S. support for the Cuban people. These included the resumption of direct flights to Cuba (which had been curtailed after the February 1996 shootdown of two U.S. civilian planes), the resumption of cash remittances by U.S. nationals and residents for the support of close relatives in Cuba (which had been curtailed in August 1994 in response to the migration crisis with Cuba), and the streamlining of procedures for the commercial sale of medicines and medical supplies and equipment to Cuba.

In January 1999, President Clinton announced several additional measures to support the Cuban people. These included a broadening of cash remittances to Cuba, so that all U.S. residents (not just those with close relatives in Cuba) could send remittances to Cuba; an expansion of direct passenger charter flights to Cuba from additional U.S. cities other than Miami (direct flights later in the year began from Los Angeles and New York); and an expansion of people-to-people contact by loosening restrictions on travel to Cuba for certain categories of travelers, such as professional researchers and those involved in a wide range of educational, religious, and sports activities.

Bush Administration Policy

The Bush Administration essentially continued the two-track U.S. policy of isolating Cuba through economic sanctions while supporting the Cuban people through a variety of measures. However, within this policy framework, the Administration emphasized stronger enforcement of economic sanctions and further tightened restrictions on travel, remittances, and humanitarian gift parcels to Cuba. There was considerable reaction to the Administration's June 2004 tightening of restrictions for family visits and other categories of travel, and to the Administration's February 2005 tightening of restrictions on payment terms for U.S. agricultural exports to Cuba. Nevertheless, the Bush Administration did not completely eliminate the easing of sanctions that occurred under the Clinton Administration. For example, Americans may travel to Cuba to participate in educational activities, but these now need to be part of a structured academic program. Direct flights to Cuba also still run from Miami and New York, although flights from Los Angeles were curtailed for economic reasons in the aftermath of the tightening of travel restrictions in 2004 that reduced the number of Americans visiting Cuba.

Commission for Assistance to a Free Cuba

In October 2003, President Bush called for the establishment of an interagency Commission for Assistance to a Free Cuba, a Cabinet-level commission chaired by then - Secretary of State Colin Powell. The Commission, which had its first meeting in December 2003, was tasked with the objectives of 1) identifying additional means to help the Cuban people bring about an expeditious end to Cuba's dictatorship and 2) considering the requirements for U.S. assistance to a post- dictatorship Cuba.[32]

In May 2004, President Bush endorsed the recommendations of the Commission's first report, which made recommendations for immediate measures to "hasten the end of Cuba's dictatorship" as well as longer-term recommendations to help plan for Cuba's transition from communism to democracy in various areas. The President directed that up to $59 million be committed to implement key recommendations of the Commission, including support for democracy-building activities and for airborne broadcasts of Radio and TV Marti to Cuba. The report's most significant recommendations included a number of measures to tighten economic sanctions on family visits and other categories of travel and on private humanitarian assistance in the form of remittances and gift parcels. Subsequent regulations issued by the Treasury and Commerce Departments in June 2004 implemented these new sanctions. (The full Commission report is on the State Department website at http://www.state.gov/p/wha/rt/cuba/commission/2004/.) In February 2005, the Administration continued to tighten U.S. economic sanctions against Cuba by further restricting the process of how U.S. agricultural exporters may be paid for their cash sales, a move opposed by many U.S. agricultural exporters (For more, see "Agricultural Exports and Sanctions" below.)

In July 2005, Secretary of State Condoleezza Rice appointed Caleb McCarry as the State Department's new Cuba Transition Coordinator to direct U.S. government "actions in support of a free Cuba." Secretary Rice reconvened the Commission for Assistance to a Free Cuba in December 2005 to identify additional measures to help Cubans hasten the transition to democracy and to develop a plan to help the Cuban people move toward free and fair elections.

In July 2006, the Commission issued its second report, making recommendations to hasten political change in Cuba toward a democratic transition. (The full report is available at http://www.cafc.gov/rpt/.)

In the report, the Commission called for the United States to provide $80 million over two years for the following: to support Cuban civil society ($31 million); to fund education programs and exchanges, including university training in Cuba provided by third countries and scholarships for economically disadvantaged students from Cuba at U.S. and third country universities ($10 million); to fund additional efforts to break the Cuban government's information blockade and expand access to independent information, including through the Internet ($24 million); and to support international efforts at strengthening civil society and transition planning ($15 million). According to the Cuba Transition Coordinator, this assistance would be additional funding beyond what the Administration is already currently budgeting for these programs.[33] Thereafter, the Commission recommended funding of not less than $20 million annually for Cuba democracy programs "until the dictatorship ceases to exist." This would roughly double the amount currently spent on Cuba democracy programs.

The report also set forth detailed plans of how the U.S. government, along with the international community and the Cuban community abroad, could provide assistance to a Cuban transition government to help it respond to critical humanitarian and social needs, to conduct free and fair elections, and to move toward a market-based economy. The report also outlined a series of preparatory steps in the areas of government organization, electoral preparation, and anticipating humanitarian and social needs that the U.S. government could take now, before Cuba's transition begins, so that it would be well prepared in the event that assistance was requested by the new Cuban government.

The Commission's second report received a mixed response from Cuba's dissident community. Although some dissidents, like former political prisoner Vladimiro Roca, maintain that they would welcome any U.S. assistance that helps support the Cuban dissident movement, others expressed concerns about the report. Dissident economist and former political prisoner Oscar Espinosa Chepe stressed that Cubans have to be the ones to solve their own problems. According to Chepe, "We are thankful for the solidarity we have received from North America, Europe, and elsewhere, but we request that they do not meddle in our country."[34] Miriam Leiva, a founding member of the Ladies in White, a human rights organization, expressed concern that the report could serve as a rationale for the government to imprison dissidents.[35] Leiva also faulted the Commission's report for presuming what a Cuban transition must be before U.S. recognition or assistance can be provided. According to Leiva, "Only we Cubans, of our own volition ... can decide issues of such singular importance. Cubans on the island have sufficient intellectual ability to tackle a difficult, peaceful transition and reconcile with other Cubans here and abroad."[36]

U.S. Reaction to Cuba's Political Succession

In response to Fidel Castro's announcement that he was temporarily ceding power to his brother Raúl, President Bush issued a statement on August 3, 2006, that "the United States is absolutely committed to supporting the Cuban people's aspiration for democracy and freedom." The President urged "the Cuban people to work for democratic change" and pledged U.S. support to the Cuban people in their effort to build a transitional government in Cuba. U.S. officials, a the time, indicated that there were no plans for the United States to "reach out" to the new leader. Secretary of State Condoleezza Rice reiterated U.S. support for the Cuban people in an August 4, 2006, statement broadcast on Radio and TV Marti. According to Secretary Rice, "All Cubans who desire peaceful democratic change can count on the support of the United States."[37]

Although there was some U.S. concern that political change in Cuba could prompt a migration crisis, there was no unusual traffic after Castro ceded provisional power to his brother. The U.S. Coast Guard had plans to respond to such a migration crisis, with support from the Navy if needed. In her August 4, 2006, message to the Cuban people, Secretary of State Rice encouraged "the Cuban people to work at home for positive change." Department of Homeland Security officials also announced several measures to discourage Cubans from risking their lives on the open seas. U.S. officials also discouraged those in the Cuban American community wanting to travel by boat to Cuba to speed political change in Cuba. (For more, see "Migration Issues" below.)

Response to Raúl's Overtures

Raúl Castro asserted in an August 18, 2006, published interview that Cuba has "always been disposed to normalize relations on an equal plane," but at the same time he expressed strong opposition to current U.S. policy toward Cuba, which he described as "arrogant and interventionist."[38] In response, Assistant Secretary of State for Western Hemisphere Affairs Thomas Shannon reiterated a U.S. offer to Cuba, first articulated by President Bush in May 2002, that the Administration was willing to work with Congress to lift U.S. economic sanctions if Cuba were to begin a political opening and a transition to democracy. According to Shannon, the Bush Administration remained prepared to work with Congress for ways to lift the embargo if Cuba was prepared to free political prisoners, respect human rights, permit the creation of independent organizations, and create a mechanism and pathway toward free and fair elections.[39]

In a December 2, 2006 speech, Raúl reiterated an offer to negotiate with the United States. He said that "we are willing to resolve at the negotiating table the longstanding dispute between the United States and Cuba, of course, provided they accept, as we have previously said, our condition as a country that will not tolerate any blemishes on its independence, and as long as said resolution is based on the principles of equality, reciprocity, non-interference, and mutual respect."[40]

On July 26, 2007, in a speech on Cuba's revolutionary anniversary (commemorating the 1953 attack on the Moncada military barracks), Raúl Castro reiterated for the third time an offer to engage in dialogue with the United States, and strongly criticized U.S. trade and economic sanctions on Cuba. A U.S. State Department spokesman responded that "the only real dialogue that's needed is with the Cuban people."[41]

In the second half of 2007, President Bush and other U.S. officials continued to call for a transition to democracy in Cuba. In a September 25, 2007 speech before the U.N. General Assembly, President Bush stated that "the long rule of a cruel dictator is nearing its end," and called on the United Nations to insist on free speech, free assembly, and free elections as Cuba "enters a period of transition."[42] U.S. Commerce Secretary Carlos Gutierrez stated in a speech on September 17 that "unless the regime changes, our policy will not," but indicated that the United States is "prepared to respond to genuine democratic change in Cuba."[43]

On October 24, 2007, President Bush made a policy speech on Cuba that reflected a continuation of the sanctions-based approach toward Cuba. According to the President: "As long as the [Cuban] regime maintains its monopoly over the political and economic life of the Cuban people, the United States will keep the embargo in place." In his speech, President Bush also sent a message to Cuban military, police, and government officials that "when Cubans rise up to demand their liberty," they have a choice to embrace the Cuban people's desire for change or "defend a disgraced and dying order by using force." The President conveyed to these officials that "there is a place for you in a free Cuba." [44]

Response to Raúl's Official Selection as President

In the aftermath of Fidel Castro's February 19, 2008 announcement that he was officially stepping down as head of state, President Bush maintained that he viewed "this as a period of transition and it should be the beginning of a democratic transition in Cuba." State Department officials made clear that U.S. policy would not change. On February 24, 2008, the day that Raúl Castro officially became Cuba's head of state, Secretary of State Condoleezza Rice issued a statement urging "the Cuban government to begin a process of peaceful, democratic change by releasing all political prisoners, respecting human rights, and creating a clear pathway towards free and fair elections."

In remarks on Cuba policy in early March 2008, President Bush maintained that in order to improve U.S.-Cuban relations, "what needs to change is not the United States; what needs to change is Cuba." The President asserted that Cuba "must release all political prisoners ... have respect for human rights in word and deed, and pave the way for free and fair elections."[45] He reiterated these words again in a speech to the Council of the Americas on May 7, 2008.[46] On May 21, 2008, President Bush called for the Cuban government to take steps to improve life for the Cuban people, including opening up access to the Internet. He also announced that the United States would change regulations to allow Americans to send mobile phones to family members in Cuba.[47]

Obama Administration Policy

During the electoral campaign, President Obama had pledged to lift restrictions on family travel to Cuba as well as restrictions on Cuban Americans sending remittances to Cuba. At the same time, he also pledged to maintain the embargo as a source of leverage to bring about change in Cuba. However, Obama also asserted that if the Cuban government takes significant steps toward democracy, beginning with the freeing of all political prisoners, then the United States would take steps to normalize relations and ease the embargo. He also maintained that, after careful preparation, his Administration would pursue direct diplomacy with Cuba without preconditions, but only when there is an opportunity to advance U.S. interests and advance the cause of freedom for the Cuban people.[48]

During her Senate Foreign Relations Committee confirmation hearing for Secretary of State on January 15, 2009, Senator Hillary Clinton reiterated President Obama's pledge to lift restrictions on family travel and remittances. She indicated that the Administration did not yet have a timeline on the change, but maintained that the Administration would consult closely with Congress as it proceeds. Clinton also reiterated Obama's position that it is not time to lift the embargo since it provides an important source of leverage for further change in Cuba.

Perhaps most significantly, in response to written questions for the record regarding U.S. agricultural sales to Cuba, Cuba's retention on the State Department's state sponsors of terrorism list since 1982, and potential cooperation with Cuba on energy security and environmentally sustainable resource management, Clinton maintained that the new Administration anticipated a review of U.S. policy. She indicated that she looked forward to working with Members of Congress as the Administration moves forward in the consideration of appropriate steps to advance U.S. interests and values in the context of U.S. relations with Cuba. With regard to a question regarding a potential anti-drug agreement with Cuba, Clinton maintained the importance of anti-drug cooperation with Cuba where such cooperation is effective in stopping trafficking.

Issues in U.S.-Cuban Relations

Aftermath of 2008 Hurricanes and Tropical Storms

From mid-August through early November 2008, three hurricanes and two tropical storms caused widespread damage throughout Cuba. Tropical Storm Fay passed through central Cuba on August 18, causing severe flooding. On August 31, Hurricane Gustav struck the tobacco-growing province of Piñar del Río in western Cuba and the Isle of Youth. Tropical Storm Hanna, which did not strike Cuba directly, caused flooding in eastern Cuba in early September. Hurricane Ike made landfall in eastern Cuba on September 7 as a Category Four hurricane and severely affected both the eastern and western parts of the island, but especially the provinces of Holguin, Camaguey, and Las Tunas in the eastern part of the island. The two hurricanes caused most of the damage. Overall, just 7 people were killed, but the hurricanes severely affected the housing sector (with almost 500,000 homes damaged and over 63,000 destroyed), the power grid, and the agricultural sector. [49] On November 8, 2008, Hurricane Paloma struck Cuba, devastating the town of Santa Cruz del Sur. Initially damages from the storms in August and September were estimated to amount to $5 billion, but Raúl Castro noted in the aftermath of Hurricane Paloma that overall damages from the storms since August amounted to some $10 billion.[50]

The U.S. Chief of Mission at the U.S. Interests Section in Havana, Jonathan Farrar, issued a disaster declaration for Cuba on September 3, 2008, and the U.S. Agency for International Development (USAID) approved the release of $100,000 in emergency relief funds to nongovernmental organizations in Cuba in response to Hurricane Gustav.[51] On September 12, in response to Hurricane Ike, the U.S. government provided another $100,000 in cash assistance to relief organizations on the ground in Cuba. The State Department maintains that the United States offered to send a humanitarian assessment team to Cuba to determine additional assistance needs, but that the Cuban government rejected the offer. U.S. officials subsequently offered a $5 million aid package for disaster relief for Cuba on September 13 that was also rejected by the Cuban government. USAID Administrator Henrietta Fore reportedly maintained that $2 million in plastic sheeting, hygiene kits, and other relief items would have been provided directly to the Cuban government, but that about $3 million in cash would still be provided through NGOs.[52] The State Department made a new offer to Cuba on September 19 to supply some $6.3 million in corrugated zinc roofs, nails, tools, lumber, sheeting, and light shelter kits that would help some 48,000 people, but the Cuban government did not accept the offer.[53]

In addition, according to the State Department, the U.S. government increased authorizations for U.S.-based non-governmental organizations (NGOs) to provide larger amounts of assistance to Cuba in the aftermath of the hurricanes, including expedited authorization over 90 days for up to $10 million per NGO.[54]

In response to the U.S. offer to send a disaster assessment team, the Cuban government maintained that it already had a sufficient number of well-trained experts in Cuba, and noted that other countries worldwide were sending humanitarian aid without inspecting the affected areas. Instead, Cuba asked the United States to allow U.S. companies 1) to sell needed relief supplies to Cuba for the repair of housing and electrical networks; and 2) to grant private commercial credit to Cuba in order to buy food in the United States.[55] In response to the U.S. offer to send $2 million in supplies to the Cuban government, the Cuban Interests Section in Washington rejected the request and called for the United States to allow U.S. companies to sell relief supplies to Cuba, if not on a permanent basis, then at least for the next six months.[56]

Legislative Initiatives

In the aftermath of the hurricanes, a number of observers, including some Members of Congress, called for the temporary relaxation of restrictions on family travel and remittances (limited to $300 per quarter) as well as on the provision of gift parcels[57] to Cuba, but the Administration did not take any of these actions. Some observers also called for temporary changes to the U.S. embargo regulations to allow for unrestricted U.S. cash sales to Cuba of food and medicines, farm machinery or equipment, and relief supplies, including building materials and electrical supplies. On September 5, 2008, Chairman of the House Foreign

Affairs Committee Howard Berman asked President Bush to suspend for 90 days restrictions on family visits, remittances, and gift parcels.

Several legislative initiatives were introduced in the 110th Congress that would have temporarily eased U.S. embargo restrictions in several areas. On September 15, 2008, Senator Dodd offered S.Amdt. 5581 to the Department of Defense authorization bill (S. 3001) that would have, for a 180-day period: allowed unrestricted family travel; eased restrictions on remittances by removing the limit and allowing any American to send remittances to Cuba; expanded the list of allowable items that may be included in gift parcels; and allowed for unrestricted U.S. cash sales of food, medicines, and relief supplies to Cuba. The amendment was not considered, and therefore not part of the final bill.

In the House, two legislative initiatives were introduced. On September 16, 2008, Representative Flake introduced H.R. 6913, which would have prohibited any funds from going to the Department of Commerce to implement, administer, or enforce tightened restrictions on the contents of gift parcels to Cuba that were introduced in June 2004. On September 18, 2008, Representative Delahunt introduced H.R. 6962, the Humanitarian Relief to Cuba Act, which would have, for a 180-day period: allowed unrestricted family travel; eased restrictions on remittances by removing the limit and allowing any American to send remittances to Cuba; and expanded the list of allowable items that may be included in gift parcels.

Restrictions on Travel and Remittances

Restrictions on travel to Cuba have been a key and often contentious component of U.S. efforts to isolate the communist government of Fidel Castro for much of the past 40 years. Over time there have been numerous changes to the restrictions and for five years, from 1977 until 1982, there were no restrictions on travel. Restrictions on travel and remittances to Cuba are part of the CACR, the overall embargo regulations administered by the Treasury Department's Office of Foreign Assets Control (OFAC).

Major arguments made for lifting the Cuba travel ban are that it contributes to the suffering of Cuban families; it hinders efforts to influence conditions in Cuba and may be aiding Castro by helping restrict the flow of information; it abridges the rights of ordinary Americans; and Americans can travel to other countries with communist or authoritarian governments. Major arguments in opposition to lifting the Cuba travel ban are that more American travel would support Castro's rule by providing his government with potentially millions of dollars in hard currency; that there are legal provisions allowing travel to Cuba for humanitarian purposes that are used by thousands of Americans each year; and that the President should be free to restrict travel for foreign policy reasons.

Under the former Bush Administration, enforcement of U.S. restrictions on Cuba travel increased, and restrictions on travel and on private remittances to Cuba were tightened. In March 2003, the Administration eliminated travel for people-to-people educational exchanges unrelated to academic course work. In June 2004, the Administration significantly restricted travel, especially family travel, and the provision of private humanitarian assistance to Cuba in the form of remittances and gift parcels. In April 2005, OFAC cracked down on certain religious organizations promoting licensed travel to Cuba and warned them not to abuse their license by taking individuals not affiliated with their organizations. OFAC's actions were prompted by reports that groups practicing the Afro-Cuban religion Santería had been taking large groups to Cuba as a means of skirting U.S. travel restrictions.[58] In 2006, the Administration suspended the licenses of several travel service providers, including one of the largest such providers in Florida, La Estrella de Cuba. Several religious organizations also had their licenses suspended, and church groups and several Members of Congress expressed concern about more restrictive licenses for religious travel.[59]

Among the June 2004 restrictions that remain in place are the following:

- Family visits were restricted to one trip every three years under a specific license and are restricted to immediate family members, with no exceptions. Under previous regulations, family visits could occur once a year under a general license, with travel more than once a year allowed, but under a specific license. Previously travel had been allowed to visit relatives to within three degrees of relationship to the traveler.
- Cash remittances were further restricted. Quarterly remittances of $300 may still be sent, but are now restricted to members of the remitter's immediate family and may not be remitted to certain government officials and certain members of the Cuban Communist Party. The regulations were also changed to reduce the amount of remittances that authorized travelers may carry to Cuba, from $3000 to $300.
- Gift parcels were limited to immediate family members and were denied to certain Cuban officials and certain members of the Cuban Communist Party. The contents of gift parcels may no longer include seeds, clothing, personal hygiene items, veterinary medicines and supplies, fishing equipment and supplies, or soap-making equipment.
- The authorized per diem allowed for a family visit was reduced from the State Department per diem rate (currently $179 per day for Havana) to $50 per day.
- With the exception of informational materials, licensed travelers may not purchase or otherwise acquire merchandise and bring it back into the United States. Previous regulations allowed visitors to Cuba to import $100 worth of goods as accompanied baggage.
- Fully-hosted travel, by a person not subject to U.S. jurisdiction, was prohibited as a permissible category of travel.
- Travel for educational activities was further restricted, including the elimination of educational exchanges sponsored by secondary schools.

There was mixed reaction to the tightening of Cuba travel and remittance restrictions. Supporters maintain that the increased restrictions deny the Cuban government dollars that help maintain its repressive control. Opponents argue that the tightened sanctions are anti-family and only result in more suffering for the Cuban people. There were also concerns that the new restrictions were drafted without considering the full consequences of their implementation. For example, the elimination of fully-hosted travel raised concerns about the status of 70 U.S. students receiving full scholarships at the Latin American School of Medicine in Havana. Members of the Congressional Black Caucus, who were instrumental in the establishment of the scholarship program for U.S. students, expressed concern that the students may be forced to abandon their medical education because of the new OFAC regulations. As a result of these concerns, OFAC ultimately licensed the medical students in August 2004 to continue their studies and engage in travel-related transactions.

On July 19, 2007, the U.S. International Trade Commission issued a report, requested by the Senate Committee on Finance, maintaining that lifting travel restrictions would result in travel by U.S. citizens to Cuba rising to between 550,000 and 1 million from an estimate of 171,000 in 2005.

As noted above, during the electoral campaign, President Obama pledged to lift restrictions on family travel to Cuba as well as restrictions on Cuban Americans sending remittances to Cuba. Senator Hillary Clinton reiterated President Obama's pledge during her confirmation hearing for Secretary of State on January 15, 2009, but indicated that the Administration did not yet have a timeline on the change.

Legislative Initiatives

From 2000-2004, one or both houses of Congress approved amendments to appropriations bills that would have eased restrictions on travel to Cuba in various ways, but these provisions ultimately were stripped out of final enacted measures. The Bush Administration regularly threatened to veto legislation if it contained provisions weakening Cuba sanctions.

In the 110th Congress, several House and Senate appropriations bills had provisions that would have eased restrictions on travel to Cuba in various ways (H.R. 2829, S. 1859, H.R. 7323, S. 3260, and , S. 3289), but none of these provisions were included in final enacted measures. A number of other legislative initiatives were introduced in the 110th Congress that would have eased Cuba travel restrictions in various ways, including bills that would have temporarily eased restrictions on travel and remittances in the aftermath of the 2008 storms, but no action was taken on these measures.

In the 111th Congress, several measures have been introduced that would ease or eliminate restrictions on travel to Cuba. H.R. 332 (Lee) would ease restrictions on educational travel to Cuba. H.R. 188 (Serrano), would lift overall economic sanctions on Cuba, including restrictions on travel and remittances. Identical bills, H.R. 874 (Delahunt) and S. 428 (Dorgan), would prohibit the President from regulating or prohibiting, directly or indirectly, travel to or from Cuba by U.S. citizens or legal residents, or any of the transactions incident to such travel

The FY2009 omnibus appropriations bill, H.R. 1105, has three provisions that would ease Cuba sanctions, including two related to travel. Section 620 of Division D would amend the Trade Sanctions Reform and Export Enhancement Act of 2000 to require the Secretary of the Treasury to issue regulations for travel to, from, or within Cuba under a general license for the marketing and sale of agricultural and medical goods. This means that there would be no requirement to obtain special permission from the Treasury Department's OFAC. Such travel currently requires a specific license from OFAC, issued on a case by case basis.

Section 621 of Division D would prohibit funds from being used to administer, implement, or enforce family travel restrictions that were imposed by the Bush Administration in June 2004. As noted above, those 2004 restrictions, currently in force, allow family travel only to visit immediate family (grandparents, grandchildren, parents, siblings, spouses, and children) once every three years for a period not to exceed 14 days. Under the 2004 restrictions, a specific license is required from OFAC for such travel; the authorized amount that family travelers can spend while in Cuba is limited to $50 a day; and the amount of remittances that such travelers may carry to Cuba is limited to $300. Prior to the 2004 tightening of the restrictions, family visits could occur once a year under a general license, there was no limit on the duration of the trip, and family travelers could spend up to the State Department per diem rate (currently $179 a day). Travel more than once a year also was allowed, but under a specific license from OFAC. Previously, travel also had been allowed to visit relatives to within three degrees of relationship to the traveler (e.g. great-grandparents and second cousins).

(For additional information, see CRS Report RL31139, *Cuba: U.S. Restrictions on Travel and Remittances*.)

Agricultural Exports and Sanctions

U.S. commercial agricultural exports to Cuba have been allowed for several years, but with numerous restrictions and licensing requirements. The 106th Congress passed the Trade Sanctions Reform and Export Enhancement Act of 2000 or TSRA (P.L. 106-387, Title IX) that allows for one-year export licenses for selling agricultural commodities to Cuba, although no U.S. government assistance, foreign assistance, export assistance, credits, or credit guarantees are available to finance such exports. TSRA also denies exporters access to U.S. private commercial financing or credit; all transactions must be conducted in cash in advance or with financing from third countries. TSRA reiterates the existing ban on importing goods from Cuba but authorizes travel to Cuba, under a specific license, to conduct business related to the newly allowed agricultural sales.

Since 2002, the United States has been Cuba's largest supplier of food and agricultural products.[60] Cuba has purchased almost $2.7 billion in agricultural products from the United States since late 2001. Overall U.S exports to Cuba rose from about $7 million in 2001 to $404 million in 2004. U.S. exports to Cuba declined in 2005 and 2006 to $369 million and $340 million, respectively, but increased to $447 million in 2007. In 2008, U.S. agricultural exports to Cuba rose to $718, far higher than in previous years, in part because of the rise in food prices and because of Cuba's increased food needs in the aftermath of several hurricanes and tropical storms that severely damaged Cuba's agricultural sector.[61]

In February 2005, OFAC amended the Cuba embargo regulations to clarify that TSRA's term of "payment of cash in advance" means that the payment is received by the seller or the seller's agent prior to the shipment of the goods from the port at which they are loaded. U.S. agricultural exporters and some Members of Congress strongly objected that the action constitutes a new sanction that violates the intent of TSRA and could jeopardize millions of dollars in U.S. agricultural sales to Cuba. OFAC Director Robert Werner maintained that the clarification "conforms to the common understanding of the term in international trade."[62] On July 29, 2005, OFAC clarified that, for "payment of cash in advance" for the commercial sale of U.S. agricultural exports to Cuba, vessels can leave U.S. ports as soon as a foreign bank confirms receipt of payment from Cuba. OFAC's action was aimed at ensuring that the goods would not be vulnerable to seizure for unrelated claims while still at the U.S. port. Supporters of overturning OFAC's February 22, 2005 amendment, such as the American Farm Bureau Federation, were pleased by the clarification but indicated that they would still work to overturn the February rule.[63]

Some groups favor further easing restrictions on agricultural exports to Cuba. They argue that the restrictions harm the health and nutrition of the Cuban population. U.S. agribusiness companies that support the removal of restrictions on agricultural exports to Cuba believe that U.S. farmers are missing out on a market of over $700 million annually so close to the United States. Some exporters want to change U.S. restrictions so that they can sell agriculture and farm equipment to Cuba.[64] Agricultural exporters who support the lifting of the prohibition on financing contend that allowing such financing would help smaller U.S. companies expand purchases to Cuba more rapidly.[65]

On July 19, 2007, the U.S. International Trade Commission issued a report, requested by the Senate Committee on Finance, maintaining that the U.S. share of Cuba's agricultural, fish, and forest imports would rise from one-third to between one-half and two-thirds if trade restrictions were lifted. (See the full report available at http://www.usitc.gov /ext_relations/news_release/2007/er0719ee1.htm.)

Opponents of further easing restrictions on agricultural exports to Cuba maintain that U.S. policy does not deny such sales to Cuba, as evidenced by the large amount of sales since 2001. Moreover, according to the State Department, since the Cuban Democracy Act was enacted in 1992, the United States has licensed billions of dollars in private humanitarian donations. Opponents further argue that easing pressure on the Cuban government would in effect be lending support and extending the duration of the Castro regime. They maintain that the United States should remain steadfast in its opposition to any easing of pressure on Cuba that could prolong the Castro regime and its repressive policies. Some agricultural producers that export to Cuba support continuation of the prohibition on financing for agricultural exports to Cuba because it ensures that they will be paid.

Legislative Initiatives

In the 110th Congress, several House and Senate appropriations bills included provisions that would have eased restrictions on U.S. agricultural exports to Cuba (H.R. 2829, S. 1859, H.R. 7323, S. 3260, and , S. 3289) but none of these provisions were included in final enacted measures. These included provisions that would have 1) prevented the Treasury Department from implementing the Administration's February 2005 tightening of policy that required the payment of cash in advance prior to the shipment of U.S. agricultural goods to Cuba and 2) authorized general licenses for travel to Cuba for the marketing and sale of agricultural and medical goods.

In other action during the 110th Congress, the House, on July 27, 2007, rejected (by a vote of 182- 245) H.Amdt. 707 (Rangel) to H.R. 2419, the Farm, Nutrition, and Bioenergy Act of 2007, also known as the 2007 farm bill. The amendment would have eased restrictions on the commercial sale of agricultural products to Cuba by clarifying the meaning of "payment of cash in advance" for the sale of such products; authorizing direct transfers between U.S. and Cuban financial institutions for such sales; and authorizing the issuance of U.S. visas for Cubans to conduct activities, including phytosanitary inspections, related to such sales. A number of other legislative initiatives were introduced in the 110th Congress that would have eased restrictions on U.S. agricultural exports to Cuba in various ways, but no action was taken on these measures.

In the 111th Congress, several measures have been introduced that would ease or lift restrictions on U.S. agricultural exports to Cuba. H.R. 188 (Serrano), would lift overall economic sanctions on Cuba, including restrictions on agricultural exports. Identical bills,

H.R. 874 (Delahunt) and S. 428 (Dorgan), would prohibit the President from regulating or prohibiting travel to or from Cuba by U.S. citizens or legal residents, including travel for the marketing or sale of agricultural goods.

The FY2009 omnibus appropriations bill, H.R. 1105, has three provisions that would ease Cuba sanctions, including two related to U.S. agricultural exports. Section 620 of Division D would amend the Trade Sanctions Reform and Export Enhancement Act of 2000 to require the Secretary of the Treasury to issue regulations for travel to, from, or within Cuba under a general license for the marketing and sale of agricultural and medical goods. This means that there would be no requirement to obtain special permission from the Treasury Department's Office of Foreign Assets Control. Such travel currently requires a specific license from OFAC, issued on a case by case basis. Section 622 of Division D would prohibit funds in the Act from being used to administer, implement, or enforce language added to the Cuban embargo regulations on February 25, 2005 requiring that U.S. agricultural exporters to Cuba must be paid in cash for their goods before the goods leave U.S. ports. Prior to the February 2005 change, the prior practice was for U.S. agricultural exporters to be paid in cash for their goods (as required under the Trade Sanctions Reform and Export Enhancement Act of 200), but before the actual delivery of the goods to Cuba.

Trademark Sanction[66]

For over a decade, the United States has imposed a sanction that denies protection for trademarks connected with businesses confiscated from their owners by the Cuban government. A provision in the FY 1999 omnibus appropriations measure (Section 211 of Division A, Title II, P.L. 105-277, signed into law October 21, 1998) prevents the United States from accepting payment for trademark registrations and renewals from Cuban or foreign nationals that were used in connection with a business or assets in Cuba that were confiscated, unless the original owner of the trademark has consented. The provision prohibits U.S. courts from recognizing such trademarks without the consent of the original owner. The measure was enacted because of a dispute between the French spirits company, Pernod Ricard, and the Bermuda-based Bacardi Ltd. Pernod Ricard entered into a joint venture with the Cuban government to produce and export Havana Club rum, but Bacardi, whose company in Cuba was expropriated in the 1960s, maintains that it holds the right to the Havana Club name. Although Pernod Ricard cannot market Havana Club in the United States because of the trade embargo, it wants to protect its future distribution rights should the embargo be lifted.

The European Union initiated World Trade Organization dispute settlement proceedings in June 2000, maintaining that the U.S. law violates the Agreement on Trade-Related Aspects of Intellectual Property (TRIPS). In January 2002, the WTO ultimately found that the trademark sanction violated WTO provisions on national treatment and most-favored-nation obligations in the TRIPS Agreement.

On March 28, 2002, the United States agreed that it would come into compliance with the WTO ruling through legislative action by January 3, 2003.[67] That deadline was extended several times since no legislative action had been taken to bring Section 211 into compliance with the WTO ruling. On July 1, 2005, however, in an EU-U.S. bilateral agreement, the EU agreed that it would not request authorization to retaliate at that time, but reserved the right to do so at a future date, and the United States agreed not to block a future EU request.[68] On August 3, 2006, the U.S. Patent and Trademark Office announced that Cuba's Havana Club trademark registration was "cancelled/expired," a week after OFAC had denied a Cuban government company the license that it needed to renew the registration of the trademark.[69]

Two different approaches have been advocated to bring Section 211 into compliance with the WTO ruling. Some want a narrow fix in which Section 211 would be amended so that it also applies to U.S. companies instead of being limited to foreign companies. Advocates of this approach argue that it would affirm that the United States "will not give effect to a claim or right to U.S. property if that claim is based on a foreign compensation."[70] Others want Section 211 repealed altogether. They argue that the law endangers over 5,000 trademarks of over 500 U.S. companies registered in Cuba.[71] They maintain that Cuba could retaliate against U.S. companies under the Inter-American Convention for Trademark and Commercial Protection.

Several legislative initiatives were introduced during the 110th Congress reflecting these two approaches to bring Section 211 into compliance with the WTO ruling, but no action was taken on these measures. Several of these could be re-introduced in the 111th Congress. The July 2005 EU-U.S. bilateral agreement, in which the EU agreed not to retaliate against the United States, but reserved the right to do so at a later date, reduced pressure on Congress to take action to comply with the WTO ruling.

Offshore Oil Sector Development

The issue of Cuba's development of its deepwater offshore oil reserves in the Gulf of Mexico has been a concern among some Members of Congress. According to the U.S. Energy Information Administration, industry analysts maintain that there could be at least 1.6 billion barrels of crude oil reserves in Cuba's offshore sector; the U.S. Geological Survey estimated a mean of 4.6 billion barrels of undiscovered oil.[72] In October 2008, an official of Cuba's state oil company, Cubapetroleo (Cupet), maintained there may be more than 20 billion barrels of oil in Cuba's deepwaters, but energy analysts expressed skepticism for such a claim.[73]

To date, Cuba has signed agreements for seven concessions involving eight foreign oil companies for the exploration of offshore oil and gas. Repsol (Spain), Norsk-Hydro (Norway), and ONGC (India) are partners in a joint project, while Sherritt International (Canada), ONGC (India), PdVSA (Venezuela), Petronas (Malaysia), PetroVietnam, and Petrobras (Brazil) also have additional concessions. In February 2008, Petrobras signed a wide-ranging agreement for potential exploration and production cooperation with Cuba's state oil company, Cupet. This ultimately led to an oil exploration agreement between Petrobras and Cupet signed in late October 2008. Some Members of Congress have expressed concern about oil development so close to the United States and about potential environmental damage to the Florida coast. The Repsol project has plans to drill a second well (the first was drilled in 2004) in mid-2009, and some press reports maintain that if that goes well, Cuban oil could be flowing to the market by 2013.[74]

Although there have been some claims that China is drilling in Cuba's offshore deepwater oil sector, to date its involvement in Cuba's oil sector has been focused on exploring onshore/close coastal oil extraction in Piñar del Rio province through its state-run China Petroleum and Chemical Corporation (Sinopec).[75] China does not have a concession in Cuba's offshore oil sector in the deepwaters of the Gulf of Mexico.[76]

In the 110th Congress, several legislative initiatives (H.R. 1679, S. 876, and S. 2503) would have imposed sanctions related to Cuba's offshore oil development on its northern coast, while several other initiatives (S. 1268, S. 2953, H.R. 3182, H.R. 3435, and H.R. 6735) would have allowed U.S. companies to work with Cuba for the offshore exploration and extraction of oil. No action was taken on any of these initiatives.

Drug Interdiction Cooperation

Because of Cuba's geographic location, the country's waters and airspace have been used by illicit narcotics traffickers to transport drugs for ultimate destinations in the United States. Over the past several years, Cuban officials have expressed concerns over the use of their waters and airspace for drug transit as well as increased domestic drug use. The Cuban government has taken a number of measures to deal with the drug problem, including legislation to stiffen penalties for traffickers, increased training for counternarcotics personnel, and cooperation with a number of countries on anti-drug efforts. Cuba has bilateral counternarcotics agreements with 33 countries and less formal arrangements with 16 others, according to the Department of State. For several years, Cuba's Operation Hatchet has focused on maritime and air interdiction and the recovery of narcotics washed up on Cuban shores. Narcotics smuggling through Cuban territory decreased in 2006, according to both U.S. and Cuban officials.[77] According to the Department of State, Cuba aggressively pursues an internal enforcement and investigation program against its incipient drug market with an effective nationwide drug prevention and awareness campaign, Operation Popular Shield.

Over the years, there have been varying levels of U.S.-Cuban cooperation on anti-drug efforts. In 1996, Cuban authorities cooperated with the United States in the seizure of 6.6 tons of cocaine aboard the Miami-bound *Limerick*, a Honduran-flag ship. Cuba turned over the cocaine to the United States and cooperated fully in the investigation and subsequent prosecution of two defendants in the case in the United States. Cooperation has increased since 1999 when U.S. and Cuban officials met in Havana to discuss ways of improving anti-drug cooperation. Cuba accepted an upgrading of the communications link between the Cuban Border Guard and the U.S. Coast Guard as well as the stationing of a U.S. Coast Guard Drug Interdiction Specialist (DIS) at the U.S. Interests Section in Havana. The Coast Guard official was posted to the U.S. Interests Section in September 2000, and since that time, coordination has increased.

The State Department, in its March 2008 *International Narcotics Control Strategy Report*, reported that narcotics cooperation, including operations in coordination with the Coast Guard DIS, increased in 2007. These included cooperation in the interception of a drug-laden aircraft destined for the Bahamas in February and a joint U.S.-Cuba container inspection at the port of Havana in June. The report also noted that Cuban authorities have provided the DIS more exposure to Cuban counternarcotics efforts, including investigative criminal information, debriefings on drug trafficking cases, visits to the Cuban national canine training center and anti-doping laboratory in Havana, and access to meet with the Chiefs of Cuba's INTERPOL and Customs office.

Cuba maintains that it wants to cooperate with the United States to combat drug trafficking, and on various occasions has called for a bilateral anti-drug cooperation agreement with the United States.[78] In January 2002, Cuba deported to the United States Jesse James Bell, a U.S. fugitive wanted on drug charges, and in early March 2002, Cuba arrested a convicted Colombian drug trafficker, Rafael Bustamante, who escaped from jail in Alabama in 1992. At the time, then Drug Enforcement Administration head Asa Hutchison expressed appreciation for Cuba's actions, but indicated that cooperation would continue on a case-by-case basis, not through a bilateral agreement.[79] In February 2007, Cuba extradited drug trafficker Luis Hernando Gómez Bustamante to Colombia, an action that drew praise from U.S. Assistant Secretary of State for International Narcotics and Law Enforcement Affairs Anne Patterson.[80] Gómez Bustamante was subsequently extradited to the United States in July 2007 to face drug trafficking charges.

In April 2008, John Walters, Director of the White House Office of National Drug Control Policy, lauded U.S. anti-drug cooperation with Cuba as a good example of how cooperation has been achieved despite overall political differences between the two countries.[81]

In early January 2009, Assistant Secretary of State for Western Hemisphere Affairs Tom Shannon maintained in an interview with Spain's *El País* newspaper that a drug trafficking accord with Cuba would be logical, although he could not anticipate what the next Administration would do.[82]

Legislative Initiatives

Over the past several years, House and Senate versions of Foreign Operations appropriations bills have contained contrasting provisions related to funding for cooperation with Cuba on counternarcotics efforts. House bills have generally prohibited funds for such efforts, while Senate versions would have funded such efforts. Ultimately, none of these provisions were included in enacted measures.

Most recently, in the second session of the 110th Congress, the Senate Appropriations Committee version of the FY2009 State, Department, Foreign Operations, and Related Agencies Appropriations Act, S. 3288, contained a provision (section 779) that would have provided for $1 million for preliminary work by the Department of State, or other entity designated by the Secretary of State, to establish cooperation with appropriate Cuban agencies on counternarcotics matters. The money would not be available, however, if the Secretary certified that Cuba 1) does not have in place procedures to protect against the loss of innocent life in the air and on the ground in connection with the interdiction of illegal drugs; and 2) there is credible evidence of involvement of the government of Cuba in drug trafficking during the preceding 10 years. No action was taken on the measure, and no such provision was included in the Consolidated Appropriations Act for FY2009 (P.L. 110-329) that provided foreign operations funding until March 6, 2009. Moreover, in the 111th Congress, no such provision was included in the FY2009 omnibus appropriations bill, H.R. 1105 (Obey).

Cuba and Terrorism[83]

Cuba was added to the State Department's list of states sponsoring international terrorism in 1982 because of its alleged ties to international terrorism and support for terrorist groups in Latin America. Cuba had a long history of supporting revolutionary movements and governments in Latin America and Africa, but in 1992, Fidel Castro said that his country's support for insurgents abroad was a thing of the past. Cuba's change in policy was in large part due to the breakup of the Soviet Union, which resulted in the loss of billions of dollars in annual subsidies to Cuba, and led to substantial Cuban economic decline.

Cuba remains on the State Department's terrorism list. According to the State Department's *Country Reports on Terrorism 2007* report (issued April 30, 2008), Cuba has "remained opposed to U.S. counterterrorism policy, and actively and publicly condemned many associated U.S. policies and actions." The report also noted that Cuba maintains close relationships with other state sponsors of terrorism, such as Iran and Syria, and has provided safe haven for members of several Foreign Terrorist Organizations (FTOs): the Basque Homeland and Freedom (ETA) and two Colombian insurgent groups, the Revolutionary Armed Forces of Colombia (FARC) and the National Liberation Army (ELN). Colombia has publicly acknowledged that it wants Cuban mediation with the ELN.

The 2007 report also maintained that Cuba continued to permit U.S. fugitives from justice to live legally in Cuba. Most of the fugitives entered Cuba in the 1 970s, and are accused of hijacking or committing violent actions in the United States. The State Department report noted that Cuba stated in 2006 that it would no longer provide safe haven to new fugitives who may enter Cuba. In 2006, Cuba returned a U.S. fugitive who had sequestered his son and flew a stolen plane to Cuba in September. In April 2007, Cuba returned another U.S. fugitive, Joseph Adjmi, who was convicted of mail fraud in the 1 960s, but disappeared before beginning his 10-year sentence. On June 13, 2008, Cuba's Ministry of Foreign Affairs announced that it deported another U.S. citizen, Leonard Auerbach, wanted in the United States for sexual exploitation of a minor and for child pornography, who had entered Cuba from Mexico in April.[84] More recently, press reports maintain that a number of fugitives from Florida accused of bilking the U.S. government of millions through Medicare fraud have fled to Cuba.[85]

Critics of retaining Cuba on the terrorism list maintain that it is a holdover from the Cold War. They argue that domestic political considerations keep Cuba on the terrorism list and maintain that Cuba's presence on the list diverts U.S. attention from struggles against serious terrorist threats. Those who support keeping Cuba on the terrorism list argue that there is ample evidence that Cuba supports terrorism. They point to the government's history of supporting terrorist acts and armed insurgencies in Latin America and Africa. They point to the government's continued hosting of members of foreign terrorist organizations and U.S. fugitives from justice.

Cuba as the Victim of Terrorism

Cuba has been the target of various terrorist incidents over the years. In 1976, a Cuban plane was bombed, killing 73 people. In 1997, there were almost a dozen bombings in the tourist sector in Havana and in the Varadero beach area in which an Italian businessman was killed and several others were injured. Two Salvadorans were convicted and sentenced to death for the bombings in March 1999, and three Guatemalans were sentenced to prison terms ranging from 10-15 years in January 2002. Cuban officials maintain that Cuban exiles funded the bombings.

In November 2000, four anti-Castro activists were arrested in Panama for a plot to kill Fidel Castro. One of the accused, Luis Posada Carriles, was also allegedly involved in the 1976 Cuban airline bombing noted above.[86] The four stood trial in March 2004 and were sentenced on weapons charges in the case to prison terms ranging from seven to eight years. In late August 2004, Panamanian President Mireya Moscoso pardoned the four men before the end of her presidential term. Three of the men are U.S. citizens and traveled to Florida, where they received strong support from some in the Cuban American community, while Posada reportedly traveled to another country.

On April 13, 2005, Posada's lawyer said that his client, reportedly in the United States after entering the country illegally, would seek asylum in the United States because he has a "well- founded fear of persecution" for his opposition to Fidel Castro.[87] Posada, a Venezuelan citizen, had been imprisoned in Venezuela for the bombing of the Cuban airliner in 1976, but reportedly was allowed to "escape" from prison in 1985 after his supporters paid a bribe to the prison warden.[88] He had been acquitted for the bombing but remained in prison pending a prosecutorial appeal.[89] Posada also reportedly admitted, but later denied, involvement in the string of bombings in Havana in 1997, one of which killed an Italian tourist.[90] Posada subsequently withdrew his application for asylum on May 17, 2005. Later that day, U.S. Immigration and Customs Enforcement (ICE) arrested Posada, and subsequently charged him with illegally entering the United States. A Department of Homeland Security press release indicated that ICE does not generally deport people to Cuba or countries believed to be acting on Cuba's behalf.[91] Venezuela requested Posada's extradition and pledged that it would not hand Posada over to Cuba. On September 26, 2005, however, a U.S. immigration judge ruled that Posada likely faced torture in Venezuela and could not be deported in keeping with U.S. obligations under the Convention Against Torture.[92]

ICE reviewed the case and determined on March 22, 2006, that Posada would not be freed from a federal immigration facility in El Paso, Texas.[93] In November 2006, however, a U.S. federal judge, who was considering Posada's plea that he be released, ordered the government to supply evidence, by February 1, 2007, justifying his continued detention. On January 11, 2007, a federal grand jury in Texas indicted Posada on seven counts for lying about how he entered the United States illegally in March 2005, whereupon he was transferred from immigration detention in El Paso to a county prison in New Mexico near the Texas border. The Cuban government responded by maintaining that Posada needs to be charged with terrorism, not just lying about how he entered the United States. Another grand jury in New Jersey is reportedly examining Posada's alleged role in the 1997 bombings in Cuba.[94] Press articles in early May 2007 reported that the FBI has been gathering evidence in the 1997 bombing and that FBI agents have visited Havana as part of their investigation.[95]

Posada was released from jail in New Mexico on April 19, 2007, and allowed to return to Miami under house arrest to await an upcoming trial on immigration fraud charges, but on May 9, 2007 a federal judge in Texas dismissed the charges. The judge maintained that the U.S. government mistranslated testimony from Posada and manipulated evidence.[96] On June 5, 2007, Justice Department prosecutors filed a notice of appeal with the 5th U.S. Circuit Court of Appeals in New Orleans and on November 6, 2007, federal prosecutors filed a brief requesting that the court reverse the lower court's decision.[97] On June 4, 2008, the appeals court heard arguments from both sides in the case; a ruling reportedly could take several months.[98] Both Cuba and Venezuela strongly denounced Posada's release, contending that he is a terrorist. In late June 2008, Panama's Supreme Court ruled that Posada's 2004 pardon was unconstitutional, and in July 2008, a Panamanian court initiated a request for Posada's extradition to the Panamanian government.

U.S. Funding to Support Democracy and Human Rights

Since 1996, the United States has provided assistance—primarily through the U.S. Agency for International Development (USAID), but also through the State Department and the National Endowment for Democracy (NED)—to increase the flow of information on democracy, human rights, and free enterprise to Cuba.

USAID's Cuba program has supported a variety of U.S.-based non-governmental organizations with the goals of promoting a rapid, peaceful transition to democracy, helping develop civil society, and building solidarity with Cuba's human rights activists.[99] These efforts are largely funded through Economic Support Funds (ESF) in the annual foreign operations appropriations bill. From FY200 1 -FY2007, the United States provided a total of almost $71 million in funding for Cuba democracy efforts.

For FY2008, Congress fully funded the Administration's request for $45.7 million in ESF for democracy assistance for Cuba in the Consolidated Appropriations Act for FY2008 (P.L. 110-161); an estimated $45.33 million, however, will be provided because of an overall 0.81% rescission. The amount was more than five times the amount requested in FY2007 ($9 million). According to the State Department's FY2008 Congressional Budget Justification (CBJ), the increase in assistance was in order to fulfill the recommendations of the July 2006 report of the Commission for Assistance to a Free Cuba to provide support for Cuban civil society, expand international awareness, break the regime's information blockade, and continue support for a democratic transition. That report, as described above, recommended $80 million over two years for a variety of measures to hasten Cuba's transition to democracy, and not less than $20 million annually thereafter for Cuba democracy programs.

Both the House- and Senate-passed versions of the FY2008 State, Foreign Operations, and Related Agencies Appropriations Act, H.R. 2764, fully funded the Administration's request for $45.7 million in ESF for Cuba democracy programs. The House committee-reported version of the bill would have provided just $9 million in ESF for such programs, but during June 21, 2007, floor consideration, the House approved H.Amdt. 351 (Diaz-Balart) by a vote of 254-170 that increased funding for ESF by $36.7 million in order to fully fund the Administration's request. The Senate Appropriations Committee report to the bill would have provided $15 million in ESF for Cuba democracy programs. However, during September 6, 2007, floor consideration, the Senate approved S.Amdt. 2694 (Martinez) by voice vote that increased funding for Cuba democracy programs by $30.7 million to fully fund the Administration's request.

For FY2009, the Administration requested $20 million in ESF to continue to implement the program recommendations of the Commission for Assistance to a Free Cuba. The money would assist human rights activists, independent journalists, Afro-Cubans, and women, youth, and student activists. The report to the Senate Appropriations Committee version of the

FY2009 State Department, Foreign Operations, and Related Agencies Appropriations Act, S, 3288 (S.Rept. 110- 425), recommended fully funding the Administration's request for Cuba, but also called for the State Department and USAID to conduct regular evaluations to ensure the cost effectiveness of the programs. No final action on the appropriations measure was taken in the 110th Congress, but overall foreign operations funding was continued under a short-term continuing resolution (P.L. 110-329) until March 6, 2009.

Until FY2008, NED's democratization assistance for Cuba had been funded largely through the annual Commerce, Justice, and State (CJS) appropriations measure, but is now funded through the State Department, Foreign Operations and Related Agencies appropriations measure. NED funding for Cuba has steadily increased over the past several years: $765,000 in FY2001; $841,000 in FY2002; $1.14 million in FY2003; and $1.15 million in FY2004. For FY2005, NED funded 17 Cuba projects with $2.4 million. For FY2006, NED funded 13 projects with almost $1.5 million, including $0.4 million from State Department ESF. For FY2007, NED funded 12 projects with almost $1.5 million, which included almost $1.4 million funded by the State Department.

Oversight of U.S. Democracy Assistance to Cuba

In November 2006, the Government Accountability Office (GAO) issued a report examining U.S. democracy assistance for Cuba from 1996-2005, and concluded that the U.S. program had significant problems and needed better management and oversight. According to GAO, internal controls, for both the awarding of Cuba program grants and oversight of grantees, "do not provide adequate assurance that the funds are being used properly and that grantees are in compliance with applicable law and regulations."[100] Investigative news reports on the program maintained that high shipping costs and lax oversight have diminished its effectiveness.[101] Representative William Delahunt, Chairman of the House Foreign Affairs Committee's Subcommittee on International Organizations, Human Rights, and Oversight, had requested the GAO study along with Representative Jeff Flake.

In March 2008, a White House aide to President Bush, Felipe Sixto, resigned because of alleged misuse of funds when he worked for the Center for a Free Cuba, which has been a major recipient of U.S. democracy funding.[102] On December 19, 2008, Sixto pled guilty to stealing nearly $600,000, and is expected to be sentenced in March 2009.[103] Another group, Grupo de Apoyo a la Democracia (Group in Support of Democracy), is also under investigation by USAID for misuse of funds. Historically these two groups have been the two largest recipients of U.S. democracy funding for Cuba.[104]

GAO issued a second report examining USAID's Cuba democracy program on November 24, 2008.[105] The report lauded the steps that USAID had taken since 2006 to address problems with its Cuba program and improve oversight of the assistance. These included awarding all grants competitively since 2006, hiring more staff for the program office since January 2008; and contracting for financial services in April 2008 to enhance oversight of grantees. The GAO report also noted that USAID had worked to strengthen program oversight through pre-award and follow-up reviews, improving grantee internal controls and implementation plans, and providing guidance and monitoring about permitted types of assistance and cost sharing.

The GAO report also maintained, however, that USAID had not staffed the Cuba program to the level needed for effective grant oversight. GAO also noted the difficulty of assessing USAID's action to improve its Cuba program because most of its actions to improve the program were only taken recently. Procurement reviews completed in August 2008 by the new financial services contractor identified internal control, financial management, and procurement weaknesses at three grantees. GAO recommended that USAID: 1) ensure that its Cuba program office is staffed at the level that is needed to fully implement planned monitoring activities; and 2) periodically assess the Cuba program's overall efforts to address and reduce grantee risks, especially regarding internal controls, procurement practices, expenditures, and compliance with laws and regulations.

The Cuban American National Foundation (CANF) released a report in May 2008 maintaining that a majority of the assistance for Cuba has been spent in operating expenses by U.S.-based grantees, transition studies, and U.S.-based activities. Among the recommendations in its report, the CANF called for USAID grantees to spend a minimum of 75% of government funds in direct aid to Cuban civil society. It also called for the assistance program to provide direct cash aid to independent civil society groups, dissidents, and families of political prisoners.[106]

Radio and TV Marti

U.S.-government sponsored radio and television broadcasting to Cuba—Radio and TV Martí— began in 1985 and 1990 respectively. As spelled out in the *Broadcasting Board of Governors FY2009 Budget Request*, the objectives of Radio and TV Martí are (1) to support the right of the Cuban people to seek, receive, and impart information and ideas through any media and regardless of frontiers; (2) to be effective in furthering the open communication of information and ideas through use of radio and television broadcasting to Cuba; (3) to serve as a consistently reliable and authoritative source of accurate, objective, and comprehensive news; and (4) to provide news, commentary, and other information about events in Cuba and elsewhere to promote the cause of freedom in Cuba.

Until October 1999, U.S.-government funded international broadcasting programs had been a primary function of the United States Information Agency (USIA). When USIA was abolished and its functions were merged into the Department of State at the beginning of FY2000, the Broadcasting Board of Governors (BBG) became an independent agency that included such entities as the Voice of America (VOA), Radio Free Europe/Radio Liberty (RFE/RL), Radio Free Asia, and the Office of Cuba Broadcasting (OCB), which manages Radio and TV Marti. OCB is headquartered in Miami, Florida, and operates under the BBG's International Broadcasting Bureau (IBB). Legislation in the 104th Congress (P.L. 104-134) required the relocation of OCB from Washington D.C. to south Florida. The move began in 1996 and was completed in 1998.

Radio Martí broadcasts on short and medium wave (AM) channels for 24 hours six days per week, and forl 8 hours one day per week utilizing transmission facilities in Marathon, Florida and Greenville, North Carolina, according to the BBG.

TV Martí broadcasts daily from its facilities in Cudjoe Key Florida, on the Hispasat satellite, and is available on the Internet 24 hours a day. It is also available on 176 cable stations throughout Latin America, according to the BBG. Until July 2005, TV Martí had also been broadcast via blimps from facilities in Cudjoe Key, Florida for four and one-half hours daily, but the aerostats were destroyed by Hurricane Dennis. From mid-2004 until 2006, TV

Martí programming was transmitted for several hours once a week via an airborne platform known as Commando Solo operated by the Department of Defense utilizing a C-130 aircraft. In August 2006, OCB began to use a contracted private aircraft to transmit pre-recorded TV Martí broadcasts six days weekly, and by late October 2006 the OCB inaugurated an aircraft-broadcasting platform known as Aero Martí with the capability of transmitting live broadcasts. Aero Martí transmits broadcasts five hours daily from Monday to Saturday during the evening. According to OCB, since mid-FY2007, it has had two contracted private aircraft transmitting the broadcasts.

In December 2006, the OCB contracted with two private U.S. commercial stations to transmit Radio and TV Martí.[107] It provided a six-month contract with Radio Mambí (710 AM) in Florida, at a cost of $182,500, to broadcast one hour of Radio Martí programming five days a week from midnight to 1:00 am. Radio Mambí is a popular station in south Florida, with a 50,000 watt capacity, that is well-known for its strong anti-Castro stance. A second six-month OCB contract with WPMF (Channel 38) in Miami, known as TV Azteca, at a cost of $195,000, provided for two 30-minute TV Martí newscasts at 6 pm and 11:30 pm weekdays, along with one-minute news updates hourly over a 12 hour period weekdays. OCB chose the station because it is offered on DirecTV and because it has only a small audience in Miami. In June 2007, the two contracts were extended for an additional six months with similar terms. The contract with Radio Mambí subsequently expired in early 2008, whereas TV Martí continues to be shown on Channel 38.

Controversies

Both Radio and TV Martí have at times been the focus of controversies, including questions about adherence to broadcast standards. There have been various attempts over the years to cut funding for the programs, especially for TV Martí, which has not had much of an audience because of Cuban jamming efforts. In December 2006, press reports alleged significant problems in the OCB's operations, with claims of cronyism, patronage, and bias in its coverage.[108] In February 2007, the former director of TV Martí programming pled guilty in U.S. federal court to receiving more than $100,000 in kickbacks over a three-year period from a vendor receiving OCB contracts.[109]

Over the years, there have been various government studies and audits of Radio and TV Martí, including investigations by the U.S. Government Accountability Office, by a 1994 congressionally established Advisory Panel on Radio and TV Martí, and by the State Department's and BBG's Office Inspector General offices in 1999, 2003, and 2007.[110]

The most recent State Department/BBG Office of Inspector General (OIG) report, issued in June 2007, maintained that OCB has significantly improved its operations under its current director, Pedro Roig, with an organizational realignment that has streamlined operations and has helped improve the quality of broadcasts. According to the report, "IBB quality reviews show that radio and television broadcasts have markedly improved over the past two years in production quality and content," although the report also called for greater emphasis on internal quality control to ensure that editorial standards are followed. The report lauded the introduction of new technology allowing OCB to broadcast television signals live into Cuba using airborne platforms, and maintained that there are indications that more Cubans are watching TV Martí broadcasts. It recommended that the BBG's International Broadcasting Bureau should review and assess the leases with Radio Mambí and TV Azteca at the end of the lease period to determine whether they provide additional listeners and viewers and are worth the cost, or whether they could be replaced with lease options for other stations. Looking ahead, the report maintained that OCB needs a "long-term strategic plan that anticipates the future needs of the Cuban audience, provides a template on how to compete with commercial broadcasters, and addresses what to do with OCB and its broadcasting facilities if and when uncensored broadcasting is allowed inside a democratic Cuba."[111]

One of the most controversial aspects of the OIG report, and one that has often been at the center of past congressional debate over TV Martí, is the extent to which TV Martí can be viewed in Cuba. The report maintains that there is anecdotal evidence that the Aero Martí airborne transmissions have increased viewership. The report refers to a January 2007 survey of Cuban arrivals—commissioned by Spanish Radio Productions with the cooperation of Miami Dade College—that found listening rates for Radio and TV Martí within Cuba were significantly higher than previously reported, especially for TV Martí. Although specific survey figures are not cited in the OIG report, OCB officials maintain that the survey shows that 17% of recent Cuban arrivals had watched TV Martí.[112] The OIG report also points to a February 2007 survey by the U.S. Interests Section (USINT) in Havana that reflected increased viewership. According to the BBG, that survey was completed by 500 Cuban visitors to the USINT (where TV Martí can be viewed) in January and February 2007, with 10% of the visitors indicating that they could watch TV Martí via UHF for brief periods.

Other observers contend that TV Martí can hardly be viewed in Cuba because of the government's jamming efforts. John Nichols, a Pennsylvania State University communications professor, visited Cuba in late June 2007 on a fact-finding mission sponsored by the Center for International Policy (a group that opposes current U.S. policy toward Cuba), and concluded "that the signal from the plane is essentially unusable" and that there was "no evidence of significant viewership of TV Martí."[113] In interviews with the *Associated Press*, more than two dozen Cuban immigrants to Florida contended that while Radio Martí can be heard throughout Cuba, TV Martí can rarely be seen.[114] Prior BBG commissioned phone surveys in Cuba from 2003, 2005, and November 2006 estimated past week TV Martí viewership between 0.1% and 0.3% of those surveyed and past month viewership of almost 0.5%. The November 2006 survey, reportedly designed to show the early effects of the Aero Martí transmissions that began in late October, showed no statistically significant change from the 2003 and 2005 surveys. In the same surveys, Radio Martí had listenership of between 1% to 2% in the past week and 4% to 5% in the past month.

In July 2008, GAO issued a report that criticized the IBB's and OCB's practices in awarding the two contracts to Radio Mambí and TV Azteca as lacking discipline required to ensure transparency and accountability. According to GAO, the approach for awarding the Radio Mambi and TV Azteca contracts did not reflect sound business practices.[115]

In January 2009, GAO issued a report asserting that the best available research suggests that Radio and TV Martí's audience is small, and cited telephone surveys since 2003 showing that less than 2% of respondents reported tuning in to Radio or TV Martí during the past week. The GAO report also cited concerns with adherence to relevant laws and standards, including the domestic dissemination of OCB programming, inappropriate advertisements during OCB programming, and TV Martí's interference with Cuban broadcasts.[116]

Funding

From FY1984 through FY2007, about $564 million has been spent for broadcasting to Cuba. In recent years, funding amounted to $37.5 million in FY2006, $33.9 million in

FY2007, and an estimated $33.4 million in FY2008. For FY2009, the Bush Administration requested $34.4 million for broadcasting to Cuba. Until FY2005, the Administration provided funding information for Cuba broadcasting with a breakdown of the amounts spent for Radio versus TV Martí. Since FY2005, however, the Broadcasting Board of Governors has not made such a distinction in its annual budget request.

For FY2009, the Administration requested $34.4 million for broadcasting to Cuba, slightly more than provided by Congress in FY2008. The request amount includes funding for the airborne platform that the Office of Cuba Broadcasting uses to broadcast Radio and TV Martí. The report to the Senate Appropriations Committee version of the FY2009 State Department, Foreign Operations, and Related Agencies Appropriations Act, S. 3288 (S.Rept. 110-425), recommended fully funding the Administration's request for Cuba broadcasting. The 110th Congress did not finalize FY2009 appropriations, although it did approve the Consolidated Appropriations Act for

FY2009 (P.L. 110-329) that provides funding until March 6, 2009. In the 111th Congress, the FY2009 omnibus appropriations bill, H.R. 1105, would fully fund the request for $34.4 million for Cuba broadcasting.

Migration Issues

1994 and 1995 Migration Accords

Cuba and the United States reached two migration accords in 1994 and 1995 designed to stem the mass exodus of Cubans attempting to reach the United States by boat. On the minds of U.S. policymakers was the 1980 Mariel boatlift in which 125,000 Cubans fled to the United States with the approval of Cuban officials. In response to Castro's threat to unleash another Mariel, U.S. officials reiterated U.S. resolve not to allow another exodus. Amid escalating numbers of fleeing Cubans, on August 19, 1994, President Clinton abruptly changed U.S. migration policy, under which Cubans attempting to flee their homeland were allowed into the United States, and announced that the U.S. Coast Guard and Navy would take Cubans rescued at sea to the U.S. naval base at Guantanamo Bay, Cuba. Despite the change in policy, Cubans continued fleeing in large numbers.

As a result, in early September 1994, Cuba and the United States began talks that culminated in a September 9, 1994 bilateral agreement to stem the flow of Cubans fleeing to the United States by boat. In the agreement, the United States and Cuba agreed to facilitate safe, legal, and orderly Cuban migration to the United States, consistent with a 1984 migration agreement. The United States agreed to ensure that total legal Cuban migration to the United States would be a minimum of 20,000 each year, not including immediate relatives of U.S. citizens. In a change of policy, the United States agreed to discontinue the practice of granting parole to all Cuban migrants who reach the United States, while Cuba agreed to take measures to prevent unsafe departures from Cuba.

In May 1995, the United States reached another accord with Cuba under which the United States would parole the more than 30,000 Cubans housed at Guantanamo into the United States, but would intercept future Cuban migrants attempting to enter the United States by sea and would return them to Cuba. The two countries would cooperate jointly in the effort. Both countries also pledged to ensure that no action would be taken against those migrants returned to Cuba as a consequence of their attempt to immigrate illegally. On January 31, 1996, the Department of Defense announced that the last of some 32,000 Cubans intercepted at sea and housed at Guantanamo had left the U.S. Naval Station, most having been paroled into the United States.

Coast Guard Interdictions

Since the 1995 migration accord, the U.S. Coast Guard has interdicted thousands of Cubans at sea and returned them to their country, while those deemed at risk for persecution have been transferred to Guantanamo and then found asylum in a third country or eventually the United States. Those Cubans who reach shore are allowed to apply for permanent resident status in one year, pursuant to the Cuban Adjustment Act of 1966 (P.L. 89-732). This so-called "wet foot/dry foot" policy has been criticized by some as encouraging Cubans to risk their lives in order to make it to the United States and as encouraging alien smuggling. Others maintain that U.S. policy should welcome those migrants fleeing communist Cuba whether or not they are able to make it to land.

The number of Cubans interdicted at sea by the U.S. Coast Guard has risen in recent years, from 666 in FY2002 to 2,712 in FY2005. In FY2006 and FY2007, Cuban interdictions rose to 2,810 and 2,868, respectively, but interdictions declined to 2,199 in FY2008.[117] In recent years, increasing numbers of Cuban migrants attempting to reach the United States have been intercepted in Mexico. Mexico and Cuba negotiated a migration accord in October 2008 to curb the irregular flow of migrants through Mexico.[118]

U.S. prosecution against migrant smugglers in Florida has increased in recent years with numerous convictions. There have been several violent incidents in which Cuban migrants have brandished weapons or in which Coast Guard officials have used force to prevent Cubans from reaching shore. In late December 2007, a Coast Guard official in Florida called on the local Cuban American community to denounce the smuggling and stop financing the trips that are leading to more deaths at sea.[119] The Cuban government also has taken forceful action against individuals engaging in alien smuggling. Prison sentences of up to three years may be imposed against those engaging in alien smuggling.

In the aftermath of Fidel Castro's July 2006, announcement that he was temporarily ceding political power to his brother, Department of Homeland Security officials announced several measures to discourage Cubans from risking their lives on the open seas. On August 11, 2006, Department of Homeland Security (DHS) Deputy Secretary Michael P. Jackson urged "the Cuban people to stay on the island" and discouraged "anyone from risking their life in the open seas in order to travel to the United States." At the same time, DHS announced additional measures to discourage Cubans from turning to alien smuggling as a way to enter the United States. The measures support family reunification by increasing the numbers of Cuban migrants admitted to the United States each year who have family members in the United States, although the overall number of Cubans admitted to the United States annually will remain at about 21,000. Cubans who attempt to enter the United States illegally will be deemed ineligible to enter under this new family reunification procedure. In another change of policy, Cuban medical personnel currently conscripted by the Cuban government to work in third countries are now allowed to enter the United States; their families in Cuba are also allowed to enter the United States.[120]

Migration Talks

Semi-annual U.S.-Cuban talks alternating between Cuba and the United States had been held regularly on the implementation of the 1994 and 1995 migration accords, but the State Department cancelled the 20th round of talks scheduled for January 2004, and no migration talks have been held since. According to the State Department, Cuba has refused to discuss five issues identified by the United States: (1) Cuba's issuance of exit permits for all qualified migrants; (2) Cuba's cooperation in holding a new registration for an immigrant lottery; (3) the need for a deeper Cuban port used by the U.S. Coast Guard for the repatriation of Cubans interdicted at sea; (4) Cuba's responsibility to permit U.S. diplomats to travel to monitor returned migrants; and (5) Cuba's obligation to accept the return of Cuban nationals determined to be inadmissible to the United States.[121] In response to the cancellation of the talks, Cuban officials maintained that the U.S. decision was irresponsible and that Cuba was prepared to discuss all of the issues raised by the United States.[122]

Guantanamo Naval Base

The 45-square mile U.S. Naval Station at Guantanamo Bay, Cuba, has been a U.S. base since 1903, and under a 1934 treaty that remains in force, the U.S. presence can only be terminated by mutual agreement or by abandonment by the United States. When Fidel Castro assumed power in the 1959 Cuban revolution, the new government gave assurances that it would respect all its treaty commitments, including the 1934 treaty covering the Guantanamo base. Subsequently, however, as U.S.-Cuban relations deteriorated, the Cuban government opposed the presence as illegal.

The mission of the base has changed over time. During the Cold War, the base was viewed as a good location for controlling Caribbean sea lanes, as a deterrent to the Soviet presence in the Caribbean, and as a location for supporting potential military operations in the region. In 1994- 1995, the base was used to house thousands of Cubans and Haitians fleeing their homeland, but by 1996 the last of the refugees had departed, with most Cubans paroled into the United States, pursuant to a May 1995 U.S.-Cuban migration accord. Since the 1995 accord, the U.S. Coast Guard has interdicted thousands of Cubans at sea and returned them to Cuba, while a much smaller number, those deemed at risk for persecution, have been taken to Guantanamo and then granted asylum in a third country.

Another mission for the Guantanamo base emerged with the U.S.-led global campaign against terrorism in the aftermath of the September 11, 2001, terrorist attacks in the United States. With the U.S. war in Afghanistan in 2001, the United States decided to send some captured Taliban and Al Qaeda fighters to be imprisoned in Guantanamo. Although the Cuban government has objected to the U.S. presence at Guantanamo, it did not initially oppose the new mission of housing detainees. Then Defense Minister Raúl Castro noted that, in the unlikely event that a prisoner would escape into Cuban territory, Cuba would capture the prisoner and return him to the base.[123] The Cuban government, however, has expressed concerns about the treatment of prisoners at the U.S. base and has said it will keep pressing the international community to investigate the treatment of terrorist suspects.[124] In January 2005, it denounced what it described as "atrocities" committed at the Guantanamo base.[125]

President Obama issued Executive Order 13492 on January 22, 2009 that requires the closure of the Guantanamo detention facility (not the base itself) as soon as practicable, but no later than one year. Some Members of Congress also have called for the closure of the detention facility and have introduced legislation in the 111th Congress: H.R. 374 (Harman) and S. 147 (Feinstein). Other measures have been introduced to prohibit the transfer of the enemy combatants detained at Guantanamo from being transferred to military prisons in Fort Leavenworth, Kansas, H.R. 148 (Jenkins); Charleston, South Carolina, H.R. 565 (Brown, Henry); Naval Consolidated Brig, Miramar, California or Camp Pendleton Base Brig, Camp Pendleton, California, H.R. 633(Hunter); Oklahoma, H.R. 701(Fallin), Florence Federal Correctional Complex, Colorado, H.R. 794 (Lamborn); Georgia, H.R. 817(Gingrey); North Carolina, H.R. 829, (Myrick); Arizona; H.R. 951 (Franks); and Florida, H.R. 1073(Rooney). Another initiative, S. 108 (Vitter) would prohibit the admission of an alien who was detained as an enemy combatant at Guantanamo unless the President determines that such admission is consistent with the national security of the United States. (For additional information, see CRS Report R40139, *Closing the Guantanamo Detention Center: Legal Issues*, by Michael John Garcia et al.)

With regard to the future of the Guantanamo base overall, a provision in the Cuban Liberty and Democratic Solidarity Act of 1996 (P.L. 104-114, Section 210) states that once a democratically elected Cuban government is in place, U.S. policy is to be prepared to enter into negotiations either to return the base to Cuba or to renegotiate the present agreement under mutually agreeable terms.

LEGISLATIVE INITIATIVES IN THE 111TH CONGRESS

H.R. 187 (Serrano). Waives certain prohibitions with respect to nationals of Cuba coming to the United States to play organized professional baseball. Introduced January 6, 2009; referred to Committees on Foreign Affairs and Judiciary.

H.R. 188 (Serrano). Lifts the trade embargo on Cuba. Introduced January 6, 2009; referred to Committees on Foreign Affairs, Ways and Means, Energy and Commerce, Judiciary, Financial Services, Oversight and Government Reform, and Agriculture.

H.R. 332 (Lee). Provides that no funds made available to the Department of the Treasury may be used to implement, administer, or enforce regulations to require specific licenses for travel-related transactions directly related to educational activities in Cuba.

H.R. 375 (Ros-Lehtinen). Section 209 of the bill sets forth restrictions on nuclear cooperation with countries assisting the nuclear program of Venezuela or Cuba or transferring advanced conventional weapons to Venezuela or Cuba. Introduced January 9, 2009; referred to Committee on Foreign Affairs.

H.R. 874 (Delahunt)/ S. 428 (Dorgan). Identical bills would prohibit the President from regulating or prohibiting, directly or indirectly, travel to or from Cuba by U.S. citizens or legal residents, or any of the transactions incident to such travel. H.R. 874 was introduced

February 4, 2009, and referred to the House Committee on Foreign Affairs. S. 428 was introduced February 12, 2009, and referred to the Senate Committee on Foreign Affairs.

H.R. 1105 (Obey). Omnibus Appropriations Act, 2009. Introduced February 23, 2009. Division D, Financial Services and General Government Appropriations Act, 2009, has three provisions that would ease U.S. sanctions on Cuba. These three provisions, explained below, were identical to provisions in the S. 3260, the Senate version of the Financial Services and General Government Appropriations Act, 2009, in the 110th Congress. In addition, the Joint Explanatory Statement to the bill requires the Department of the Treasury to prepare a report within 90 days on the steps that it is taking to assess the Office of Foreign Assets Control's allocation of resources for investigating and penalizing violations of the Cuba embargo with respect to the numerous other sanctions programs it administers. As part of the report, the Treasury Department is directed to provide detailed information on OFAC's Cuba-related licensing on its enforcement of the Cuba embargo.

Section 620 of Division D would amend the Trade Sanctions Reform and Export Enhancement Act of 2000 to require the Secretary of the Treasury to issue regulations for travel to, from, or within Cuba under a general license for the marketing and sale of agricultural and medical goods, meaning that there would be no requirement to obtain special permission from OFAC. Such travel currently requires a specific license from OFAC, issued on a case by case basis.

Section 621 of Division D would prohibit funds from being used to administer, implement, or enforce family travel restrictions that were imposed by the Bush Administration in June 2004. Those 2004 restrictions, currently in force, allow family travel only to visit immediate family (grandparents, grandchildren, parents, siblings, spouses, and children) once every three years for a period not to exceed 14 days. Under the 2004 restrictions, a specific license is required from OFAC for such travel; the authorized amount that family travelers can spend while in Cuba is limited to $50 a day; and the amount of remittances that such travelers may carry to Cuba is limited to $300. Prior to the 2004 tightening of the restrictions, family visits could occur once a year under a general license, there was no limit on the duration of the trip, and family travelers could spend up to the State Department per diem rate (currently $179 a day for Havana). Travel more than once a year also was allowed, but under a specific license from OFAC. Previously, travel also had been allowed to visit relatives to within three degrees of relationship to the traveler (e.g. great-grandparents and second cousins).

Section 622 of Division D would prohibit funds in the Act from being used to administer, implement, or enforce language added to the Cuban embargo regulations on February 25, 2005 requiring that U.S. agricultural exporters to Cuba must be paid in cash for their goods before the goods leave U.S. ports. Prior to the February 2005 change, the prior practice was for U.S. agricultural exporters to be paid in cash for their goods (as required under the Trade Sanctions and Export Enhancement Act), but before the actual delivery of the goods to Cuba.

Division H (Department of State, Foreign Operations, and Related Programs Appropriations Act, 2009) has two provisions related to Cuba. Section 7005 prohibits foreign assistance to the government of Cuba. Section 7015(f) provides that no funds appropriated for foreign assistance shall be obligated or expended for Cuba except as provided through the regular notification procedures of the Committees on Appropriations.

Legislation in the 110th Congress

Approved Measures

P.L. 110-161 (H.R. 2764). FY2008 Consolidated Appropriations Act. H.R. 2764 was originally introduced and reported by the House Committee on Appropriations (H.Rept. 110-197) on June 18, 2007 as the FY2008 State, Foreign Operations, and Related Agencies Appropriations Act. The House passed (241-178) the measure on June 22, 2007. The Senate Appropriations Committee reported the bill on July 10, 2007 (S.Rept. 110-128), and the Senate passed (81-12) it on September 6, 2007. On December 17, 2007, H.R. 2764 subsequently became the vehicle for the FY2008 Consolidated Appropriations Act, which included 11 FY2008 appropriations measures. President Bush signed the measure into law on December 26, 2007.

As signed into law, Division J of the Consolidated Appropriations Act covers State Department, Foreign Operations, and Related Agencies appropriations. The law has the following Cuba provisions:

- Similar to previous years, Section 607 of Division J prohibits direct funding for Cuba. This provision had been included in both the House and Senate versions of the bill.
- Section 620 of Division J adds Cuba to the list of countries requiring a special notification to the Appropriations Committees for funds obligated or expended under the act. This provision had been included in the Senate version of the bill.
- Section 691(b) of Division J provides that Cubans who supported an anti-Castro guerrilla group in the 1960s known as the Alzados are eligible for U.S. refugee status. The Senate version of the bill had included this provision.
- As set forth in the joint explanatory statement, the measure provides $45.7 million in ESF for Cuba democracy programs as requested by the Administration. Both the House- and Senate-passed versions of H.R. 2764 fully funded the Administration's request for $45.7 million in ESF for Cuba democracy programs. The House committee-reported bill would have provided $9 million in ESF for such programs, but during June 21, 2007, floor consideration, the House approved H.Amdt. 351 (Diaz-Balart) by a vote of 254-170 that increased ESF by $36.7 million in order to fully fund the Administration's request. The Senate Appropriations Committee report to the bill would have provided $15 million in ESF for Cuba democracy programs, but during September 6, 2007, floor consideration, the Senate approved S.Amdt. 2694 (Martinez) by voice vote that increased funding for Cuba democracy programs by $30.7 million to fully fund the Administration's request.
- As set forth in the joint explanatory statement, the measure provides $33.681 million for Radio and TV Marti broadcasting to Cuba, $5.019 million below the Administration's request of $38.7 million and identical to the amount provided for FY2007. Both the House and Senate committee reports to the bill had recommended $33.681 million for Cuba broadcasting. S.Amdt. 2695 (Martinez), which was withdrawn from consideration on September 6, 2007, would have increased funding by $5.019 million to fully fund the Administration's request.

- The measure does not include contrasting provisions related to counternarcotics assistance for Cuba that were included in the House and Senate versions of the bill. Section 673 of the House bill would have specifically prohibited International Narcotics Control and Law Enforcement (INCLE) assistance to the Cuban government. Section 696 of the Senate bill would have provided $1 million in INCLE assistance for preliminary work by the Department of State, or such other entity as the Secretary of State may designate, to establish cooperation with the Cuban government on counternarcotics matters.

The final enacted measure does not include provisions easing Cuba sanctions that had been included in the House and Senate-committee versions of the FY2008 Financial Services and General Government Appropriations Act or the Senate-committee reported version of the FY2008 Agriculture Appropriations bill.

P.L. 110-96 (S. 1612). International Emergency Economic Powers Enhancement Act. Introduced and reported by the Committee on Banking, Housing, and Urban Affairs on June 13, 2007 (S.Rept. 110-82). Senate approved, amended, by unanimous consent on June 26, 2007. House approved by voice vote October 2, 2007. As approved, the bill amends the International Emergency Economic Powers Act (IEEPA) to increase the potential civil penalty imposed on any person who commits an unlawful act under the act to not exceed the greater of $250,000 (from $50,000) or an amount that is twice the amount of the transaction. The bill also increases a criminal penalty to not more than $1 million and/or 20 years imprisonment.

S.Res. 573 (Martinez). Celebrates Cuba Solidarity Day, recognizes the injustices faced by the Cuban people, and stands in solidarity with the Cuban people as they continue to work towards democratic changes in their homeland. Introduced and passed by the Senate on May 21, 2008, by unanimous consent.

Additional Considered Measures with Cuba Provisions

The following measures that received consideration contained various provisions on Cuba that would have eased U.S. sanctions, but none of these provisions made it into final enacted measures. For a complete listing of additional legislative initiatives on Cuba in the 110th Congress, see CRS Report RL33819, *Cuba: Issues for the 110th Congress.*

H.R. 2419 (Peterson). Farm, Nutrition, and Bioenergy Act of 2007. Introduced May 22, 2007; House passed July 27, 2007. Senate passed December 14, 2007. During House floor consideration on July 27, 2007, the House rejected (182-245) H.Amdt. 707 Rangel, that would have clarified the meaning of "payment of cash in advance" for the sale of agricultural commodities to Cuba; authorized direct transfer between U.S. and Cuban financial institutions for a product authorized for sale under the Trade Sanctions Reform and Export Enhancement Act of 2000; and would have authorized the issuance of U.S. visas for Cubans to conduct activities, including phytosanitary inspections, related to the export of U.S. agricultural goods to Cuba.

In the Senate, S.Amdt. 3660 (Baucus), which would have eased restrictions on U.S. agricultural sales to Cuba, was proposed on December 11, 2007, but subsequently withdrawn the same day. Several amendments regarding Cuba were submitted, but never proposed: S.Amdt. 3668 (Baucus), would have eased restrictions on U.S. agricultural exports to Cuba; S.Amdt. 3796 (Nelson, Bill), would have required a certification of certain human rights conditions in Cuba before restrictions on U.S. agricultural exports to Cuba would be eased; S.Amdt. 3792 (Martinez), would have expressed the sense of the Senate regarding the human rights situation in Cuba; and S.Amdt. 3793 (Martinez), would have prevented the easing of restrictions on U.S. agricultural exports to Cuba as long as the country is identified by the Secretary of State as a "state sponsor of terror."

H.R. 2829 (Serrano). FY2008 Financial Services and General Government Appropriations Act. Introduced and reported by House Appropriations Committee (H.Rept. 110-207) June 22, 2007. Reported by Senate Appropriations Committee July 13, 2007 (S.Rept. 110-129). House passed (240-179) June 28, 2007. As approved by the House, Section 903 would have prevented Treasury Department funds from being used to implement a February 2005 regulation that requires the payment of cash in advance prior to the shipment of U.S. agricultural goods to Cuba. The House adopted the provision during June 28, 2007 floor consideration when it approved H.Amdt. 467 (Moran, Kansas) by voice vote. The Senate Appropriations Committee version had a similar provision in Section 619, as well as another provision in Section 620 that would have allowed for travel to Cuba under a general license for the marketing and sale of agricultural and medical goods. The Cuba provisions of both the House and Senate versions of the bill were not included in the final enacted version of the measure, which was included as Division D of the FY2008 Consolidated Appropriations Act (P.L. 110-161, H.R. 2764).

H.R. 3161 (DeLauro)/ S. 1859 (Kohl). FY2008 Agricultural, Rural Development, Food and Drug Administration, and Related Agencies Appropriations Act. H.R. 3161 introduced and reported by House Appropriations Committee July 24, 2007; House passed August 2, 2007. S. 1859 introduced and reported by Senate Appropriations Committee July 24, 2007 (S.Rept. 110- 134). Section 741 of the Senate bill would authorize travel to Cuba under a general license for the marketing and sale of agricultural and medical goods to Cuba. The Cuba provision in the Senate version was not included in the final enacted version of the measure, which was included as Division A of the FY2008 Consolidated Appropriations Act (P.L. 110-161, H.R. 2764).

H.R. 7323 (Serrano). FY2009 Financial Services and General Government Appropriations bill. Introduced and reported by the House Appropriations Committee on December 10, 2008 (H.Rept. 110-920). The committee had approved a draft version of the bill on June 25, 2008. The bill has several provisions that would have eased Cuba sanctions. Section 621 would have prohibited funds in the Act from being used to administer, implement, or enforce new language in the Cuban embargo regulations added on February 25, 2005 (31CFR Part 5 15.533) that requires that U.S. agricultural exports to Cuba must be paid for before they leave U.S. ports. Section 622 would have allowed for family travel once a year (instead of the current restriction of once every three years). Section 623 would have expanded family travel to visit an aunt, uncle, niece, nephew, or first cousin (instead of the current restriction limiting such travel to visit a spouse, child, grandchild, parent, grandparent, or sibling.) The report to the bill would require the Treasury Department's Office of Foreign Assets Control (OFAC) to provide detailed information on OFAC's Cuba-related licensing and enforcement actions. None of these provisions were included in the Consolidated Appropriations Act for FY2009 (P.L. 110-329) that provided funding until March 6, 2009.

S. 3001(Levin). Duncan Hunter National Defense Authorization Act for FY2009. **S.Amdt. 5581 (Dodd)**, submitted on September 15, 2008, would, for a 180-day period: allow unrestricted family travel; ease restrictions on remittances by removing the limit and allowing any American to send remittances to Cuba; expand the list of allowable items that may be included in gift parcels; and allow for unrestricted U.S. cash sales of food, medicines, and relief supplies to Cuba. The amendment was not considered and therefore not included in the final bill.

S. 3260 (Durbin). Financial Services and General Government Appropriations Act, 2009. Introduced and reported by Senate Appropriations Committee (S.Rept. 110-417) on July 14, 2008. Includes provisions easing restrictions on payment terms for the sale of agricultural goods to Cuba (section 618), travel relating to the commercial sale of agricultural and medical goods (section 619), and family travel (section 620). None of these provisions were included in the Consolidated Appropriations Act for FY2009 (P.L. 110-329) that provided funding until March 6, 2009.

S. 3288 (Leahy). Department of State, Foreign Operations, and Related Programs Appropriations Act, 2009. Introduced and reported by Senate Appropriations Committee (S.Rept. 110-425) July 18, 2008. Includes several Cuba provisions: section 706 continues a prohibition on assistance to Cuba, unless the President determines that it is in the national interest of the United States; section 719 continues the provision from FY2008 that requires that any assistance for Cuba go through the regular notification procedures of the Committees on Appropriations; section 779 provides for $1 million for preliminary work by the Department of State, or other entity designated by the Secretary of State, to establish cooperation with appropriate Cuban agencies on counternarcotics matters, although the money would not be available if the Secretary certifies that Cuba 1) does not have in place procedures to protect against the loss of innocent life in the air and on the ground in connection with the interdiction of illegal drugs; and 2) there is credible evidence of involvement of the government of Cuba in drug trafficking during the preceding 10 years. The Senate Appropriations Committee report to the bill recommended full funding for the Administration's requests of $34.392 million for Cuba broadcasting and $20 million in ESF for Cuba democracy programs, and called for the State Department and USAID to conduct regular evaluations to ensure the cost effectiveness of the programs.

S. 3289 (Kohl). Agriculture, Rural Development, Food and Drug Administration, and Related Agencies Appropriations Act, 2008. Introduced and reported by Senate Appropriations Committee (S.Rept. 110-426) July 21, 2008. Includes a provision (section 737) that would ease restrictions on travel to Cuba for the sale of agricultural and medical goods. This provision was not included in the Consolidated Appropriations Act for FY2009 (P.L. 110-329) that provided funding until March 6, 2009.

For Additional Reading

Active CRS Reports

CRS Report R40 139, *Closing the Guantanamo Detention Center: Legal Issues*, by Michael John Garcia et al.

CRS Report RL3 1139, *Cuba: U.S. Restrictions on Travel and Remittances*, by Mark P. Sullivan.

CRS Report RS22742, *Cuba's Political Succession: From Fidel to Raul Castro*, by Mark P. Sullivan.

CRS Report RL34523, *Financial Services and General Government (FSGG): FY2009 Appropriations*, coordinated by Garrett Hatch.

CRS Report RS22094, *Lawsuits Against State Supporters of Terrorism: An Overview*, by Jennifer K. Elsea.

CRS Report RL3 1258, *Suits Against Terrorist States by Victims of Terrorism*, by Jennifer K. Elsea.

CRS Report RL32014, *WTO Dispute Settlement: Status of U.S. Compliance in Pending Cases*, by Jeanne J. Grimmett.

Archived CRS Reports

CRS Report RS20450, *The Case of Elian Gonzalez: Legal Basics*, by Larry M. Eig.

CRS Report RL33622, *Cuba's Future Political Scenarios and U.S. Policy Approaches*, by Mark P. Sullivan.

CRS Report RL3225 1, *Cuba and the State Sponsors of Terrorism List*, by Mark P. Sullivan

CRS Report RL338 19, *Cuba: Issues for the 110th Congress*, by Mark P. Sullivan.

CRS Report RL32730, *Cuba: Issues for the 109th Congress*, by Mark P. Sullivan.

CRS Report RL3 1740, *Cuba: Issues for the 108th Congress*, by Mark P. Sullivan.

CRS Report RL30806, *Cuba: Issues for the 107th Congress*, by Mark P. Sullivan and Maureen Taft-Morales.

CRS Report RL30628, *Cuba: Issues and Legislation In the 106th Congress*, by Mark P. Sullivan and Maureen Taft-Morales.

CRS Report RL30386, Cuba-U.S. Relations: Chronology of Key Events 1959-1999, by Mark P. Sullivan.

CRS Report RS20468, *Cuban Migration Policy and Issues*, by Ruth Ellen Wasem.

CRS Report RL33499, *Exempting Food and Agriculture Products from U.S. Economic Sanctions: Status and Implementation*, by Remy Jurenas.

CRS Report RS22094, *Lawsuits Against State Supporters of Terrorism: An Overview*, by Jennifer K. Elsea.

CRS Report RL32826, *The Medical Device Approval Process and Related Legislative Issues,* by Erin D. Williams.

CRS Report 94-636, *Radio and Television Broadcasting to Cuba: Background and Issues Through 1994*, by Susan B. Epstein and Mark P. Sullivan.

CRS Report RS21764, *Restricting Trademark Rights of Cubans: WTO Decision and Congressional Response*, by Margaret Mikyung Lee.

End Notes

1 For more on Cuba's political succession, see CRS Report RS22742, *Cuba's Political Succession: From Fidel to Raul Castro*, by Mark P. Sullivan.

2 Daniel Dombey, Richard Lapper, and Andrew Ward, "A Family Business, Cuban-Americans Look Beyond the Havana Handover," Financial Times, February 27, 2008.

3 Pablo Bachelet, "New Cuban Leader Adds Military Loyalists to Team," *Miami Herald*, February 25, 2008.

4 "Cuba: Full Text of Raúl Castro's National Assembly Address," *Cubavisión*, Havana (as translated by Open Source Center) February 24, 2008.

5 "Text of Fidel Castro's Online Essay," *Associated Press Newswires*, January 22, 2009.

6 Frances Robles, "Raúl Castro May Usher in More Economic Reforms," *Miami Herald*, January 15, 2009.

7 For further discussion of potential Cuban political scenarios in the aftermath of Fidel Castro's stepping down from power in 2006 because of poor health, see CRS Report RL3 3622, *Cuba's Future Political Scenarios and U.S. Policy Approaches*, by Mark P. Sullivan.

8 Organization of American States, Inter-American Commission on Human Rights, "Annual Report of the IACHR 2007," December 29, 2007, "Chapter IV, Cuba" available at http://www.cidh.org/annualrep/2007eng/Chap.4b.htm.

9 Comision Cubana de Derechos Humanos y Reconciliacion Nacional, "Cuba en el año 2009: la situacíon de derechos civiles, políticos y económicos," February 2, 2009.

10 Anita Snow, "Cuban Rights Group: Political Prisoners Down, But Brief Detentions of Activists Up," *Associated Press Newswires*, February 2, 2009; "Cuba Has Fewer Political Prisoners, Report Says," *Reuters News*, February 2, 2009; and Isabel Sanchez, "Cuba's Raúl Castro Marks 100 Days in Power," *Agence France-Presse*, June 2, 2008.

11 James C. McKinley, Jr, "Cuban Signs Rights Pacts That It Long Had Fought," *New York Times*, March 1, 2008.

12 Frances Robles, "Cuban Police Are Detaining Activists Prior to Human Rights Day," *Miami Herald*, December 11, 2008.

13 The website of the Damas de Blanco is available at http://www.damasdeblanco.com/.

14 Frances Robles, "Jailed Cuban Journalist Wins Prize," *Miami Herald*, December 5, 2008; and "Cuba's Repression," *Miami Herald*, November 24, 2008.

15 Marco Sibaja, "Raul Castro Offers To Free Dissidents in Exchange for Alleged Cuban Spies Jailed in U.S.," *Associated Press Newswires*, December 18, 2008.

16 For further information, see the website of Oswaldo Payá, at http://www.oswaldopaya.org/es/.

17 "Text of Jimmy Carter's Speech, Broadcast Live to Cuban People," Associated Press, May 15, 2002.

18 "Cuba Country Report," *Economist Intelligence Unit*, February 2009.

19 Frances Robles, "Venezuelan Oil Subsidies to Cuba Balloon," *Miami Herald*, August 2, 2007.

20 "Cuba Country Report," *Economist Intelligence Unit*, February 2009.

21 "Infant Mortality, 5.3 in 2007!" *Granma Internacional*, January 4, 2008.

22 Larry Luxner, "New Decree Limits Dollar Transactions as Cuba Tightens Controls Once Again," *CubaNews*, April 2004.

23 Larry Luxner, "Cuba's 'Convertible Peso' No Longer Linked to U.S. Dollar," *CubaNews*, April 2005, p. 3.

24 Manuel Roig-Franzia, "Cuba's Call for Economic Detente," *Washington Post,* July 27, 2007.

25 Frances Robles, "Cubans Urged to Vent Views," *Miami Herald*, October 2, 2007.

26 "Cuba: Full Text of Raúl Castro's National Assembly Address," *Cubavisión*, Havana (as translated by Open Source Center) February 24, 2008.

27 Marc Frank, "Raúl Castro Overhauls Cuba's Farm Bureaucracy," *Reuters News*, May 1, 2008.

28 U.S. Department of State, "Country Reports on Human Rights Practices 2007, Cuba," March 11, 2008.

29 "Cuba: Raúl Castro's 26 July Rebellion Day Speech," Havana Cubavisión (Open Source Center), July 26, 2006.

30 "Cuba: Text of Raúl Castro's 11 July National Assembly Speech," Havana Cubavisión (Open Source Center), July 11, 2008.

[31] "Cuba: Bringing Cuba in from the cold," *Latin American Regional Report, Caribbean & Central America*, December 2008.
[32] U.S. Department of State, "Commission for Assistance to a Free Cuba," White House Fact Sheet, December 8, 2003.
[33] U.S. Department of State, Second Report of the Commission for Assistance to a Free Cuba, Briefing, July 10, 2006.
[34] Nicholas Kralev, "Bush OKs Initiative to Support Opposition," *Washington Times*, July 11, 2006.
[35] Frances Robles and Pablo Bachelet, "Plan for Change in Cuba Gets OK," *Miami Herald,* July 11, 2006.
[36] Miriam Leiva, "We Cubans Must Decide," *Miami Herald*, July 15, 2006.
[37] U.S. Department of State, "Secretary of State Condoleezza Rice Message to the People of Cuba," August 4, 2006.
[38] "No Enemy Can Defeat Us," interview of Raúl Castro by Laszar Barredo Medina, *Diario Granma,* August 18, 2006.
[39] U.S. Department of State, "U.S. Policy Toward Cuba," Thomas Shannon, Assistant Secretary for Western Hemisphere Affairs, August 23, 2006.
[40] "English Transcript of Raul Castro's Speech," *Miami Herald*, December 2, 2006.
[41] Frances Robles, "Raúl Again Offers 'Olive Branch' to U.S.," *Miami Herald,* July 27, 2007; "U.S. Government Rejects Dialogue with Cuba," *EFE*, July 27, 2007.
[42] White House, Office of the Press Secretary, "President Bush Addresses the United Nations General Assembly," September 25, 2007.
[43] U. S . Department of Commerce, "Commerce Secretary Carlos M. Gutierrez Remarks at the Heritage Foundation," September 17, 2007.
[44] White House, "President Bush Discusses Cuba Policy," October 24, 2007.
[45] White House, "President Bush Delivers Remarks on Cuba," March 7, 2008.
[46] "Text of Bush Speech to Council of the Americas," *Miami Herald*, May 9, 2008.
[47] White House, "President Bush Discusses Cuba, Marks Day of Solidarity," May 21, 2008.
[48] "Remarks of Senator Barack Obama, Renewing U.S. Leadership in the Americas," May 23, 2008, and "Renewing U.S. Leadership in the Americas," Factsheet, June 6, 2008, BarackObama.com
[49] U.N. Office for the Coordination of Humanitarian Affairs (OCHA), "Situation Report 17 – Caribbean Hurricane Season," September 22, 2008.
[50] ""Paloma Brings 2008 Hurricane Season to a Close; Damages Exceed $10 Billion,"," *CubaNews*, December 2008.
[51] USAID, Bureau for Democracy, Conflict, and Humanitarian Assistance (DCHA), Office of U.S. Foreign Disaster Assistance (OFDA), "Latin America and the Caribbean – Hurricane Season 2008, Fact Sheet #3, FY2008," September 10, 2008.
[52] Frances Robles, "Cuba Rejects U.S. Supplies, Asks for Suspension of Trade Embargo," *Miami Herald*, September 16, 2008.
[53] Frances Robles, "U.S. Offers $6.3M in Construction Materials to Cuba," *Miami Herald*, September 22, 2008; Joshua Partlow, "Hurricanes Shift Debate on Embargo Against Cuba," *Washington Post*, September 24, 2008.
[54] U.S. Department of State, "Humanitarian Assistance to the Cuban People Following Hurricanes Gustav and Ike," September 15, 2008.
[55] Cuban Ministry of Foreign Affairs, "Cuba Asks Washington to Lift Commercial Restrictions," September 11, 2008; and "Statement by the Ministry of Foreign Affairs," September 6, 2008.
[56] Karen DeYoung, "U.S. Urges Cuba to Accept Aid; Storm Relief Would Be Sent Directly to Havana Government," *Washington Post*, September 16, 2008.
[57] In June 2004, the Department of Commerce's Bureau of Industry and Security (BIS) published changes to the Export Administration Regulations that placed new limits on gift parcels sent to Cuba. This included prohibiting the inclusion of previously-allowed items such as seeds, clothing, personal hygiene items, veterinary medicines and supplies, fishing equipment and supplies, and soap-making equipment. (*Federal Register*, June 22, 2004, pp. 34565-34567).
[58] Oscar Corral, "Is Santería Used as Ploy to Skirt Travel Rules?," *Miami Herald*, February 27, 2005.
[59] Oscar Corral, "Feds Lay Down the Law on Cuba to Travel Agents," *Miami Herald*, April 29, 2006; Pablo Bachelet, "New Rules Impede Religious Travel," *Miami Herald*, March 16, 2006.
[60] U.S. Department of Agriculture, Foreign Agricultural Service, Office of Global Analysis, "Cuba's Food & Agriculture Situation Report," March 2008.
[61] World Trade Atlas, which uses Department of Commerce Statistics.
[62] U.S. Department of the Treasury, Testimony of Robert Werner, Director, OFAC, before the House Committee on Agriculture, March 16, 2005.
[63] Christopher S. Rugaber, "Treasury Clarifies Cuba Farm Export Rule, and Baucus Relents on Nominees," *International Trade Reporter*, August 4, 2005.
[64] "Ag Groups Split Over Trade With Cuba," *Congress Daily AM*, National Journal, February 11, 2003.
[65] "Farm Equipment Exports Likely to Face Tough Opposition from White House, Congress," *Cuba Trader*, Vol. III, No. 7, February 17, 2003.

[66] For additional information, see CRS Report RS2 1764, *Restricting Trademark Rights of Cubans: WTO Decision and Congressional Response*, by Margaret Mikyung Lee.

[67] "U.S., EU Agree on Deadline for Complying with Section 211 WTO Finding," *Inside U.S. Trade*, April 12, 2002.

[68] "Japan, EU Suspend WTO Retaliation Against U.S. in Two Cases," *Inside U.S. Trade*, July 15, 2005.

[69] "PTO Cancels Cuban 'Havana Club' Mark; Bacardi Set to Sell Rum Under Same Mark," *International Trade Daily*, August 10, 2006.

[70] Brian Lehman, testimony before the Senate Committee on the Judiciary, hearing on "An Examination of Section 211 of the Omnibus Appropriations Act of 1998," July 13, 2004.

[71] "USA-Engage Joins Cuba Fight," *Cuba Trader*, April 1, 2002.

[72] U.S. Energy Information Administration , "Country Analysis Briefs: Caribbean," September 2007; U.S. Geological Survey, "Assessment of Undiscovered Oil and Gas Resources of the North Cuban Basin, Cuba, 2004," Fact Sheet 2005-3009, February 2005.

[73] Jeff Franks, "Cuba Oil Claims Raise Eyebrows in Energy World," October 24, 2008; and Larry Luxner, "Cuba May have 20 Billion Barrels of Oil But Cash Crunch Threatens Investment," *CubaNews*, November 2008.

[74] Jorge Piñon, "Cuba's Energy Future," Canadian Foundation for the Americas, *FocalPoint*, April 2007, Vol. 6, No. 3; "PetroVietnam Gets Go-Ahead to Explore Seven Cuban Oil Fields," *Dow Jones International News*, November 20, 2007; and Larry Luxner, "Cuba May have 20 Billion Barrels of Oil But Cash Crunch Threatens Investment," *CubaNews*, November 2008.

[75] Domingo Amuchastegui, "Cuban Again Invites U.S. Oil Giants to Invest in Oil Sector," *CubaNews*, May 2007.

[76] Lesley Clark and Erika Bolstad, "China-Cuba Rumors Fuel Renewed Offshore Drilling Debate, Rumors of China Drilling in Cuban Waters Are Rallying Support for Drilling off Florida's Coast, But Experts Say They're Untrue," *Miami Herald*, June 12, 2008.

[77] Frances Robles, "Drug-Trafficking at 11-Year Low, Cuba Says," *Miami Herald*, March 3, 2007; U.S. Department of State, International Narcotics Control Strategy Report, March 2007, p. 188.

[78] On March 12, 2002, Cuba's Ministry of Foreign Affairs and the Cuban Interests Section in Washington delivered three diplomatic notes to the U.S. Interests Section in Havana and the State Department in Washington proposing agreements on drug interdiction, terrorism, and migration issues. See "Statement from the Ministry of Foreign Affairs: Prominent Drug Trafficker Arrested in our Country," Information Office, Cuban Interests Section, March 17, 2002; "Cuba Offers to Sign Anti-Drug Pact," *Miami Herald*, April 8, 2006.

[79] Anthony Boadle, "U.S. Thanks Cuba, But Declines Anti-Drug Accord," Reuters, March 19, 2002.

[80] U.S. Department of State, Release of the 2007 International Narcotics Control Strategy Report, Anne W. Patterson, Assistant Secretary of State for International Narcotics and Law Enforcement Affairs, On-The-Record Briefing, March 1, 2007.

[81] "White House Office of National Drug Control Policy Director Waters Holds News Briefing on Emerging Transatlantic Drug Threats at the Foreign Press Center," *Newsmakers Transcripts, CQ.com*, April 28, 2008.

[82] José Manuel Calvo, "Thomas Shannon Secretario de Estado adjunto para Latinoamérica: "Sería un acuerdo contra el narcotráfico entre Cuba y EE UU," *El País*, January 11, 2009.

[83] For further information, see CRS Report RL32251, *Cuba and the State Sponsors of Terrorism List*, by Mark P. Sullivan.

[84] Patricia Grogg, "Cuba: Government Deports U.S. Citizen Charged with Child Abuse," *Inter Press Service*, June 16, 2008.

[85] Jay Weaver, "Fugitives Flee South Florida with Medicare Millions," *Miami Herald*, January 2, 2009.

[86] Frances Robles, "An Old Foe of Castro Looks Back on His Fight," *Miami Herald*, September 4, 2003.

[87] Alfonso Chardy and Nancy San Martin, "Lawyer Expects Posada to Show Soon," *Miami Herald*, April 14, 2005.

[88] Ann Louise Bardach, "Our Man's in Miami. Patriot or Terrorist?," *Washington Post*, April 17, 2005.

[89] Although Posada was acquitted by a military court, a higher court ordered a new civilian trial. Reportedly a first set of prosecutors recommended against charging Posada, but a second set of prosecutors took the case to trial, and Posada escaped during that time in 1985. See Oscar Corral, "Debate Focuses on Escape," *Miami Herald*, June 19, 2005.

[90] Oscar Corral and Alfonso Chardy, "Victim's Kin Oppose Posada Bid for Asylum," *Miami Herald*, May 7, 2005.

[91] Department of Homeland Security, Office of Public Affairs, Statement, May 17, 2005.

[92] Alicia Caldwell, "Judge Says Cuban Militant Can't Be Deported to Venezuela," *Associated Press*, September 28, 2005.

[93] Oscar Corral, "Cuban Exile Militant Luis Posada Denied Release," *Miami Herald*, March 22, 2006.

[94] Alfonso Chardy and Jay Weaver, "Posada a Target of New Federal Probes," *Miami Herald*, November 12, 2006, and "Grand Jury Indicts Cuban Exile Militant Luis Posada Carriles," *Miami Herald*, January 12, 2007.

[95] Alfonso Chardy, Oscar Corral, and Jay Weaver, "FBI, Cuba Cooperating on Posada," *Miami Herald*, May 3, 2007; "U.S., Cuba Unite to Investigate Former CIA Op," National Public Radio, Morning Edition, May 4, 2007.

[96] Carol J. Williams, "Pressure Grows to Prosecute Cuban Exile," *Los Angeles Times*, May 10, 2007.

[97] The federal prosecutors' brief is available at http://media 5CA_07- 50737_electronic_copy. source.prod_affiliate.56.pdf.

[98] Michael Kunzelman, "Appeals Court Hears Cuban Militant's Immigration Case," *Associated Press*, June 4, 2008.
[99] See USAID's Cuba program website: http://www.usaid.gov/locations/latin_america_caribbean/country/cuba/.
[100] U.S. Government Accountability Office, U.S. Democracy Assistance for Cuba Needs Better Management and Oversight, GAO-07-147, November 2006.
[101] Oscar Corral, "Federal Program to Help Democracy in Cuba Falls Short of Mark," *Miami Herald*, November 14, 2006, and "Is U.S. Aid Reaching Castro Foes?" *Miami Herald*, November 15, 2006.
[102] Alfonso Chardy and Pablo Bachelet, "Cuban Exile Activist Felt 'Betrayal' by Employees," *Miami Herald,* April 24, 2008.
[103] Jesse J. Holland, "Former Bush Aide Pleads Guilty to Stealing from Anti-Castro Cuban Democracy Advocates," *Associated Press Newswires*, December 19, 2008.
[104] Frances Robles, "Hold on Funds for Cuba Democracy Project Lifted," *Miami Herald*, July 23, 2008.
[105] U.S. Government Accountability Office, *Foreign Assistance: Continued Efforts Needed to Strengthen USAID's Oversight of U.S. Democracy Assistance for Cuba*, GAO-09-165, November 2008.
[106] Alfonso Chardy, "Exile Group: Not Enough Money Getting to Cuban Dissidents," *Miami Herald*, May 15, 2008; Cuban American National Foundation, "Findings and Recommendations on the Most Effective Use of USAID-CUBA Funds Authorized by Section 109(a) of the Cuban Liberty and Democratic Solidarity (Helms-Burton) Act of 1996," March 2008.
[107] Christina Hoag, "Radio, TV Martí To Be Aired Locally," *Miami Herald*, December 19, 2006.
[108] Oscar Corral, "Radio, TV Martí Face Another Government Audit," *Miami Herald*, December 18, 2006, and "Problems Dog Broadcaster," *Miami Herald*, December 19, 2006.
[109] Jay Weaver, "TV Martí Executive Admits Taking Kickbacks," *Miami Herald*, February 14, 2007.
[110] See the following reports and audits: U.S. General Accounting Office (GAO), Broadcasts to Cuba, TV Marti Surveys are Flawed, GAO/NSIAD-90-252, August 1990; U.S. GAO, TV Marti, Costs and Compliance with Broadcast Standards and International Agreements, GAO/NSIAD-92-199, May 1992; U.S. GAO, Letter to Hon. Howard L. Berman and Hon. John F. Kerry regarding Radio Marti broadcast standards, GAO/NSIAD-93-126R, February 17, 1993; Advisory Panel on Radio and TV Marti, Report of the Advisory Panel on Radio and TV Marti, Three Volumes, March 1994; U.S. GAO, Radio Marti, Program Review Processes Need Strengthening, GAO/NSIAD-94-265, September 1994; U.S. GAO, U.S. Information Agency, Issues Related to Reinvention Planning in the Office of Cuba Broadcasting, GAO/NSIAD-96-1 10, May 1996; U.S. Department of State, Office of the Inspector General, Review of Polices and Procedures for Ensuring that Radio Marti Broadcasts Adhere to Applicable Requirements, 99-IB-010, June 1999; U.S. Department of State and the Broadcasting Board of Governors, Office of Inspector General, Review of the Effectiveness and Implementation of Office of Cuba Broadcasting's New Program Initiatives, Report No. IBO-A03-01, January 2003, and Report of Inspection, Office of Cuba Broadcasting, Report No. ISP-IB 07-35, June 2007.
[111] The State Department originally issued a two-page summary of the report on its website on June 5, 2007, and pointed out that the full report received only "limited official distribution." On July 31, 2007, the State Department issued the entire 43-page report on its website, with certain sections redacted. That version is available at http://oig.state.gov/lbry/.
[112] Pablo Bachelet, "Martí Extending Its Reach, U.S. Says," *Miami Herald*, June 20, 2007.
[113] Vanessa Bauza, "TV Martí Signal Weak in Cuba, Broadcast Specialist Says," *South Florida Sun-Sentinel*, July 31, 2007.
[114] Laura Wides-Muñoz, "Despite Expenditures, TV Martí Still Tough to See in Cuba," Associated Press, July 30, 2007.
[115] U.S. Government Accountability Office, "Broadcasting to Cuba, Weaknesses in Contracting Practices Reduced Visibility into Selected Award Decisions," GAO-08-764, July 2008.
[116] U.S. Government Accountability Office, "Broadcasting to Cuba, Actions Are Needed to Improve Strategy and Operations," GAO-09-127, January 2009.
[117] U.S. Coast Guard, Alien Migrant Interdiction, Coast Guard Office of Law Enforcement, "Total Interdictions, Fiscal Year 1982 to Present," October 15, 2008.
[118] Diego Cevallos, "Migration: More and More Cubans Entering U.S. Through Mexico," *Inter Press Service News Agency*, June 17, 2008.
[119] Laura Morales, "Exiles Urged to Stem Tide of Cubans," *Miami Herald*, December 29, 2007.
[120] Department of Homeland Security, "DHS Announces Additional Measures to Combat Alien Smuggling of Cubans," and "USCIS Will Further Strengthen Measures that Support the Reunification of Families Separated by the Castro Regime," Press Releases, August 11, 2006; Pablo Bachelet, "U.S. Program for Defecting Cuban Doctors a Success," *Miami Herald*, March 12, 2007.
[121] U.S. Department of State. State Department Regular Briefing, Richard Boucher. January 7, 2004.
[122] "Migration Talks Cancelled," *Miami Herald*, January 8, 2004.
[123] "Cuba Would Hand Over Escapees, Raúl Castro Says," *Miami Herald*, January 20, 2002.
[124] For information on terrorist suspects held at Guantanamo, see CRS Report RL3 1367, *Treatment of "Battlefield Detainees" in the War on Terrorism*, by Jennifer K. Elsea; and CRS Report RS22 173, *Detainees at Guantanamo Bay*, by Jennifer K. Elsea.

[125] Ana Radelat, "Cuba Turns Up Rhetoric on Guantanamo as UN Condemns Human Rights Abuses," *CubaNews*, April 2005.

In: Politics and Economics of Latin America. Volume 6 ISBN: 978-1-61668-014-5
Editor: Samantha R. Dawes

Chapter 2

CHINA'S FOREIGN AID ACTIVITIES IN AFRICA, LATIN AMERICA, AND SOUTHEAST ASIA*

Thomas Lum, Hannah Fische, Julissa Gomez-Granger and Anne Leland

SUMMARY

In the past several years, the People's Republic of China (PRC) has bolstered its diplomatic presence and garnered international goodwill through its financing of infrastructure and natural resource development projects, assistance in the carrying out of such projects, and large economic investments in many developing countries. This chapter examines China's economic impact in three regions — Africa, Latin America (Western Hemisphere), and Southeast Asia — with an emphasis on bilateral foreign assistance.

China's foreign aid is difficult to quantify. The PRC government does not release or explain Chinese foreign aid statistics and much of PRC foreign aid does not appear to be accounted for in the scholarly literature on foreign aid. Some Chinese foreign assistance partially resembles *official development assistance* (ODA) as defined by the Organization for Economic Cooperation and Development (OECD), but in other aspects shares characteristics of foreign investment. In terms of development grants, the primary form of assistance provided by major OECD countries, China is a relatively small source of global aid. However, when China's concessional loans and state-sponsored or subsidized overseas investments are included, the PRC becomes a major source of foreign aid.

This chapter is based on research done by the New York University Robert F. Wagner Graduate School of Public Service in 2007-2008. The Wagner School study, while not comprehensive, suggests a dramatic increase in PRC foreign aid and related activity. According to the research, which is largely based upon news reports of Chinese foreign economic activity, PRC foreign assistance and government-supported economic projects in

* This is an edited, reformatted and augmented version of a CRS Report for Congress publication dated February 2009.

Africa, Latin America, and Southeast Asia grew from less than $1 billion in 2002 to $27.5 billion in 2006 and $25 billion in 2007. Aid and related investment to Africa showed the most significant increase. These totals, however, should be interpreted with caution. Some aggregate values may be inflated: Some PRC loans or aid pledges may not have been fulfilled and some aid pledges that include multiple projects or that span several years may have been counted more than once. Some PRC investment activities may more closely resemble FDI than aid. In other ways, totals may be undervalued, such as when economic projects or data have not been reported or when the values of Chinese materials and labor have not been included.

Overall, China's foreign assistance during the past several years has been driven primarily by Beijing's desire to secure and transport natural resources and secondarily for diplomatic reasons. According to the NYU Wagner School study, during the 2002-2007 period, Africa received the greatest amount of loans and development assistance, followed by Latin America and Southeast Asia. The study suggests that China's foreign aid activities in Africa and Latin America serve the PRC's immediate economic interests, while those in Southeast Asia relate to longer term diplomatic or strategic objectives. In Africa and Southeast Asia, Chinese infrastructure and public works projects constitute the most common form of aid, while in Latin America, where some countries are more developed, PRC-sponsored natural resource development activities are more prominent.

China is fast becoming a top trading partner to Africa and Southeast Asia, and it is second to the United States as a market for Latin American commodities and goods. Although the PRC's aid projects are a highly visible reminder of China's growing "soft power," other countries and regions, such as the European Union, the United States, and Japan, continue to dominate foreign direct investment in Africa, Latin America, and Southeast Asia.

INTRODUCTION

This chapter examines China's aid-related activities in Africa, Latin America, and Southeast Asia.[1] In the past several years, China's growing "soft power" — primarily diplomatic and economic influence in the developing world — has become a concern among many U.S. foreign policy leaders, including Members of Congress.[2] One of the most important ways in which the People's Republic of China (PRC) has bolstered its economic presence and garnered international goodwill has been through its offers of financing or concessional loans for infrastructure projects, large economic investments, and the signing of trade agreements. Many observers have praised

Chinese aid and investment as filling unmet development needs, particularly in countries that have been relatively neglected by major aid donors. Others have criticized China for failing to promote democracy, equitable and sustainable development, and environmental preservation in these countries. Some U.S. policy-makers and others have expressed frustration that because of China's policy of providing foreign assistance without conditions, they are losing the ability to influence the behaviors of aid recipients regarding human rights and economic reforms. Some reports indicate, however, that PRC foreign aid, investment, and trade activities may begin to contract as the global economic crisis unfolds.

MEASURING CHINA'S FOREIGN AID

PRC foreign assistance is difficult to quantify. Still a developing country itself, China appears to administer foreign aid in an ad hoc fashion, without a centralized system, foreign aid agency and mission, or regularized funding schedule.[3] Nor does Beijing publicly release foreign aid-related data. Some analysts surmise that the Chinese leadership is reluctant to be perceived as a major aid donor, since the PRC itself continues to be a recipient of foreign assistance and because the government fears that its citizens may object to lavish spending on economic projects abroad.

Estimates of China's foreign assistance, which consists mainly of concessional or low-interest loans and government-backed or subsidized investments in infrastructure and natural resources, vary widely due to the different definitions of aid. A relatively small portion of Chinese aid includes what typically is characterized as "official development assistance" (ODA) by the world's major aid donors, such as development grants, humanitarian assistance, social welfare programs, and food aid. China also provides relatively little military and security-related assistance. Few of China's foreign aid activities fit the Organization for Economic Co-operation and Development's (OECD) definition of ODA — "flows of official financing to developing countries provided by official agencies which have a clear development or anti-poverty purpose and are at least partially concessional in nature," with a grant element of at least 25%.[4]

China's aid projects to a large extent serve its own development needs, facilitating the export of raw materials to China, and requiring that 50% of project materials and services are to be sourced in the PRC. By contrast, the foreign aid programs of the United States, European countries, and most other major aid donors are not directly or strongly linked to their own economies. Furthermore, they often include objectives or conditions related to political development and democratic reform. Among OECD countries, Japan's history of ODA, with its relatively large loan component (from 60% in the mid-1990s to roughly 25% a decade later),[5] emphasis on infrastructure projects, and links to its own economy, may come closest to providing a model for China's foreign assistance.[6]

China reportedly has taken some tentative steps toward making its foreign aid process more centralized and transparent, coordinating its programs with other aid providers, and offering more development-oriented assistance, while continuing to eschew the label of major ODA donor. The PRC has begun sending abroad "youth volunteers," similar to U.S. Peace Corps volunteers, engaged in teaching and training in such subjects as Chinese language and medicine, computer skills, agricultural technologies, and sports.[7]

Many forms of Chinese foreign assistance that are included in this chapter share only some characteristics with traditional development assistance as provided by major aid donors, and have often been overlooked in the literature on global foreign aid. Although they often do not fit the OECD's narrow definition of development assistance, many of China's economic activities in developing countries are supported by the PRC government and provide benefits to recipient countries that otherwise may not be available. Furthermore, many PRC economic investments abroad can be counted as aid rather than foreign direct investment (FDI) because they are secured by official bilateral agreements, do not impose real financial risks upon the PRC companies involved, or do not result in Chinese ownership of foreign assets. See **Table 1**.

Table 1. Similarities and Differences between OECD-Defined "Official Development Assistance" (ODA) and "Chinese Aid"

	Government to Government	Financing through Development Agency	Strong Links to Donor Country Economy	Concessional or Favorable Lending Terms	Receives Payment of Debt in Kind	Grant Element of at Least 25%	Private or Corporate Financing
OECD Aid Donor	yes [a]	yes	no	yes	no	yes	no
China	yes	no [b]	yes[c]	yes	yes[d]	no	no

Sources: Penny Davies, "China and the End of Poverty in Africa," August 2007; "Building Bridges: China's Growing Role as Infrastructure Financier for Sub-Saharan Africa," The World Bank, No. 5 (2008).

a. Grants may be awarded to NGOs based in either the donor country or recipient country.

b. PRC aid is provided largely in the form of concessional loans administered by the China Eximbank.

c. Aid projects facilitate the export of natural resources and commodities to China and utilize PRC companies, materials, and labor.

d. In some cases, aid recipients make payments on loans from China with oil or minerals.

Many estimates of China's foreign assistance in PRC official publications and in the existing scholarly literature do not appear to capture much of PRC aid activity. The *China Statistical Yearbook 2003-06* reportedly released an annual aid figure of $970 million. According to other sources, annual PRC foreign assistance ranges from $1.5 billion to $2 billion.[8] These figures would place China's aid levels comparable to those of Australia, Belgium, or Denmark.[9] However, many analysts, applying more flexible definitions of foreign aid, consider actual PRC aid numbers to be far higher. Some of the discrepancy may be caused by regarding many Chinese economic activities abroad as foreign investment rather than aid. In 2006 and 2007, according to various sources referring to PRC official statistics, China's annual FDI outflows totaled roughly $21 billion annually.[10] Counting some of these outflows as aid would raise PRC foreign assistance estimates; however, doing so also would lower calculations of China's outward investment levels, which are small compared to those of the United States ($216 billion in 2006).

The NYU Wagner School study on China's foreign aid tabulated PRC foreign assistance and related activities — pledges of aid or loans and government-sponsored investment projects — that had been reported in 62 African, Latin American, and Southeast Asian countries between 2001 and 2008. In 2007, the last full year for which Chinese aid-related activities were examined in the study, the Wagner School research team found projects worth up to $25 billion in aggregate. Of this amount, $16.6 billion, or 66%, was provided in the form of loans (concessional loans or credit lines), $7.2 billion, or 29%, represented state-sponsored investment, and the remaining 5% included grants, debt cancellation or debt relief, and in-kind aid.[11]

Although the NYU Wagner School study strongly indicates that China has been providing significant and growing amounts of economic assistance to developing countries — if not ODA as defined by the OECD — the totals should be interpreted with caution. Some values may be inflated: Many loans represent offers or pledges that may not have been fulfilled; some projects have been cancelled; some aid endeavors involving several activities or taking several years to complete may have been counted more than once; and some PRC investments that were counted as aid may actually be FDI. In other ways, however, totals may be undervalued, such as when projects or data have not been reported or when Chinese materials and labor have not been included.

In terms of official development assistance as defined by the OECD, United States ODA is the largest among OECD member countries, followed by Japan, the United Kingdom, France, and Germany. The United States' foreign operations budget (bilateral development, economic, security, and military assistance, multilateral assistance, and food aid) was estimated at $24 billion in FY2008.[12]

China's Foreign Aid Impact

In addition to their actual monetary value, Chinese assistance and related economic activities often garner appreciation disproportionate to their size, for several reasons:

- They often are made available relatively quickly and easily — without the political, economic, social, and environmental conditions and safeguards and bureaucratic procedures that major OECD aid donors, multilateral financial institutions, and multinational corporations typically impose.[13]
- China often promotes economic projects in countries, areas, and sectors that developed country governments and multinational corporations have avoided because they have determined them to be unfriendly, too arduous, or infeasible.
- Many PRC funded or built public works in foreign countries, such as national cultural centers, stadiums, and highways, are highly visible and provide tangible, short-term benefits.
- Such aid and investment activities are often announced at bilateral summit meetings with great fanfare, powerfully symbolizing the friendship between China and other developing countries.

Major Findings of the NYU Wagner School Study

The NYU Wagner School research may serve as a basis for conducting further research and thinking about U.S. policy responses to China's growing foreign aid and investment. The study's findings are not meant to be exhaustive, but may suggest the broad contours and trajectory of Chinese aid and related activities in Africa, Latin America, and Southeast Asia:

- China's foreign aid is driven primarily by the need for natural resources and secondarily by diplomatic objectives, such as the objectives of isolating Taiwan and garnering support in international organizations such as the United Nations. Beijing also aims to open up foreign markets for Chinese goods and help PRC companies invest, set up manufacturing plants, and develop markets overseas.

- Unlike major aid donors, China lacks a centralized aid agency affiliated with its foreign affairs ministry. PRC assistance consists primarily of concessional loans administered by the Ministry of Commerce through its Department of Aid to Foreign Countries. To lesser extents, the Export-Import Bank of China (Eximbank) the Ministry of Finance, and the Ministry of Foreign Affairs also play roles.
- Reported Chinese aid activities to the three regions grew from $1.5 billion in 2003 to $27.5 billion in 2006 and $25 billion in 2007. Africa received the largest year-on-year increases and showed the clearest growth trend. See **Figure 1** and **Table 2.**
- In terms of financing, the NYU Wagner research team found that most aid to the three regions is provided in the form of state-sponsored investment. During the 2002-2007 period, PRC government-backed investments made up 53% of reported aid activity, concessional loans constituted 42%, and grants and debt cancellations accounted for the remaining 5%. See **Figure 2** and **Table 3.**
- Of the loans, infrastructure projects, and other aid provided by China to the three regions between 2002 and 2007, 44% was allocated to Africa, 36% to Latin America, and 20% to Southeast Asia. See **Table 4**.
- During the same period (2002-2007), 44.5% of aid and investment was directed at the natural resources and agricultural sectors while 43% supported infrastructure development. See **Table 5**.

Table 2. Reported PRC Aid by Year, 2002-2007 (Million US$).

2002 Year	51 Total
2003	1,482
2004	10,485
2005	10,106
2006	27,518
2007	25,098

Source: NYU Wagner School, *Understanding Chinese Foreign Aid: A Look at China's Development Assistance to Africa, Southeast Asia, and Latin America*, April 25, 2008.

Notes: Annual totals represent announced loans and other reported aid and economic projects using PRC financing.

Table 3. Reported PRC Aid by Funding Source and Region, 2002-2007 (Million US$).

Africa			
Govt.-Sponsored Investment	8,042	24,389 Latin America	7,429 Southeast Asia
Concessional Loan	22,379	1,950	7,114
Grant	1,851	421	231
Debt Cancellation	850	0	60
In-kind Aid	21	1	0

Source: NYU Wagner School, *Understanding Chinese Foreign Aid: A Look at China's Development Assistance to Africa, Southeast Asia, and Latin America*, April 25, 2008.

Notes: Annual totals represent announced loans and other reported aid and economic projects using PRC financing.

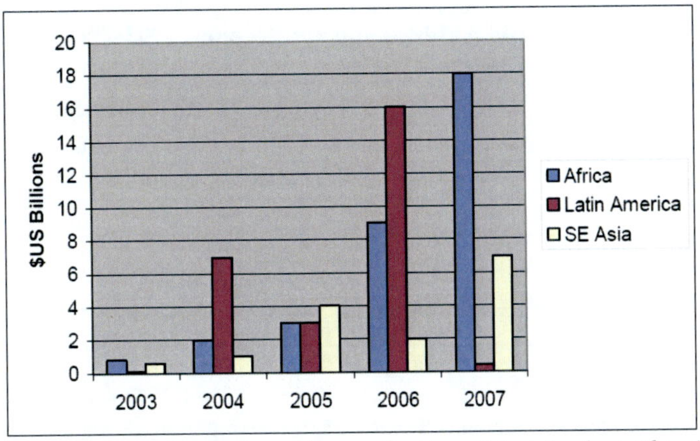

Source: NYU Wagner School, *Understanding Chinese Foreign Aid: A Look at China's Development Assistance to Africa, Southeast Asia, and Latin America*, April 25, 2008.

Notes: Annual totals represent announced loans and other reported aid and economic projects using PRC financing.

Figure 1. Reported PRC Aid by Year and Region, 2003-2007

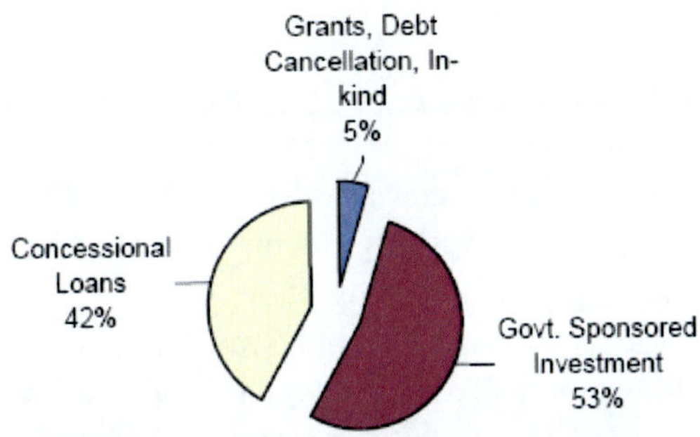

Source: NYU Wagner School, *Understanding Chinese Foreign Aid: A Look at China's Development Assistance to Africa, Southeast Asia, and Latin America*, April 25, 2008.

Notes: Annual totals represent announced loans and other reported aid and economic projects using PRC financing.

Figure 2. Reported PRC Foreign Aid by Funding Source

Table 4. Reported PRC Aid by Year and Region, 2002-2007 (Million US$

	Africa	Latin America	Southeast Asia
2002	10	4	36
2003	838	1	644
2004	2,292	7,000	1,193
2005	2,953	2,931	4,221
2006	9,088	16,425	2,004
2007	17,962	401	6,735

Source: NYU Wagner School, *Understanding Chinese Foreign Aid: A Look at China's Development Assistance to Africa, Southeast Asia, and Latin America*, April 25, 2008.

Notes: Annual totals represent announced loans and other reported aid and economic projects using PRCfinancing.

Table 5. Reported PRC Aid by Type and Region, 2002-2007 (Million US$)

	Africa	Latin America	Southeast Asia
Natural Resources Extraction/Production	9,432	18,585	4,788
Infrastructure/Public Works	17,865	7,535	6,438
Not Specified/Other	5,024	608	2,276
Humanitarian	802	32	159
Military	4	0	170
Technical Assistance	10	1	3

Source: NYU Wagner School, *Understanding Chinese Foreign Aid: A Look at China's Development Assistance toAfrica, Southeast Asia, and Latin America*, April 25, 2008.

Notes: Annual totals represent announced loans and other reported aid and economic projects using PRCfinancing.

REGIONAL HIGHLIGHTS

Africa

In the past several years, China's aid to Africa has grown dramatically. During the 1970s and 1980s, China provided assistance in the form of infrastructure projects, public works, technical and public health assistance, and scholarships to study in China. Its motivations were largely diplomatic: to forge friendships among "non-aligned" nations and to compete with Taiwan (the Republic of China) for recognition. Only four of 48 sub-Saharan African countries (Burkina Faso, Sao Tome, Gambia, and Swaziland) still maintain official relations with Taiwan. In 2007, China reportedly offered Malawi aid and investment worth $6 billion in major economic sectors. In January 2008, Malawi switched diplomatic relations to the PRC. However, in 2008, China reportedly offered Malawi only $287 million in aid.[14] While traditional types of aid activities remain staples of Chinese assistance in the region, many of them now complement much grander development projects that serve China's direct economic interests.[15]

According to some of the more conservative definitions and estimates, China's foreign aid on the continent ranges from roughly $1.4 billion annually to $2.7 billion, with outstanding concessional loans of $8 billion-$9 billion.[16] More inclusive totals from the World Bank and PRC government refer to "infrastructure financing" ($7 billion) and "economic cooperation" ($9.5 billion) in Africa in 2006.[17] In 2007, the China Development Bank reportedly set up a $5 billion China-Africa Development Fund to finance infrastructure, industrial, and agricultural projects.[18] The NYU Wagner School research team found PRC aid and state-sponsored investment projects in Africa reported during the 2002-2007 period that amounted to several billion dollars annually ($6.6 billion on average). These aid activities included financing (concessional loans), grants, debt cancellations, and economic investments. However, as explained above, these totals may be inflated or represent the high end of a possible range of estimates.

The following data from OECD countries provide an indication of ODA levels to Africa. They are not meant to be directly compared to estimates of Chinese assistance to the region, which are based upon different definitions of aid. U.S. assistance to Sub-Saharan Africa, the second-largest regional recipient of U.S. foreign assistance after the Near East and the largest recipient of U.S. development assistance, totaled an estimated $5.2 billion in 2008 and $4.7 billion in 2007.[19] The United States, the United Kingdom, and France are the largest bilateral donors of ODA to Africa, providing $5.8 billion, $5.4 billion, and $5.1 billion, respectively, in assistance in 2006.[20]

Estimates of PRC direct investment in Africa range from under $500 million to roughly $1 billion annually. Historically, Europe (UK, France, and Germany), Japan, and the United States have been the principal sources of FDI on the continent. Some studies indicate that India has more cumulative investment in Africa ($1.8 billion in 2004) than China ($1.3 billion in 2005) and is a major source of infrastructure financing.[21] According to some estimates, in 2005, Chinese FDI flows to Africa totaled $392 million or 3% of total PRC outward investment.[22] Other studies report that China had $2.6 billion in cumulative FDI and over $0.5 billion in annual investment in Africa in 2006. Higher estimates include figures of nearly $1 billion in PRC annual direct investment in Africa during 2000-2006.[23] By contrast, in 2006, the United States reportedly invested $1.5 billion in Africa out of a total of $36 billion in global FDI received by Africa that year.[24] OECD countries reportedly pledged $5 billion in ODA for infrastructure projects in Sub- Saharan Africa in 2006.[25]

China has exerted growing influence as a trading partner. As part of its integrated approach, China's diplomatic outreach to the region is accompanied by aid, investment, and trade. China is Africa's third largest trading partner after the European Union and the United States.[26] PRCAfrica trade reportedly was worth $106.6 billion in 2008 compared to U.S.-Africa trade of $142 billion.[27]

China's aid to Africa is driven largely by its objective of securing access to oil and minerals for its growing economy. African oil reportedly accounts for 80% of China's trade in the region and about one-third of its oil imports.[28] Nearly 70% of PRC infrastructure financing on the continent reportedly is concentrated in Angola, Nigeria, Ethiopia, and Sudan, all of which have oil fields.[29] Angola, Congo, and Sudan have major oil fields and pay for much of their assistance or loans from China with oil. Sudan reportedly sends 60% of its crude oil to China.[30] However, Europe and the United States remain the largest buyers of African petroleum (33% and 36% of Africa's oil exports, respectively).[31] Estimates of China's share of the African oil market range from 10%- 16%, although the PRC reportedly plays a larger role in the continent's minerals markets.[32] See **Table 6**.

China's aid to Africa is dominated by concessional loans and export credits provided through the Ministry of Commerce and Eximbank. PRC loans to Africa, which reportedly grew by 35% annually between 2001 and 2005, have been used chiefly to finance infrastructure projects in over 35 African countries (mainly hydropower and transportation).[33] See **Table 7**. The NYU Wagner School research team compiled a list of PRC aid and related investment projects or offers in Africa reported during the 2002-2007 period. The combined values amounted to $33 billion.[34] In dollar terms, 54% was related to infrastructure and other public works projects, 28.5% to the extraction or production of natural resources, and 2.5% to humanitarian activities, technical assistance, and military assistance (15% was unspecified). In many cases, especially when the recipient country has poor credit, loans are to be repaid in kind (oil or commodities). The China Eximbank reported in 2007 that its outstanding loans to the continent totaled $8 billion-$9 billion.[35] According to the Wagner School study, examples of PRC development and humanitarian aid in the region include the construction of schools and hospitals, medical training and equipment, agricultural technical assistance, food aid, and disaster assistance.

Table 6. Selected African Countries with Large Reported Aid and Investment Projects, 2002-2007

Country	Main Exports to China	Pledged Aid, Loans, Credit Lines, and Investments	Major Types of Financing (as Reported)	Major Types of Projects Financed (as Reported)
Angola [a b c]	oil	$7.4 billion	loans, interest-free loans, credit lines	infrastructure (railways)
Congo (DRC)[a b c]	oil, minerals	$5 billion	loans	infrastructure, mining
Sudan [a b c]	oil	$4.2 billion	investment, loans, grants	oil refining; infrastructure, hydro power, humanitarian
Gabon [d]	oil, minerals	$3 billion	investment, grants	iron ore mining, infrastructure, port facilities, hydro power
Mozambique	wood, ores	$2.4 billion	debt cancellation, concessional loans, grants	dam construction, infrastructure, national stadium
Equatorial Guinea b c	oil	$2 billion	concessional loans, credit lines	not specified
Ethiopia	oil drilling rights	$2 billion (includes 2008 aid of $150 million)	loans, grants, investment	infrastructure, telecommunications, public buildings, hydropower, light industry
Nigeria [a b]	oil	$1.6 billion	debt cancellation, investment, grants	offshore oil development, infrastructure (railways), medical

Source: NYU Wagner School, *Understanding Chinese Foreign Aid: A Look at China's Development Assistance to Africa, Southeast Asia, and Latin America*, April 25, 2008.

a. major African trading partner of China

b. loan payments in oil

c. major African oil supplier of China

d. loan payments in minerals

Table 7. Selected Major PRC Financing and Aid-Related Economic Projects in Africa

Amount	Funding (Year)	Project Type(s)	Country
$5 billion	loan (2007)	transportation infrastructure	Congo
$4 billion	investment (2007)	oil production	Sudan
$3 billion	investment (2006)	port, railway, hydropower, mining (iron)	Gabon
$2.5 billion	loan (credit line) (2007)	unspecified	Angola
$2.3 billion	loan (2006)	hydropower (dam)	Mozambique
$2 billion	loan (credit line) (2006)	unspecified	Equatorial Guinea
$2 billion		uns	

Source: NYU Wagner School, *Understanding Chinese Foreign Aid: A Look at China's Development Assistance to Africa, Southeast Asia, and Latin America*, April 25, 2008.

Latin America

China's growing engagement with Latin America and the Caribbean (the Western Hemisphere) lacks the deep historical ties of its relations with Southeast Asia and legacy of its Cold War friendships in Africa. China's growing interest in the region appears to be principally linked to its objective of gaining broader access to natural resources and agricultural commodities, such as oil, ores, and soybeans. Beijing also aims to fully isolate Taiwan — 12 Latin American and Caribbean nations still maintain diplomatic relations with Taiwan — and bolster China's diplomatic presence in the region. China's recent aid to Costa Rica reportedly was directly linked to the Central American country's establishment of diplomatic relations with the PRC (and termination of relations with Taiwan) in 2007. Other goals include opening up alternative markets and opportunities for Chinese goods and investment. According to many analysts, however, Beijing acknowledges that the United States remains the dominant economic and political influence in the Western Hemisphere.[36]

The PRC is not a major foreign investor in the region. The European Union (EU) is the largest source of FDI in Latin America, with $620 billion invested in the region in 2006, followed by the United States with $350 billion. According to PRC official data, Latin America had received $22 billion in cumulative PRC investment at the end of 2006, about 25% of PRC total overseas investment. However, the vast majority of PRC FDI in the region reportedly goes to off-shore financial havens such as the Cayman Islands and the Virgin Islands, to be reinvested in China (thereby taking advantage of tax breaks for "foreign companies"). When these destinations are excluded, only about $1.9 billion remains.[37] According to some sources, in 2006, PRC direct investment flows to the Western Hemisphere totaled roughly $100 million, less than its outbound investment to Africa ($500 million).[38] Conversely, Latin American companies have made sizable investments in China with $20 billion in cumulative FDI.[39]

China's trade with Latin America grew ten-fold between 2000 and 2007 and reached $142 billion in 2008. China's total trade with the region is only about one-fifth that of the United States ($664 billion in 2008), but growing at a faster rate.[40] The United States reportedly imports 12 times more oil from Venezuela than does China.[41] Nonetheless, China has become an important trading partner to major countries in the region, and is second only to the United States as an importer of commodities and goods from Latin America. China's largest trading partners in the region are Brazil, Mexico, Chile, Argentina, and Peru.[42]

The NYU Wagner School research team compiled a list of PRC aid and related investment projects or offers in the Western Hemisphere reported during the 2002-2007 period. The combined values amounted to $26.7 billion.[43] Over two-thirds of these projects were in natural resource sectors, while 28% were related to infrastructure and public works, 1% involved humanitarian activities and technical assistance, and 2% of aid was unspecified. In the past several years, Chinese humanitarian assistance has included infrastructure repair in Costa Rica, hospitals in Cuba, funding to the Bolivian Red Cross for mudslide victims, and help to people affected by an earthquake in Peru and flood in Uruguay. In 2008, China joined the Inter American Development Bank and committed $350 million for public and private sector projects.[44] The emphasis on natural resources implies a strongly commercial nature to China's aid in Latin America, less oriented toward infrastructure development than China's foreign assistance to Africa and Southeast Asia. See **Table 8** and **Table 9**.

Table 8. Selected Latin American Countries with Large Reported Aid and Investment Projects, 2002-2007

Country	Main Exports to China	Pledged Aid, Loans, Credit Lines, and Investments	Major Types of Financing (as Reported)	Major Types of Projects Financed (as Reported)
Venezuela	oil	$16.4 billion	investment	oil, gas exploration and production; transportation; telecom; light industry
Brazil	iron ore, agricultural commodities, oil	$8.2 billion	investment, loans	infrastructure (ports, aviation, rail)
Chile	minerals, ores	$0.5 billion	investment	natural resources (copper)
Columbia	iron, oil	$0.4 billion	investment	steel,, oil exploration,, mining
Costa Rica	electrical	$0.4 billion	grants, loans	humanitarian, infrastructure

Source: NYU Wagner School, *Understanding Chinese Foreign Aid: A Look at China's Development Assistance to Africa, Southeast Asia, and Latin America*, April 25, 2008.

Table 9. Selected Major PRC Financing and Aid-Related Economic Projects in Latin America

Amount	Funding (Year)	Project Type(s)	Country
$9 billion	investment (2006)	infrastructure (railways), telecom, mining, agriculture	Venezuela
$7 billion	investment (2004)	infrastructure (port, railways, aviation), steel	Brazil
$5 billion	20		Venezuela

Source: NYU Wagner School, *Understanding Chinese Foreign Aid: A Look at China's Development Assistance to Africa, Southeast Asia, and Latin America*, April 25, 2008.

In terms of official development assistance as measured by the OECD, which often refers to different types of aid than that typically provided by China, the EU, the United States, and Japan are the largest providers in the region. U.S. foreign assistance to the Western Hemisphere, including regional assistance, was an estimated $1.46 billion in 2008 and $1.55 billion in 2007.[45]

Southeast Asia

China has become an important source of infrastructure financing in Southeast Asia. While China is not counted as a major regional provider of ODA as defined by the OECD, some reports and observations suggest that the PRC is one of the largest sources of economic assistance in Southeast Asia. Although access to natural resources plays a prominent role in China's engagement in the region, strategic interests are likely to influence China's activities in Southeast Asia to a greater extent than they do in Africa and Latin America. Many of China's aid activities in the region appear to provide relatively greater long-term diplomatic benefits and comparatively few short-term economic ones.

China has a large economic presence in Southeast Asia, owing in part to its proximity and historical ties to the region. Southeast Asia's largest sources of FDI in 2006 (net inflow) were the EU ($13.3 billion), Japan, ($10.8 billion), the United States ($3.8 billion), South Korea ($1 billion), and China ($900 million).[46] The EU, the United States, Japan, and China are the largest trading entities in the region. In 2008, China's trade with the Association of Southeast Asian Nations (ASEAN) countries, at $230 billion, was larger than its trade with Africa ($106 billion) and Latin America ($142 billion).[47]

China and the least developed countries of mainland Southeast Asia are becoming increasingly economically integrated, although each of these countries also has sought to hedge against the PRC's rising influence. China is considered the "primary supplier of economic and military assistance" to Burma (Myanmar), Cambodia, and Laos and provides them with an "implicit security guarantee," according to some analysts.[48] In recent years, PRC government entities have financed many infrastructure, energy-related (especially hydro power), agricultural, and other high profile development projects in these countries, which also rely upon Chinese construction materials, equipment, technical expertise, and labor. There are some indications that Chinese aid in this part of the region is diversifying, including support for counter-trafficking in persons and counter-narcotics efforts, programs involving Chinese youth volunteers (Laos), elections (Cambodia), and historical preservation (Cambodia). The PRC also has financed railway construction, hydro power development, and ship building facilities in Vietnam.[49]

In the past few years, China has become a major financer and investor in infrastructure, energy, agriculture, and mining in the Philippines. According to one source, in 2006, China was the third largest source of bilateral development assistance to the Philippines after Japan and the United Kingdom.[50] The Philippines reportedly is the largest recipient of PRC loans in Southeast Asia, which totaled $2 billion in 2007, of which about half has been disbursed.[51] One of the largest PRC-funded projects in the country is the $1 billion North Rail line.[52]

The NYU Wagner School research team compiled a list of PRC aid and related investment projects or offers in Southeast Asia reported during the 2002-2007 period. The combined values amounted to $14.8 billion.[53] Of this amount, 43% was channeled toward infrastructure and public works projects, 32% to natural resource extraction or development, 3% to military, humanitarian, and technical assistance activities, and 22% to purposes not specified. See **Table 10** and **Table 11**.

In terms of official development assistance as measured by the OECD, which often refers to different types of aid than that typically provided by China, Japan remains the largest bilateral aid donor in Southeast Asia, providing $2 billion in 2006.[54] The United States funded an estimated $517 million in aid programs in Southeast Asian countries in 2008.[55] Since 2001, Indonesia and the Philippines have received the largest increases in U.S. foreign assistance in the region, chiefly for counter-terrorism programs. Vietnam has also received large increases in U.S. ODA, including significant funding for HIV/AIDS programs.

Table 10. Selected Southeast Asian Countries with Large Reported Aid and Investment Projects, 2002-2007

Country	Main Exports to China	Pledged Aid, Loans, Credit Lines, and Investments	Major Types of Financing (as Reported)	Major Types of Projects Financed (as Reported)
Philippines	ores, copper	$5.4 billion	loans, grants	infrastructure (railways), mining, non-lethal military
Vietnam	oil, rubber, wood, ores	$3.4 billion	loans, investment	infrastructure (power), shipya mining
Burma	ores	$3.1 billion		

Source: NYU Wagner School, *Understanding Chinese Foreign Aid: A Look at China's Development Assistance to Africa, Southeast Asia, and Latin America*, April 25, 2008.

Table 11. Selected Major PRC Financing and Aid-Related Economic Projects in Southeast Asia

Amount	Funding (Year)	Project Type(s)	Country
$2.4 billion	Investment (2005)	steel plant	Thailand
$2 billion	Loan (2007)	infrastructure	Philippines
$2 billion	Investment (2006- 2007)	infrastructure, hydropower, oil pipeline	Burma
$1.6 billion	Investment (2007)	mining	Vietnam
$1 billion	Loan (2005)	power plant	Vietnam

Source: NYU Wagner School, *Understanding Chinese Foreign Aid: A Look at China's Development Assistance toAfrica, Southeast Asia, and Latin America*, April 25, 2008.

APPENDIX: RECENT PRC FOREIGN ASSISTANCE AND INVESTMENT PROJECTS (2008)

Table A-1. Selected PRC Aid and Investment Projects in 2008 (Announced or Begun): Africa

Country	Type of Assistance or Investment	Funding Source	Description	Value in $US (b = billion m = million)
Angola	Development	Govt-Sponsored Investment	housing and related infrastructure	$3.5 b
Congo	Infrastructure/Public Works	Concessional Loan	optical cable network	$35 m
Congo	Infrastructure/Public Works; Natural Resources	Govt-Sponsored Investment; Concessional Loan	transportation, mining sector	$9 b
Ethiopia	Infrastructure/Public Works	Grant/Donation	construction of African Union Hall	$150 m

Ethiopia	Infrastructure/Public Works	In-kind	vehicles and office equipment	not specified
Ethiopia	Infrastructure; Development	Govt-Sponsored Investment	industrial park	$713 m
Gabon	Infrastructure/Public Works	Concessional Loan	hydroelectric dam	$83 m
Kenya	Infrastructure/Public Works	Concessional Loan	road construction	$120 m
Liberia	Infrastructure/Public Works	Grant; In-kind	hospital and medical supplies	$10 m
Madagascar	Humanitarian; Development	Grant	medical aid team	not specified
Niger	Natural Resources	Govt-Sponsored Investment	oil drilling,, refinery	$5 b
Nigeria	Infrastructure/Public Works	Govt-Sponsored Investment	road construction	$1 b
Nigeria	Infrastructure/Public Works	Govt-Sponsored Investment	power plant	$2.4 b
Rwanda	Infrastructure/Public Works	Grant	hospitals	$1.5 m
Sierra Leone	Infrastructure/Public Works	Concessional Loan	telecommunications network	$20 m
Sudan	Humanitarian	Grant; In-kind	de-mining training, mine sweeping equipment	not specified
Sudan	Humanitarian	Grant; In-kind	housing shelters, health equipment	$11 m
Uganda	Military	Grant; In-kind	military training, trucks and equipment	not specified
Uganda	Development	Grant	upgrade health centers	$15 m
Uganda	Infrastructure/Public Works	Grant/Donation	government office complex	$20 m
Country	**Type of Assistance or Investment**	**Funding Source**	**Description**	**Value in $US (b = billion m = million)**
Zambia	Infrastructure/Public Works	Govt-Sponsored Investment; Concessional Loan	power station expansion	$400 m
Zambia	Infrastructure/Public Works	Grant/Donation	sports stadium	$65 m

Source: various international news reports

Table A-2. Selected PRC Aid and Investment Projects in 2008 (Announced or Begun): Latin America

Country	Type of Assistance or Investment	Funding Source	Description	Value in $US (b = billion m = million)
Brazil	Infrastructure/Public Works	Govt-Sponsored Investment	power plant	$850 m
Brazil	Natural Resources	Concessional Loan	oil exploration	$10 b

Table A-2 (Continued)				
Chile	Infrastructure/Public Works; Natural Resources	Concessional Loan (joint credit lines)	ports, shipping, mining	$100 m
Costa Rica	Infrastructure/Public Works; Natural Resources	Grant/Donation	stadium, oil refinery	$130 m
Cuba	Humanitarian	Concessional Loan	hurricane relief – repair of hospitals	$70 m
Grenada	Infrastructure/Public Works	Concessional Loan	tourist marina	$83 m
Venezuela	Infrastructure/Public Works; Development; Natural Resources	Concessional Loan	infrastructure, electricity, health, and education	$4 b (to be paid back in oil)

Table A-3. Selected PRC Aid and Investment Projects in 2008 (Announced or Begun): Southeast Asia

Country	Type of Assistance or Investment	Funding Source	Description	Value in $US (b = billion m = million)
Cambodia	Infrastructure/Public Works	Grant; Concessional Loan	road construction	$ 215 m
Laos/Thailand	Infrastructure/Public Works	Govt-Sponsored Investment	construction of China-Laos-Thailand railroad	$3 b
Myanmar (Burma)	Natural Resources	Govt-Sponsored Investment	nickel mining	not specified (profit sharing arrangement)
Myanmar (Burma)	Natural Resources	Govt-Sponsored Investment	2 oil and gas pipelines	$350 m
Indonesia	Infrastructure/Public Works	Concessional Loan	power plants	$615 m

Source: various international news reports

End Notes

[1] This chapter is based on research done by the New York University Robert F. Wagner Graduate School of Public Service, *Understanding Chinese Foreign Aid: A Look at China's Development Assistance to Africa, Southeast Asia, and Latin America*, April 25, 2008. For questions or further information, please contact Thomas Lum of the Congressional Research Service who served as project manager for this study.

[2] For a discussion of China's soft power, see CRS Report RL34620, *Comparing Global Influence: China's and U.S. Diplomacy, Foreign Aid, Trade, and Investment in the Developing World*, section by Thomas Lum.

[3] Carol Lancaster, "The Chinese Aid System," Center for Global Development, June 2007 http://www.cgdev.org.

[4] OECD Glossary of Statistical Terms, http://stats.oecd.org/glossary/index.htm.

[5] Japan's Official Development Assistance White Paper 2007; "Japan Urged to Improve Quality of Foreign Aid," *Inter Press Service News Agency*, August 18, 2005; "Japan and Asia: Developing Ties," *OECD Observer*, 2008; Japan Ministry of Foreign Affairs.

[6] Edward J. Lincoln, "Japan: Using Power Narrowly," Council on Foreign Relations, Winter 2003.

[7] China reportedly has youth volunteers in 50 countries, mostly in Africa and Southeast Asia, and has begun to send volunteers to Latin America. The Chinese government has pledged to send 300 volunteers to Africa by 2009. "China to Send Youth Volunteers to Africa this Year," *The Ethiopian Herald*, February 17, 2007.

[8] Lancaster, op. cit.; See also Phillip C. Saunders, "China's Global Activism: Strategy, Drivers, and Tools," Institute for National Strategic Studies, National Defense University, 2006.

[9] Organization for Economic Co-operation and Development (OECD) data. See http://www.globalissues.org/.

[10] CRS Report RL34620, *Comparing Global Influence: China's and U.S. Diplomacy, Foreign Aid, Trade, and Investment in the Developing World*, op. cit., section by Dick Nanto; "Chinese Investment Pouring into Thailand's Neighbors," *The Nation (Thailand)*, December 4, 2007.

[11] Because of the lack of official data, either from China or recipient countries, the NYU Wagner School research team relied largely upon the international press and scholarly research. Sources included allAfrica.com, the Economist Intelligence Unit (EIU), International Relations and Security Network, the PRC Ministry of Commerce, ReliefWeb (United Nations), Reuters, Xinhua, and other news agencies.

[12] CRS Report RL34552, *State, Foreign Operations, and Related Programs: FY2009 Appropriations*, by Susan B. Epstein and Kennon H. Nakamura.

[13] China's conditions on aid are often international rather than domestic —— requiring aid recipients to support the "one- China" principle regarding Taiwan and China's agenda in the United Nations.

[14] Pilirani Semu-Banda, "NGO Keeping an Eye on Malawi's New Best Friend, China," Inter Press Service News Agency, May 26, 2008, http://allafrica.com/; Mabvuto Banda, "Malawi Leader Says China to Give $287 Min in Aid," *Reuters News*, April 4, 2008.

[15] For further discussion of Chinese influence in Africa, see Congressional Research Service, "China's Foreign Policy and 'Soft Power' in South America, Asia, and Africa: A Study Prepared for the Committee on Foreign Relations, United States Senate," April 2008, section by Nicolas Cook.

[16] Deborah Brautigam, "China's Africa Aid," The German Marshall Fund of the United States, April 2008; Penny Davies, "China and the End of Poverty in Africa," August 2007; China Exim Bank.

[17] Nick Tattersall, "Chinese Firm to Build $1 Bln Road in Nigeria Oil Hub," *Reuters News*, July 13, 2008; China National Bureau of Statistics.

[18] Tom Miller, "U.S. $5 b Fund to Make First Forays into Africa," *South China Morning Post*, January 8, 2009.

[19] Congressional Budget Justification for Foreign Operations, FY2008.

[20] Organization for Economic Co-operation and Development, *OECD and Africa*, March 2008.

[21] "U.S.-African Trade Profile," U.S. Department of Commerce, International Trade Administration (2008); Harry G. Broadman, "China and India Go to Africa," *Free Republic*, March 16, 2008.

[22] Leonard K. Cheng and Zihui Ma, "China's Outward FDI: Past and Future," July 2007; Jian-Ye Wang, "What Drives China's Growing Role in Africa," IMF Working Paper, October 2007; Mauro De Lorenzo, "China and Africa: A New Scramble?" *American Enterprise Institute*, April 6, 2007.

[23] Jian-Ye Wang, "What Drives China's Growing Role in Africa," op. cit.

[24] Hany Besada, Yang Wang, and John Whalley, "China's Growing Economic Presence in Africa," *Policy Brief*, The Centre for International Governance Innovation, No. 6 (October 2008); CRS Report RL34620, *Comparing Global Influence: China's and U.S. Diplomacy, Foreign Aid, Trade, and Investment in the Developing World*, op. cit., section by Dick Nanto (data excludes Egypt).

[25] "Building Bridges: China's Growing Role as Infrastructure Financier for Sub-Saharan Africa," The World Bank, No. 5 (2008); China National Bureau of Statistics.

[26] Jian-Ye Wang and Abdoulaye Bio-Tchane, "Africa's Burgeoning Ties with China," *Finance and Development*, International Monetary Fund, http://www.imf.org/external/pubs/ft/fandd/2008/03/wang.htm.

[27] World Trade Atlas.

[28] Building Bridges, op. cit.; "Africa Accounts For 30 Percent Of China's Oil Imports: Official," *People's Daily Online,* http://english.peopledaily.com.cn, October 19, 2006.

[29] "Building Bridges," op. cit.

[30] Stephanie Hanson, "China, Africa, and Oil," *Council on Foreign Relations Backgrounder*, June 6, 2008.

[31] Zong He, "Some Responses to the 'China Threat in Africa,'" *China Daily*, November 7, 2007.

[32] "Building Bridges," op. cit.

[33] "Building Bridges," op. cit.; Brautigam, "China's Africa Aid," op. cit.; World Bank, "Press Release: New Financiers are Narrowing Africa's Infrastructure Deficit," July 10, 2008.

[34] This aggregate number may include some double counting of aid that involved multiple projects or spanned several years. The figure is not based upon a precise definition of aid and does not represent an exact aid total.

[35] Davies, "China and the End of Poverty in Africa," op. cit.

[36] Peter Brookes, "Russia, China, Move In on Latin America," Heritage Foundation, November 27, 2008; Cynthia A. Watson, "U.S. Responses to China's Growing Interests in Latin America: Dawning Recognition of a Changing Hemisphere," in *Enter the Dragon? China's Presence in Latin America*, Woodrow Wilson International Center for Scholars, February 2007. For further discussion of Chinese influence in Latin America and the Caribbean, see Congressional Research Service, "China's Foreign Policy and 'Soft Power' in South America, Asia, and Africa," op. cit., section by Mark P. Sullivan.

[37] Daniel P. Erikson, "The New Challenge: China and the Western Hemisphere," Testimony before the House Committee on Foreign Affairs, Subcommittee on the Western Hemisphere, June 11, 2008.

[38] CRS Report RL34620, *Comparing Global Influence: China's and U.S. Diplomacy, Foreign Aid, Trade, and Investment in the Developing World*, op. cit., section by Dick Nanto.

[39] Erikson, "The New Challenge," op. cit.

[40] Frank Bajak, "Slowdown Doesn't Shrink China's LatAm Ambitions," *Associated Press*, November 17, 2008; World Trade Atlas.

[41] CRS Report RL34620, *Comparing Global Influence: China's and U.S. Diplomacy, Foreign Aid, Trade, and Investment in the Developing World*, op. cit., section by Dick Nanto.

[42] He Li, "China's Growing Interest in Latin America," *The Journal of Strategic Studies*, Vol. 30, No. 4-5 (August-October 2007); Global Trade Atlas.

[43] This aggregate number may include some double counting of aid that involved multiple projects or spanned several years. The figure is not based upon a precise definition of aid and does not represent an exact aid total.

[44] "China Makes IDB Aid Commitment to Bolivia, Guyana, Haiti, Honduras," *BBC Monitoring Americas*, October 23, 2008.

[45] Congressional Budget Justification for Foreign Operations, FY2008.

[46] ASEAN Foreign Direct Investment Database, August 2007.

[47] World Trade Atlas; "China, ASEAN become 4th-Largest Trade Partners," *Xinhua*, March 1, 2008. Data among different sources varies.

[48] Catherin E. Dalpino, "Consequences of a Growing China," *Statement before the Senate Committee on Foreign Relations Subcommittee on East Asian and Pacific Affairs*, June 7, 2005; Heritage Foundation, "Southeast Asia's Forgotten Tier: Burma, Cambodia and Laos," July 26, 2007; Marvin C. Ott, "Southeast Asian Security Challenges: America's Response? *Strategic Forum*, October 1, 2006; Joshua Kurlantzick, "China's Charm Offensive in Southeast Asia," *Current History*, Vo. 105, no. 692 (September 2006).

[49] For further information, see CRS Report RL34620, *Comparing Global Influence: China's and U.S. Diplomacy, Foreign Aid, Trade, and Investment in the Developing World*, op. cit., section by Bruce Vaughn, Thomas Lum, and Wayne Morrison.

[50] Michelle Remo, "RP Should Look to China for its Infra Funding Needs," *Philippine Daily Inquirer*, March 9, 2008.

[51] Katrice R. Jalbuena, "Ties with PRC, Now Most Important to RP, Also Involves Security Matters," *Manila Times*, June 29, 2008.

[52] Walter Lohman, "Off the Rails in the Philippines," Heritage Foundation, Web Memo no. 1856, March 14, 2008; Darwin G. Amojelar, "Chinese Loans to RP Rising," *The Manila Times*, December 3, 2007.

[53] This aggregate number may include some double counting of aid that involved multiple projects or spanned several years. The figure is not based upon a precise definition of aid and does not represent an exact aid total.

[54] Organization for Economic Cooperation and Development (OECD), http://www.oecd.org/home/.

[55] Congressional Budget Justification for Foreign Operations, FY2008; Japan's Official Development Assistance White Paper 200

In: Politics and Economics of Latin America. Volume 6
Editor: Samantha R. Dawes
ISBN: 978-1-61668-014-5

Chapter 3

MERIDA INITIATIVE FOR MEXICO AND CENTRAL AMERICA: FUNDING AND POLICY ISSUES*

Clare Ribando Seelke

SUMMARY

Increasing violence perpetrated by drug trafficking organizations, gangs, and other criminal groups is threatening citizen security in Mexico and Central America. Drug-related violence claimed more than 5,300 lives in Mexico in 2008, and several Central American countries have some of the highest homicide rates in the world. Mexican drug cartels dominate the illicit drug market in most regions of the United States and are expanding their operations by forming partnerships with U.S. gangs. As a result, some of the drug-related violence in Mexico has begun to spillover into the United States.

On October 22, 2007, the United States and Mexico announced the Mérida Initiative, a multi-year proposal for $1.4 billion in U.S. assistance to Mexico and Central America aimed at combating drug trafficking and organized crime. The Administration requested $500 million for Mexico and $50 million for Central America in FY2008 supplemental appropriations, and another $450 million for Mexico and $100 million for Central America in the FY2009 budget request. While the Bush Administration did not request any additional funding for domestic programs to complement the Mérida Initiative, U.S. officials pledged to step up efforts to prevent arms, precursor chemicals, and bulk cash flows from the United States into Mexico, and to reduce U.S. drug demand.

In June 2008, the 110th Congress appropriated $465 million in FY2008 and FY2009 supplemental assistance for Mexico and Central America in the FY2008 Supplemental Appropriations Act, H.R. 2642 (P.L. 110-252). In the act, Mexico receives $352 million in FY2008 supplemental assistance and $48 million in FY2009 bridge fund supplemental assistance, while Central America, Haiti, and the Dominican Republic receive $65 million in

* This is an edited, reformatted and augmented version of a CRS Report for Congress publication dated January 2009.

FY2008 supplemental assistance. The 110th Congress did not include funding for Mérida in a continuing resolution (P.L. 110-329) providing FY2009 funding through March 6, 2009 at FY2008 levels.

The 111th Congress may examine the Mérida Initiative as it considers the Bush Administration's pending FY2009 foreign aid request, as well as the FY20 10 budget to be submitted by the Obama Administration. Policy debates that may emerge during congressional consideration of Mérida may include what levels and types of funding should be provided to Mexico and Central America; how well the interagency community, in coordination with its counterparts in partner countries, is implementing the Initiative; and the degree to which the nations involved, including the United States, are fulfilling their domestic obligations under Mérida. Congress may also maintain a keen interest in enforcement of Mérida's human rights conditions. This chapter provides an overview of the funding provided for the Mérida Initiative and a discussion of some policy issues that Congress may consider as it oversees implementation of the Initiative. For related information, see CRS Report RL32724, *Mexico-U.S. Relations: Issues for Congress*, by Mark P. Sullivan and June S. Beittel.

In October 2007, the United States and Mexico announced the Mérida Initiative, a three-year proposal for $1.4 billion in U.S. assistance to Mexico and Central America[1] aimed at combating drug trafficking, gangs, and organized crime.[2] Named for the location of a March 2007 meeting between Presidents George W. Bush and Felipe Calderón of Mexico, the Mérida Initiative seeks to expand bilateral and regional anticrime and counterdrug cooperation. In June 2008, the 110th Congress appropriated $465 million in supplemental assistance for Mexico, Central America, Haiti, and the Dominican Republic in the FY2008 Supplemental Appropriations Act (P.L. 110- 252). On December 3, 2008, the United States and Mexico signed a Letter of Agreement, allowing $197 million in Mérida funds to be disbursed.[3]

The Bush Administration requested a second installment of Mérida funding – $450 million for Mexico and $100 million for Central America – in its FY2009 budget request. Congress did not include funding for the Mérida Initiative in a continuing resolution (P.L. 110-329) providing FY2009 funding through March 6, 2009 at FY2008 levels.[4] For that reason, early in its first session, the 111th Congress may consider what level and types of funding should be provided for Mérida in the FY2009 and FY20 10 budgets.

This chapter provides an overview of the funding provided for Mérida, as well as a discussion of several issues that Congress may consider as it oversees implementation of the Initiative.

BACKGROUND

The stated objective of the Mérida Initiative, according to the U.S. and Mexican government joint statement of October 2007, is to maximize the effectiveness of efforts against drug, human, and weapons trafficking. The joint statement highlights counterdrug and anticrime efforts of both countries, including Mexico's 24% increase in security spending in 2007 under President Felipe Calderón and U.S. efforts to reduce weapons, human, and drug trafficking along the Mexican border.[5] The Central America portion of the Initiative aims to bolster the capacity of governments to inspect and interdict unauthorized drugs, goods, arms, and people and to support regional anti- gang efforts.

The Mérida Initiative is not only the largest foreign aid package for the Western Hemisphere since Plan Colombia,[6] it is, according to its proponents, a new kind of partnership between the United States, Mexico and Central America. Analysts and U.S. officials have said that in order for the Initiative to be successful, all the countries involved will have to accept their "shared responsibility" to tackle domestic problems contributing to drug trafficking and crime in the region, including U.S. drug demand.[7] Since President Calderón took office in December 2006, Mexico has, for its part, increased security spending (to some $4 billion in 2008), mobilized thousands of soldiers and police to drug trafficking "hot-spots" throughout the country, and extradited record numbers of drug traffickers to the United States.

Drug trafficking organizations (DTOs) and other organized criminal groups pose an increasing security threat to Mexico and Central America. In 2008, the Calderón government's crackdown on the cartels, as well as rivalries and turf wars among Mexico's drug cartels fueled an escalation in violence throughout the country, including northern states along the U.S.-Mexico border. Some 5,376 Mexicans died in the first 11 months of 2008, many as a result of drug-related violence.[8] Mexico and Central American security officials lack the training and equipment needed to deal with DTOs and other criminal groups who are securing illicit arms and cash resources from the United States and elsewhere. In addition, Mexico and Central America continue to have problems with impunity, police corruption, and human rights abuses by security forces that have hindered the performance and reputation of their law enforcement and judicial systems.

FUNDING FOR THE MÉRIDA INITIATIVE

The Bush Administration designed the Mérida Initiative as a three-year counterdrug and anticrime package for Mexico and Central America that would begin in FY2008 and last through FY2010. Prior to the FY2008 supplemental request for Mérida, neither Mexico nor the countries of Central America had received large amounts of U.S. counternarcotics (CN) assistance.[9] In FY2007, Mexico received $14.6 million in CN assistance and the only Central American countries to receive CN funds were Guatemala ($1. 9 million) and Panama ($3.3 million).

This section of the report briefly discusses Mérida authorization legislation that was considered, but not enacted, during the 110th Congress. It then compares the FY2008 supplemental request for Mérida with the FY2008 supplemental funds that were enacted by Congress in June 2008. This is followed by a brief summary of the Bush Administration's pending FY2009 request for Mérida, which may be taken up by the 111th Congress. **Table 3**, included at the end of this funding section, provides a country-level breakdown of all Mérida requests and appropriations.

Mérida Authorization Legislation

While several Members of Congress initially expressed concern that they were not adequately consulted by the Administration during the development of the Mérida Initiative, a majority of House Members subsequently voted to authorize the aid package. On June 11, 2008, the House approved H.R. 6028 (Berman), the Merida Initiative to Combat Illicit Narcotics and Reduce Organized Crime Authorization Act of 2008 by a vote of 311 to 106, demonstrating bipartisan support for the proposed assistance. The Senate did not take any action on the measure so legislative attention turned to consideration of appropriations for the Mérida Initiative.

As passed by the House, H.R. 6028 would have authorized $1.6 billion over three years, FY2008- FY2010, for both Mexico and Central America, $200 million more than originally proposed by President Bush.[10] Of that amount, $1.1 billion would have been authorized for Mexico, $405 million for the countries of Central America, and $73.5 million for activities of the U.S. Bureau of Alcohol, Tobacco, Firearms, and Explosives (ATF) to reduce the flow of illegal weapons from the United States to Mexico. Among the bill's various conditions on providing the assistance, the measure would have required that vetting procedures be in place to ensure that members or units of military or law enforcement agencies receiving assistance were not involved in human rights violations.

FY2008 Supplemental Request and Appropriations for Mérida

The Bush Administration requested $500 million for Mexico and $50 million for Central American countries in its FY2008 supplemental appropriations request.[11] All of the funding was requested through the International Narcotics Control and Law Enforcement (INCLE) account, administered by the State Department's Bureau of International Narcotics and Law Enforcement Affairs (INL). Administration officials justified inclusion of the Mérida request in an emergency supplemental request rather than the FY2009 regular foreign aid budget request, which was not submitted until February 2008, because of the gravity of the security situation in Mexico.

In the FY2008 supplemental request, the size, goals, and composition of the Mexican and Central American portions of the Mérida Initiative differed markedly. Prior to the October 2007 joint announcement of the proposed aid package, U.S. and Mexican officials had met over many months to craft the Mexican portion of the Initiative. As a result, the FY2008 supplemental budget request for Mexico was 10 times as large, and much further along in its development than the initial Mérida request for Central America. The largest category of assistance to Mexico would fund equipment and technology infrastructure improvements for military and law enforcement agencies. Another category of assistance would fund such items as inspection scanners, x-ray ions, computer equipment, and security equipment. A third category would fund institution-building and justice sector projects, while the final category of assistance would fund program support.

The Central America portion of the Initiative would bolster the capacity of governments to inspect and interdict unauthorized drugs, goods, arms, and people. It would also support implementation of the U.S. Strategy for Combating Criminal Gangs from Central America and Mexico, announced at a July 2007 U.S.-Central American Integration System (SICA) summit. In contrast to the Mexico request, which focused on providing training and equipment to fight drug trafficking, the majority of proposed funding for Central America would fund programs to improve policing and support anti-gang efforts, including prevention programs. Limited funding would also support judicial and police reform, as well as efforts to improve countries' capacity to share information on gang members and other criminals, interdict illicit goods on land and at sea, and curb weapons trafficking.

FY2008 supplemental funding for the Mérida Initiative was considered as part of a broader FY2008 Supplemental Appropriations Act, H.R. 2642 (Edwards). Originally introduced June 11, 2007 as the FY2008 Military Construction and Veterans Affairs Appropriations Act, this bill subsequently became the vehicle for the second FY2008 supplemental appropriations measure. On June 19, 2008, the House approved an amended version of the FY2008 Supplemental Appropriations Act, H.R. 2642, that provides $465 million in FY2008 and FY2009 supplemental assistance for Mexico and Central America. The Senate approved the compromise House version of H.R. 2642 on June 26, 2008. The bill was then signed into law by President Bush on June 30, 2008 (P.L. 110-252).

In the act, Mexico receives $352 million in FY2008 supplemental assistance and $48 million in FY2009 bridge fund supplemental assistance, while Central America, Haiti, and the Dominican Republic receive $65 million in FY2008 supplemental assistance. The measure has human rights conditions softer than compared to earlier House and Senate versions, largely because of Mexico's objections that some of the original conditions, particularly those in the Senate version of the bill, would violate its national sovereignty. The language in the final enacted measure reduced the amount of funding subject to human rights conditions, from 25% to 15%, removed conditions that would have required the Mexican government to try military officials accused of abuses in civilian courts and to enhance the power of its National Human Rights Commission, and softened the language in other conditions. (See **Appendix** for the final language of the human rights conditions included in P.L. 110-252).

The State Department subsequently developed a spending plan for how it and the other U.S. agencies involved will spend the FY2008 supplemental funding and FY2009 bridge funding appropriated for the Mérida Initiative.[12] In its plan, the State Department elected to break its program descriptions out by funding account, rather than by the program components it had included in the FY2008 supplemental request.

Mexico

In contrast to the Administration, which requested all Mérida funding in the INCLE account, Congress divided the funding for Mexico in P.L. 110-252 between the ESF, INCLE, and FMF aid accounts. Additionally, while the vast majority of funds provided ($352 million) were labeled as FY2008 supplemental assistance, Congress provided another $48 million in FY2009 bridge fund assistance. As noted above, Congress made 15% of INCLE and FMF funds contingent upon human rights conditions. Another significant change that Congress made to the Administration's request was to limit the amount of FMF and INCLE available to provide equipment to the Mexican Army/Air Force and Navy. As a result, the FY2008 State Department spending plan includes $94 million less funding for the Mexican armed forces than the FY2008 supplemental request. Due to other funding limitations, some border security and justice sector reform programs also had to be scaled back from the budget request. Congress provided $24 million for program and staff support for the Mérida

Initiative, $13 million less than the Administration's request. In addition to these aid cuts, Congress included a $73.5 million earmark for judicial reform, institution building, rule of law, and anti-corruption activities, as well as $18 million in other earmarks.[13]

According to the State Department's spending plan, ESF funds will support implementation of Mexico's recently enacted judicial reforms, as well as efforts to provide human rights training to Mexican police, military, and judicial officials. ESF funds will also seek to build civil society's capacity to monitor and document human rights abuses. FMF funds will be used to purchase two aircraft, up to five helicopters, and ion scanners for the Mexican armed forces. The majority of INCLE funds ($180 million total, of which $34 million is FY2009 bridge funding) will provide equipment and programs to strengthen the Mexican government's capacity to interdict drugs, arms, and people. Another $59.5 million in INCLE funds (of which $14 million is FY2009 bridge funding) will support Mexico's law enforcement and judicial systems.

Central America

[14]As with Mexico, Congress divided the funding for Central America between several different aid accounts. In addition to changing the account structure, Congress shifted the bulk of funding for Central America from public security and law enforcement programs to institution building, rule of law, and development programs. It did so by earmarking $25 million in ESF funds for the creation of an Economic and Social Development Fund for Central America. Of the ESF funds provided, $20 million are to be administered by the U.S. Agency for International Development (USAID) for youth violence prevention, community policing, and community development programs in violence-prone areas. The other $5 million in ESF funds are to fund educational and cultural exchange programs administered by the State Department. Congress also earmarked $1 million to support the International Commission against Impunity in Guatemala (CICIG).[15]

Due to the aforementioned shifts in the type of funds provided by Congress, the State Department had to scale back some of its proposed law enforcement programs supported by INCLE funding. As compared to the FY2008 supplemental request, the FY2008 spending plan included less funding devoted to transnational anti-gang units, police equipment, and police training provided at the International Law Enforcement Academy.

Table 1. FY2008 Mérida Funding for Mexico by Aid Account ($ in millions)

Account	FY2008 Supplement al Funds	FY2009 Bridge Funds
Economic Support Fund (ESF)	20.0	0.0
International Narcotics Control and Law Enforcement (INCLE)	215.5	48.0
Nonproliferation, Anti-Terrorism, Demining and Related Programs (NADR)	0.0	0.0
Foreign Military Financing (FMF)	116.5	0.0
Total	352.0	48.0

Source: U.S. Department of State, FY2008 Supplemental Appropriations Spending Plan

Table 2. FY2008 Mérida Funding for Central America by Aid Account ($ in millions)

Account	FY2008 Supplemental Funds
Economic Support Fund	25.0
International Narcotics Control and Law Enforcement	24.8
Nonproliferation, Anti-Terrorism, Demining and Related Programs	6.2
Foreign Military Financing	4.0
Total	60.0

Source: U.S. Department of State, FY2008 Supplemental Appropriations Spending Plan.

Congress did provide close to full funding for counternarcotics and border security programs requested by the Bush Administration. Those programs include efforts to include information- sharing and data collection among the Central American countries; programs to improve port, airport, and border security; and regional arms trafficking and maritime interdiction programs. These programs will be supported by a combination of INCLE, FMF, and NADR funding.

According to the State Department spending plan, some 40% of the Mérida funding appropriated for Central America will be used to support regional programs. Among the Central American countries, those with the highest violent crime rates and greatest prevalence of gangs and organized criminal groups – El Salvador, Guatemala, and Honduras – will receive the most bilateral funding (see **Table 3** for Mérida funding by country).

Table 3. Estimated Mérida Requests and Appropriations by Country ($ in millions).

Country	FY2008 Supp. Request	FY2008 Supp. App. Act P.L. 110-252	FY2009 Request
Mexico	500.0	400.0	450.0
Belize	1.9	1.5	5.8
Costa Rica	4.3	4.3	9.5
El Salvador	7.1	6.1	17.3
Guatemala	11.1	10.6	17.7
Honduras	10.8	7.3	12.4
Nicaragua	3.7	2.4	6.7
Panama	3.9	2.0	8.9
Central America (Regional)	7.2	24.9	21.7
Central America (total)	50.0	60.0	100.0
Haiti	0.0	2.5	0.0
Dominican Republic	0.0	2.5	0.0
Total	550.0	465.0	550.0

Source: U.S. Department of State briefing papers provided to Congressional offices; FY2008 Supplemental Appropriations Spending Plan

Haiti and the Dominican Republic

Although not included in the original Mérida request, Congress dedicated $2.5 million in INCLE funding for Haiti and $2.5 million for the Dominican Republic, two major drug transit countries in the Caribbean. In Haiti, Mérida funds will be used to install a secure communications network for the Haitian National Police (HNP), to support the HNP's drug interdiction efforts and to provide training for Haitian judicial officials. In the Dominican Republic, Mérida funds will be used to support police professionalization programs, to provide logistical support to interdiction units, and to train judicial authorities in implementing the new criminal procedure code. A portion of the Mérida funds for each country will also support the U.N. Stabilization Mission in Haiti (MINUSTAH), which has been providing joint counternarcotics and border security training to Haitian and Dominican security officials.

FY2009 Budget Request

In the FY2009 foreign aid request, the Bush Administration asked for another $550 million for the Mérida Initiative – $450 million for Mexico and $100 million for Central American countries. All of the funding was requested through the INCLE account, administered by the State Department's Bureau of International Narcotics and Law Enforcement Affairs (INL). As in the FY2008 supplemental request, no Mérida funding was requested for Haiti or the Dominican Republic. (See Appendix for a description of the FY2009 request by program components).

Mexico

In the FY2009 request, the Administration placed more emphasis on assistance to non-military agencies. The FY2009 request included $118 million to improve infrastructure and information systems at non-military agencies, including Mexico's immigration agency, the Attorney General Office's (PGR), the intelligence service (CISEN), the postal service, and customs. With respect to military agencies, the FY2009 request included $100 million to support aircraft for surveillance and counternarcotics interception missions carried out by the Mexican Navy and $20 million in inspection equipment for use at Army checkpoints. For FY2009, the Administration requested $158.5 million in public security and law enforcement assistance. Most of the assistance, $147.6 million, would go to support the Mexican federal police. The Administration requested significantly less funding for institution building programs in FY2009 than in the FY2008 supplemental, $30.7 million, with $23.4 million to improve the justice system; $8.5 million to support the PGR's Forensic Institute; and $9.4 million to support improved data collection and analysis. The FY2009 request included $22.5 million to cover the cost of U.S. personnel, administration, and budget services related to the proposed aid package.

Central America

For FY2009, the Administration requested $40 million for border security and counterdrug programs. More than half of that money, $25.8 million, would go to land and maritime interdiction assistance, as well as to a regional arms tracking program. The FY2009 request included $13 million to implement the U.S. anti-gang strategy, with $7.5 million of that for prevention programs, up from $5 million in the FY2008 supplemental request. It also included $13 million for police modernization and technical assistance and $6 million to support the International Law Enforcement Academy in El Salvador. The Administration's FY2009 budget request for institution-building programs rose to $23 million. The largest increases from the FY2008 supplemental request were for courts management programs and training to improve prosecutorial capacity. The FY2009 budget request also included $2 million for juvenile justice systems and rehabilitation programs and $1 million for programs to build public confidence in the justice system, two components not included in the FY2008 supplemental request.

The FY2009 budget request also included $5 million in unspecified program support.

Legislative Action on the FY2009 Request for Mérida

The 110th Congress did not conclude its consideration of the Bush Administration's FY2009 foreign aid budget request. Instead, Congress passed a continuing resolution (P.L. 110-329) providing FY2009 funding through March 6, 2009 at FY2008 levels. Since the initial pot of Mérida Initiative funding in FY2008 was provided through a supplemental assistance measure rather than the regular FY2008 foreign aid funding measure, the continuing resolution does not fund the Mérida Initiative for FY2009. As a result, the 111th Congress may consider what level of funding to include for the Mérida Initiative in the FY2009 budget.

POLICY ISSUES

A broad consensus appears to be shared by Congress and the policy community on the need for the United States to support neighboring governments in Mexico and Central America that are struggling to address drug-related violence. The 111th Congress may consider the efficacy of U.S. and regional counterdrug and anticrime efforts as it provides funding and oversight of the Mérida Initiative. Congress may also choose to examine how well the U.S. government is demonstrating its "shared responsibility" to tackle domestic problems contributing to drug trafficking and crime in the region, including U.S. drug demand. This section of the report raises some questions and policy issues for Congress to consider at it oversees implementation of the Mérida Initiative.

Is Mérida the Right Drug Control Approach?[16]

Unless programs like the Mérida Initiative are woven into a more holistic U.S. drug policy focusing on reducing supply and demand, many analysts predict that they are unlikely to have a significant impact on drug flows in the region. Analysts from a range of organizations, including the Brookings Institution, the Inter-American Dialogue, the Heritage Foundation, and the Washington Office on Latin America (WOLA), have called for a new comprehensive U.S. counternarcotics policy that attacks the drug problem in source, transit, and, perhaps most importantly, consumer countries. As a comparison, many recent studies, including an October 2008 report by the Government Accountability Office, have concluded that while Plan Colombia has improved security conditions in Colombia, it has not significantly reduced the amount of drugs flowing into the United States.[17] Other recent assessments of U.S. drug policy's historic and current tendency to focus on eradication, interdiction, and extraditions of drug traffickers have been even more pessimistic.[18]

Assessments of the likely impact of the Mérida Initiative are varied. Mérida supporters describe the initiative as a security cooperation partnership against drug traffickers and organized criminal groups, rather than a foreign assistance program. They emphasize the importance of fully funding Mérida in order to build up the capacity of both military and civilian institutions in partner nations so that bilateral and regional counterdrug efforts can be more successful.[19] The Heritage Foundation supports the Mérida Initiative and recommends that the next Congress provide funding above the $1.4 billion originally proposed by the Bush Administration if the Initiative has positive results. At the same time, it maintains that "the U.S. needs to do more to secure the border [and] reduce the flow of illegal arms and illicit cash" to Mexico.[20] WOLA, the Council on Foreign Relations, and others maintain that fighting the drug trade will require more than providing equipment and training for Mexican (and Central American) military and police forces. They assert that Mérida needs to include more funding to address the weak civilian judicial and police institutions, as well as the underlying societal problems, such as poverty, underdevelopment, and corruption, that have allowed the drug trade to flourish in Mexico and Central America. They also emphasize the importance of addressing U.S. and European drug demand.[21]

Monitoring Progress

In the last year, several think tanks held forums addressing the issue of how to monitor progress in implementing the Mérida Initiative. Many analysts maintain that it is crucial for both the U.S. and Mexican executive branches to manage legislative and popular expectations for the Initiative. They argue that it is important that the goals for the Initiative be realistic, and that progress made towards meeting those goals be regularly communicated to legislators and to the general public in both countries. For example, in this vain, an achievable goal would not be to end drug trafficking through Mexico, but to reduce trafficking and related violence to a public security issue, rather than a national security threat. Some contend that it is likely to take much longer than three fiscal years for the Mérida Initiative to help partner governments make real headway in achieving that goal.[22] A recent press report describes how difficult it is proving to be for the United States and Mexico to overcome decades of mistrust in order to work together to implement Mérida.[23]

U.S. and Mexican security experts have also urged Congress to look at a range of indicators when evaluating the Mérida Initiative, rather than merely measuring its effects on drug seizures and flows. Perhaps in response to that advice, Congress asked the State Department to include a list of performance measures for each portion of the Mérida Initiative in its FY2008 supplemental spending plan. For example, one indicator that is to be used to measure improvements in the Mexican justice system would be the percentage change in the Mexican federal criminal case backlog.

Balancing "Hard-Side" and "Soft-Side" Assistance

During the 110th Congress, there was ongoing debate between some in Congress and the Bush Administration over what levels and types of assistance should be provided to countries in Latin America. The most vigorous debates centered on what type of assistance should be provided to large aid recipients like Colombia and, more recently, Mexico.[24] The Bush Administration tended to favor "hard-side" security-related assistance, whereas a majority in Congress sought to balance security assistance with "soft-side" rule of law, human rights, and development assistance programs.[25] These debates may continue in the 111th Congress.

With respect to Mérida, debates emerged within the human rights community and Congress about the balance of security vs. institution-building funding in the Bush Administration's FY2008 supplemental request for Mexico.[26] Several Members of Congress opposed the request's apparent emphasis on providing expensive equipment to the Mexican military, with its poor human rights record. In response, Administration officials contended that the Calderón government specifically requested security assistance from the United States because Mexican law enforcement and military forces were being outgunned by the drug cartels. They assured Members of Congress that military and police units receiving U.S. equipment and training would be properly vetted.[27]

As noted above, Congress employed a variety of measures to ensure that various "soft-side" programs received support from the Mérida Initiative. These included limiting the FMF and INCLE funds available to provide equipment to the Mexican military, as well as earmarking $73.5 million in FY2008 supplemental assistance for institution building, rule of law, and anticorruption activities in Mexico. Congress reduced border security and counterdrug assistance for Central America in order to free up $25 million in ESF funds for the creation of an Economic and Social Development Fund for the subregion.

Interagency Coordination

In the last few years, several studies have noted the proliferation of U.S. agencies engaged in foreign assistance activities, as well as the challenges of getting those agencies to work together in a coordinated fashion.[28] Each federal agency tends to have its own mission, priorities, and operating style. Instead of working together to implement a particular policy or initiative, agencies often engage in "turf battles" as they compete for leadership roles and budgetary resources.

Interagency coordination may prove particularly difficult during implementation of the Mérida Initiative since its diverse program components are being carried out by a wide range of U.S. agencies under the leadership of the State Department. Like many other foreign aid programs in Latin America, most Mérida programs are being administered by the State Department and USAID. However, since border security is a key component of Mérida, the Department of Homeland Security (DHS) is to also have a major role to play in its implementation. Within DHS, officials from Immigration and Customs Enforcement (ICE), Customs and Border Protection (CBP), and the U.S. Coast Guard are to provide training and logistical support to their counterparts in Mexico and Central America.[29] Additionally, the Department of Justice is to have agents from the Drug Enforcement Administration (DEA) and the Federal Bureau of Investigations (FBI) working with their counterparts in partner countries. According to a press report from late 2008, some Members of Congress have complained about the lack of coordination, turf battles, and general confusion among the various federal agencies implementing the Initiative.[30]

Similar "turf battles" may also play out in the congressional committees that have an interest in overseeing Mérida. Since it is a foreign assistance program, primary oversight responsibilities for Mérida is to rest with the Senate Foreign Relations and House Foreign Affairs Committees. However, other committees, such as the Senate and House Homeland Security Committees, may seek to weigh in on how Mérida funding is being spent, how its progress is being evaluated, and how Mérida-funded programs are dovetailing with U.S. homeland security programs.

Role of the Department of Defense

Since the terrorist attacks of September 11, 2001, the Department of Defense (DOD) has become increasingly involved in funding counterterrorism and other foreign assistance programs around the world.[31] In Latin America, DOD, acting through its Southern Command (Southcom), has expanded its definition of security threats to include nontraditional threats such as international crime, public health crises, radical populism, and even poverty and inequality. Human rights groups have tracked DOD's expanding role in providing foreign aid in Latin America, alleging DOD's "mission creep" into programs and activities they feel are best funded and administered by the State Department or USAID.[32] Many analysts have expressed similar concerns about Mexico and some of the Central American countries' increasing reliance on military forces to perform anticrime and counternarcotics activities traditionally handled by civilian law enforcement personnel.

When the Mérida Initiative was first announced, analysts from across the political spectrum praised the fact that it did not appear to involve an active role for U.S. military forces in Mexico or Central America.[33] Some were pleased that civilian officials from the Central American Integration System (SICA) and the State Department designed the Central American portion of the proposal, rather than military personnel from the Central American Armed Forces Conference (CFAC) and Southcom.[34] Although DOD may not have taken a leadership role in designing Mérida, it will be administering assistance provided to Mexico through the FMF aid account, as well as a maritime assistance package in Central America. DOD also has programs in the works to complement the Mérida Initiative, such as a proposed Regional Aircraft Modernization Program (RAMP) for Central America that reportedly may cost as much as $300 million.[35]

U.S. Pledges under the Mérida Initiative

In the U.S. and Mexico joint statement announcing the Mérida Initiative, the United States government pledged to "intensify its efforts to address all aspects of drug trafficking (including demand-related portions) and continue to combat trafficking of weapons and bulk currency to Mexico."[36] Many security experts argue that this pledge may be even more important to the success of regional counterdrug and anticrime efforts than any amount of U.S. foreign aid provided to Mexico or Central America.[37] However, Mérida was proposed and funded as a foreign assistance package without any companion legislation on the domestic side. As such, it may prove difficult for Congress to monitor the degree to which the U.S. government is fulfilling its domestic pledges under the Mérida Initiative.

Weapons Trafficking

U.S. officials maintain that 90%-95% of the guns used in Mexico's drug violence have been traced to the United States.[38] Mexican drug cartels and enforcer gangs are reportedly buying semiautomatic versions of AK-47 and AR-15 style assault rifles, and other military-style firearms in the United States. The cartels often obtain their weapons through a series of "straw purchases," whereby guns are legally purchased from licensed gun dealers or at gun shows in border states and then sold to a third party, who smuggles the guns across the border. In November 2008, the Mexican government announced that it made the largest seizure of drug-cartel weapons in Mexican history when it discovered a cache of 540 rifles, 165 grenades, 500,000 rounds of ammunition, and 14 sticks of TNT at a house in the border town of Reynosa, Mexico.[39]

During FY2006 and FY2007, the Bureau of Alcohol, Tobacco, Firearms, and Explosives (ATF) dedicated approximately 100 special agents and 25 industry operations investigators (IOIs) to a new Southwest border initiative known as Project Gunrunner. The initiative aims to deny firearms to criminal organizations in Mexico, and to combat firearms-related violence affecting communities on both sides of the border. In FY2007, ATF agents investigated 187 firearms trafficking cases and recommended 465 defendants for prosecution. As of November 2008, 146 special agents and 68 IOIs had been deployed to the Southwest border to bolster Project Gunrunner. In addition to these efforts along the U.S.-Mexico border, ATF has deployed eTrace firearms tracking technology to U.S. Consulates in Mexico to help with arms trafficking investigations.[40]

In response to the increasing flow of high-caliber weapons from the United States to Mexico, ICE, in collaboration with Mexican law enforcement agencies, has launched a new bilateral program against weapons smuggling, known as *Armas Cruzadas*. Among other things, the program is to involve intelligence sharing and joint law enforcement efforts with vetted Mexican units.[41]

Gun control advocates have suggested that the U.S. government could further expand its efforts against gun trafficking to Mexico. They have advocated for, among other things, improving regulations to combat "straw purchases," better regulating how weapons that are particularly attractive to criminal groups (such as "vest-buster" handguns and anti-armor rifles) are marketed, and enacting an effective assault weapons ban.[42]

Drug Demand

In 2007, more than 35 million people in the United States reported using illicit drugs or abusing prescription drugs. U.S. drug demand fuels a multi-billion dollar illicit industry that has enhanced the power of DTOs and other allied gangs and organized criminal groups. Some 90% of the cocaine consumed in the United States is now trafficked from South America through the Mexico-Central America corridor. Mexico is also a major supplier of marijuana, methamphetamines, and heroin. Mexican DTOs have become the leading drug distributors of cocaine, heroin, and other illicit drugs in the United States, with supply networks established in at least 230 U.S. cities.[43]

Studies have shown that addressing drug demand through a combination of treatment programs for heavy users and prevention programs is more successful and cost-effective than through supply reduction programs.[44] Nevertheless, the U.S. drug control budget has continued to emphasize supply-side programs, including drug crop eradication in source countries, interdiction, and domestic law enforcement efforts, rather than demand reduction efforts. Since FY2002, funding for supply-side programs reportedly has increased by almost 57%, whereas support for demand reduction efforts has increased by less than 3%.[45] Supply reduction efforts now account for nearly two-thirds of the federal drug control budget.

It remains to be seen whether U.S. pledges to intensify domestic demand reduction efforts in order to complement the Mérida Initiative will be reflected in new budgetary priorities. For example, in the Bush Administration's FY2009 budget request, which was submitted after Mérida was announced, funding for drug prevention programs was cut by 25% as compared to the previous year. Ongoing debates about the proper balance of funding for supply reduction vs. demand reduction programs are likely to continue during the 111th Congress.[46]

Bulk Cash Smuggling

Each year Mexican drug trafficking organizations repatriate huge amounts of illicit revenues from drug sales in the United States to Mexico, perhaps totaling some $15 to 20 billion annually.[47] In order to address this problem, the DEA has carried out bulk cash seizure investigations with the FBI, ICE, and CBP. In 2005, ICE and CBP launched a program known as "Operation Firewall," which resulted in increased operations against bulk cash smuggling in the U.S.-Mexico border region. Many operations have been carried out in coordination with Mexican customs and the Mexican money laundering vetted unit. In 2008, ICE created a Trade Transparency Unit (TTU) in Mexico. Mexican TTU representatives are receiving training and technical support from ICE officials in how to identify cross-border trade anomalies that could be indicative of bulk cash smuggling.

Mexico Policy Issues[48]

As Congress oversees implementation of the Mérida Initiative, it is likely to maintain an interest in what the Mexican government is doing to combat the drug cartels and reform its law enforcement and judicial systems. Congress may want to ensure that U.S. and Mexican counternarcotics programs are complementing, rather than duplicating each other's efforts. Congress may also to monitor the Mexican government's anti-corruption efforts, as well as its ability to hold police and military forces accountable for human rights abuses.

Domestic Counterdrug Eefforts

President Calderón has made combating drug cartels a top priority of his administration. He has increased Mexico's security budget from roughly $2 billion in 2006, to some $4 billion in 2008. He has mobilized thousands of soldiers and federal police to arrest drug traffickers, establish check points, burn marijuana and opium plants, and interdict drug shipments. According to the U.S. State Department, Mexican authorities seized more than twice the amount of cocaine in 2007 than they did in 2006.[49] A recent U.S. government report credits Mexico's recently established import restrictions on products containing methamphetamine precursors with reducing Mexican methamphetamine shipments to the United States.[50] President Calderón has also used extradition as a major tool to combat drug traffickers, extraditing 83 alleged criminals to the United States in 2007 and a record 85 individuals in 2008.

While a majority of Mexicans still support President Calderón, some predict that popular frustration with his government may soon mount if his two-year campaign against the drug cartels fails to produce measurable results.[51] Drug seizures and extraditions have increased, but drug- related violence has reached record levels. As of early December 2008, drug violence had claimed some 5,300 lives, with police and military frequently targeted by drug traffickers. More than 500 police and military members have been slain since late 2006.[52] Some have expressed concerns about the militarization of Mexican law enforcement. Calderón officials, however, maintain that the military has to be used for counterdrug efforts due to the corruption of state and local police by the cartels, and because the police cannot compete with the type of heavy weaponry that the drug cartels are using.[53] Others assert that Calderón has not devoted enough resources to addressing issues that are closely linked to the drug trade, such as money laundering. Still others are concerned about ongoing corruption, impunity, and human rights abuses by military and police forces.

Police Reform and Anti-Corruption Efforts

Instances of corruption of law enforcement and government officials have been a significant problem that has made the campaign against drug cartels more difficult. In late October 2008, for example, an elite unit within the federal Attorney General's office known as SIEDO was implicated in a scandal involving payoffs for sensitive information about antidrug activities, with at least 35 officials and agents fired or arrested.[54] In August 2008, six members of SIEDO reportedly had been arrested on suspicion of leaking information to drug traffickers.

President Calderón has taken steps to reform the country's federal, state, and municipal police forces and to crack down on corruption within the police and other government institutions. Calderón has reorganized the two federal police agencies under a single commander, established a new police training institute, and created a national database through which police can share information and intelligence. His government has begun to test the competency of state and local police forces and to reward units whose officers meet certain standards with higher budgets. Only roughly 50% of officers tested in 2008 are said to have met the minimum standards. President Calderón has also purged hundreds of corrupt police officers. In late December 2008, he asserted that some 11,500 law enforcement and other government employees had been fined for corruption in the past two years, with fines totaling close to $300 million.[55]

The State Department's 2007 human rights report, issued in March 2008, recognized the Mexican government's efforts to reform and professionalize the police force, although it highlighted that corruption and impunity, particularly at the state and local levels, remain endemic problems. Analysts have suggested that the Calderón government consider implementing other reforms, including, but not limited to, strengthening police professionalization programs, establishing a career track within federal and state police forces, and developing internal and external review mechanisms for police performance.[56]

Implementation of Judicial Reforms

The Mexican judicial system has been widely criticized for being opaque, inefficient, and corrupt. It is plagued by long case backlogs, a high pre-trial detention rate (some 40% of Mexican inmates are simply awaiting trials), and an inability to secure convictions. In June 2008, President Calderón signed a judicial reform decree after securing the approval of Congress and Mexico's states for an amendment to Mexico's Constitution. Under the reform, Mexico will have eight years to replace its trial procedures, moving from a closed door process based on written arguments to a public trial system with oral arguments and the presumption of innocence until proven guilty. In addition to oral trials, the judicial system is to adopt more alternative means of dispute resolution (ADR), which should help make it more flexible and efficient.

Implementing these judicial reforms is likely to bring with it a series of challenges that will have to be addressed. Many observers hope that the federal government can learn how to identify and overcome those challenges by looking at the experiences that states such as Chihuahua and Oaxaca have had in adopting an accusatorial justice system and in using ADR.[57] Some of those challenges may include the need to update law school curricula, retrain current legal professionals, build new courtrooms, improve forensic technology, and encourage the use of ADR. USAID has been supporting state-level judicial reform programs in Mexico since the mid- 1990s, and will now be supporting implementation of the federal judicial reform.

Protection of Human Rights

Both the Mexican police and military have poor human rights records. According to the State Department's most recent human rights report, there were credible reports of police involvement in extrajudicial killings, kidnappings for ransom, and torture. On July 1, 2008, the media's release of videos reportedly showing police from an elite squad in the city of León, Mexico, practicing torture techniques provoked strong expressions of concern by Mexican and international human rights organizations. An American instructor was seen in the videos. A spokesman for the U.S. Embassy in Mexico City maintained that the "U.S. government was not involved in the training in any way."[58]

There is increasing concern that the Mexican military, which has less human rights training and is less accountable to civilian authorities than the police, will commit more human rights abuses as it is tasked with law enforcement and duties for which it is ill-trained and ill-suited.[59] Between December 2006 and May 2008, Mexico's Human Rights Commission (the CNDH) received 634 reports of human rights abuses by Mexican military forces. In July 2008, the CNDH issued a report recommending that, among other measures, the military should conduct investigations into each of the cases, punish those who are found guilty of abuses, pay damages to victims, and develop plans to prevent future abuses. There are also concerns that the desertion rate among military members is increasing, with a number of those deserters leaving to join the cartels. Some have urged the Calderón government to develop a time-table for when Mexico's military will disengage from law enforcement efforts. In the meantime, many experts maintain that there needs to be greater oversight of the military by civilian institutions, particularly the Congress.[60]

Central America Policy Issues

A number of policy issues may emerge as Congress considers the Central American portion of the Mérida Initiative including concerns about:

- **Funding:** When the Mérida Initiative was first announced, Central American leaders and some Members of Congress expressed concerns about the funding disparity between the Mexican and Central American portions of the Initiative.[61] Depending upon how much funding Central America receives in the FY2009 and FY2010 budgets for Mérida, there may be lingering questions about the adequacy of the funds provided, as well as how much of those funds should be spent on regional programs versus bilateral programs in the seven Central American countries.

- **Type of Funds Provided:** In the FY2008 Supplemental Appropriations Act, Congress reduced the funds appropriated for law enforcement programs in Central America in order to increase funding for institution-building, rule of law, and development programs. Members are likely to continue to debate how funding should be balanced between the various program components, particularly how much funding should support law enforcement programs and drug interdiction efforts versus institution-building and rule of law activities.

- **Interagency Coordination:** Debates are likely to continue concerning what U.S. agency is best equipped to oversee Mérida programs, including the issue of whether there is a role for the U.S. Southern Command in anticrime efforts, and how U.S. programs should be coordinated with those funded by other donors.

- **Domestic Efforts by Partner Governments:** Congress and the Obama Administration are likely to monitor the political will among the Central American governments to combat corruption and impunity, address crime and violence in a holistic way, and to complement U.S. funding with support from their national budgets, the private sector, and other international donors.

- **Anti-gang Policies:** There is ongoing disagreement over the level and combination of preventive and suppressive policies that should be used in Central America to address the gang problem. Proponents of law enforcement solutions maintain that Central American law enforcement officials lack the capacity and resources to target gang leaders effectively, share data, and conduct thorough investigations that lead to successful prosecutions. Human rights groups tend to emphasize the importance of prevention and rehabilitation programs.

- **U.S. Deportation Procedures:** Congress may also maintain an interest in how U.S. deportation procedures for individuals with criminal records might be improved and whether U.S. assistance should be provided to help receiving governments reintegrate deportees.

Haiti and the Dominican Republic

The Bush Administration originally conceived the Mérida Initiative as a foreign assistance package for Mexico and Central America, the countries through which the bulk of cocaine heading to the United States now flows. However, some Members of Congress felt that the Initiative should also include funding for the Caribbean drug transit countries of Haiti and the Dominican Republic. If not, they argued, drug traffickers are likely to return to the Caribbean transit zone rather than the Mexico-Central America drug transit corridor. As a result, the 110th Congress included Haiti and the Dominican Republic in Mérida authorizations and appropriations legislation. The 111th Congress may consider whether to insert additional Mérida funding for Haiti and the Dominican Republic in the pending FY2009 budget request. Similarly, the Obama Administration may or may not include Haiti and the Dominican Republic in its FY2010 request for Mérida.

Some favor including Haiti and the Dominican Republic in the Mérida Initiative since both countries are key transhipment points for cocaine bound from South America to the United States and Europe. They point out that both countries have experienced a surge in air smuggling of cocaine from Venezuela since 2007.[62] Haiti, the poorest and most unstable country in the Western Hemisphere, is particularly attractive to narcotics traffickers since its coasts and border with the Dominican Republic are largely uncontrolled.

Others oppose providing additional Mérida funds for Haiti and the Dominican Republic since there are only limited funds available for the Initiative. Haiti and the Dominican Republic already receive U.S. counternarcotics assistance through other foreign aid accounts. Moreover, they argue, both countries are also receiving counternarcotics training and support from the U.N. Stabilization Mission in Haiti.

Appendix: Conditions on FY2008 Supplemental Assistance for Merida

Mexico

The FY2008 Supplemental Appropriations Act (P.L. 110-252), which includes the first tranche of funding provided for the Mérida Initiative, has human rights conditions softer than compared to earlier House and Senate versions, in large part because of Mexico's objections that some of the conditions would violate its national sovereignty. The Secretary of State, after consultation with Mexican authorities, is required to submit a report on procedures in place to implement Section 620J of the Foreign Assistance Act (FAA) of 1961. That section of the FAA "prohibits assistance to any unit of the security forces of a foreign country if the Secretary of State has credible evidence that such unit has committed gross violations of human rights." An exception to this prohibition is provided in Section 620J if the Secretary of State determines and reports to Congress that the government of such country is taking effective measures to bring the responsible members of the security forces unit to justice.

In P.L. 110-252, human rights conditions require that 15% of INCLE and FMF assistance be withheld until the Secretary of State reports in writing that Mexico is taking action in four human rights areas:

- improving transparency and accountability of federal police forces;
- establishing a mechanism for regular consultations among relevant Mexican government authorities, Mexican human rights organizations, and other relevant Mexican civil society organizations, to make consultations concerning implementation of the Mérida Initiative in accordance with Mexican and international law;
- ensuring that civilian prosecutors and judicial authorities are investigating and prosecuting, in accordance with Mexican and international law, members of the federal police and military forces who have been credibly alleged to have committed violations of human rights, and the federal police and military forces are fully cooperating with the investigations; and
- enforcing the prohibition, in accordance with Mexican and international law, on the use of testimony obtained through torture or other ill-treatment.

Central America, Haiti and the Dominican Republic

P.L. 110-252 includes similar conditions on assistance provided to Central America, Haiti and the Dominican Republic. As with Mexico, The Secretary of State is required to submit a report on procedures in place to implement Section 620J of the Foreign Assistance Act (FAA) of 1961 in order for Mérida funding to be released.

Other human rights conditions require that 15% of INCLE and FMF assistance be withheld until the Secretary of State reports in writing that the governments of the countries in Central America, Haiti, and the Dominican Republic are taking action in three areas:

- establishing police complaints commissions with authority and independence to receive complaints and carry out effective investigations;
- implementing reforms to improve the capacity and ensure the independence of the judiciary; and
- investigating and prosecuting members of the federal police and military forces who have been credibly alleged to have committed violations of human rights.

End Notes

[1] The Central American countries include Belize, Costa Rica, El Salvador, Guatemala, Honduras, Nicaragua, and Panama.

[2] For background information on conditions in Mexico and Central America, see CRS Report RL32724, *Mexico-U.S. Relations: Issues for Congress*, by Mark P. Sullivan and June S. Beittel; CRS Report RL34215, *Mexico's*

Drug Cartels, by Colleen W. Cook, and CRS Report RL341 12, *Gangs in Central America*, by Clare Ribando Seelke.

[3] The $197 million is from the International Narcotics Control and Law Enforcement (INCLE) foreign aid funding account, and will fund equipment, training, and technology programs. More than $136 million under the Mérida Initiative from the Foreign Military Financing (FMF) and Economic Support Funds (ESF) accounts was already being used to support antidrug and anticrime programs. See Embassy of the United States in Mexico, Press Release, "Mérida Initiative Monies Released; Letter of Agreement signed," December 3, 2008. Letters of Agreement are being negotiated with the Central American countries, Haiti, and the Dominican Republic.

[4] Since the initial pot of Mérida Initiative funding in FY2008 was provided through a supplemental assistance measure rather than the regular FY2008 foreign aid funding measure, the continuing resolution does not fund the Mérida Initiative for FY2009.

[5] Although the statement did not announce additional funding for U.S. domestic efforts, it cited several examples of such efforts to combat drugs and crime that are already in place. Those examples included the 2007 Southwest Border Counternarcotics Strategy and the 2008 National Drug Control Strategy. See U.S. Department of State and Government of Mexico, "Joint Statement on the Mérida Initiative," October 22, 2007.

[6] Developed by former Colombian President Andrés Pastrana (1998-2002), Plan Colombia sought to end Colombia's military conflict, eliminate drug trafficking, and promote economic and social development. Since FY2000, Congress has appropriated more than $6 billion to support Plan Colombia, largely through the Andean Counterdrug Program account.

[7] Eric L. Olson, "Six Key Issues in U.S.-Mexico Security Cooperation,"Woodrow Wilson Center, July 2008; Statement by Thomas Shannon, Assistant Secretary of State for Western Hemisphere Affairs at a briefing entitled, "The Merida Initiative: Our Partnership Moves Forward," States News Service, July 9, 2008.

[8] These Mexican government statistics were cited in "Mexico Says Gang Killings More Than Double in 2008," Associated Press, December 8, 2008. The figure cited for the same period in 2007 was 2,477.

[9] For an evaluation of recent U.S. counternarcotics assistance to Mexico, see Government Accountability Office, "U.S. Assistance Has Helped Mexican Counternarcotics Efforts, but Tons of Illicit Drugs Continue to Flow into the United States," August 17, 2007.

[10] In H.R. 6028, the term "countries of Central America" is defined to include Haiti and the Dominican Republic, along with Belize, Costa Rica, El Salvador, Guatemala, Honduras, Nicaragua, and Panama.

[11] For a detailed description of the Bush Administration's FY2008 supplemental assistance proposal for the Mérida Initiative, see CRS Report RS22837, *Merida Initiative: U.S. Anticrime and Counterdrug Assistance for Mexico and Central America*, by Colleen W. Cook and Clare Ribando Seelke.

[12] U.S. Department of State, FY2008 Supplemental Appropriations Spending Plan: Mexico, Central America, Haiti, and the Dominican Republic, September 9, 2008.

[14] As with Mexico, Congress divided the funding for Central America between several different aid accounts. In addition to changing the account structure, Congress shifted the bulk of funding for Central America from public security and law enforcement programs to institution building,

[13] Aside from the broad $73.5 million earmark, Congress earmarked $3 million to support the creation a national police registry, $10 million for drug demand reduction programs, and $5 million for police education and training programs.

[14] For information on the Mérida funds provided for anti-gang programs, see CRS Report RL341 12, *Gangs in Central America*, by Clare Ribando Seelke.

[15] In December 2006, the United Nations and the Guatemalan government signed an agreement to establish the International Commission against Impunity in Guatemala (CICIG) to investigate illegal security groups and clandestine organizations, some of which have been tied, directly or indirectly, to the Guatemalan state. In August 2007, the Guatemalan Congress ratified the UN-Guatemala agreement allowing the creation of the CICIG. The CICIG was inaugurated on January 11, 2008.

[16] For more information on U.S. international drug control policy, see CRS Report RL34543, *International Drug Control Policy*, by Liana Sun Wyler.

[17] Government Accountability Office, "Plan Colombia: Drug Reduction Goals Were Not Fully Met, But Security Has Improved; U.S. Agencies Need More Detailed Plans for Reducing Assistance," October 2008, GAO-09-7.

[18] Michael Shifter, "Latin America's Drug Problem," Current History, February 2007; International Crisis Group, "Latin American Drugs II: Improving Policy and Reducing Harm," March 14, 2008; Brookings Institution, "Re- Thinking U.S.-Latin American Relations: A Hemispheric Partnership for a Turbulent World," November 24, 2008.

[19] American Enterprise Institute, "Five Perspectives on the Mérida Initiative: What it is and why it Must Succeed," March 4, 2008.

[20] Heritage Foundation, "Executive Summary: Mexico, Drug Cartels, and the Merida Initiative: A Fight We Cannot Afford to Lose," by Ray Walser, July 23, 2008.

[21] Washington Office on Latin America (WOLA), "The Mérida Initiative and Citizen Security in Mexico and Central America," March 19, 2008; Council on Foreign Relations, "Task Force Report: U.S.-Latin America Relations: A New Direction for a New Reality," May 2008.

[22] See, for example, comments made at the Woodrow Wilson Center Event, "U.S.-Mexico Security Cooperation: The Mérida Initiative and Beyond," February 8, 2008. Available at [http://www.wilsoncenter.org/index.cfm?topic_id=5949&fuseaction=topics.event_summary&event_id=370648].

[23] Josh Meyer, "Mistrust Bedevils War on Mexican Drug Cartels," Los Angeles Times, December 31, 2008.

[24] For example, the FY2008 Consolidated Appropriations Act (P.L. 110-161) cut security-related aid to Colombia significantly from the Administration's request, and increased funding for alternative development, human rights, and institution-building programs.

[25] In Mexico and Central America, "hard-side" assistance generally refers to counterdrug and anti-terror assistance provided to police and military forces, while "soft-side" assistance refers to rule of law, human rights, and economic and social development programs. In Andean drug-producing countries like Colombia, the "hard-side/soft-side" dichotomy is not just about security vs. development assistance, but also an allusion to crop eradication ("hard-side) vs. alternative development ("soft-side") programs.

[26] WOLA, "The Mérida Initiative and Citizen Security in Mexico and Central America," March 19, 2008; Center for International Policy Americas Policy Program,"A Primer on Plan Mexico" by Laura Carlsen, updated July 10, 2008.

[27] Senate Foreign Relations Committee, "Hearing on Mexico and Central America Counternarcotics Aid," November 15, 2007.

[28] See, for example, Ann Van Dusen and Carol Lancaster, Organizing U.S. Foreign Aid: Confronting the Challenges of the 21st Century, Washington, D.C.: Brookings Institution, 2005.

[29] Testimony of Paul Rosenzweig, Acting Assistance Secretary of the Office of International Affairs, Department of Homeland Security, before the House Homeland Security Subcommittee on Border, Maritime, and Global Counterterrorism, June 6, 2008.

[30] Josh Meyer, "Mexico Under Siege; Mistrust Bedevils War on Cartels" Los Angeles Times, December 31, 2008.

[31] For more information, see CRS Report RL34639, *The Department of Defense Role in Foreign Assistance: Background, Major Issues, and Options for Congress*, coordinated by Nina M. Serafino.

[32] WOLA, Center for International Policy, and Latin America Working Group Education Fund, "Ready, Aim, Foreign Policy: How the Pentagon Takes Over More and More Areas of Foreign Policy," April 20, 2008.

[33] Heritage Foundation, July 2008; WOLA, March 2008.

[34] U.S. Department of State, Office of Language Services Translating Division, "Not All That is Gold Glitters and Not All That Glitters is Gold," by Joel Fyke and Maureen Meyer, originally published in Foreign Affairs en Español, vol. 8, no. 1.

[35] See "House Foreign Affairs Committee, Subcommittee on the Western Hemisphere Holds a Hearing on Central America and the Mérida Initiative," CQ Transcriptions, May 8, 2008.

[36] U.S. Department of State and Government of Mexico, "Joint Statement on the Mérida Initiative," October 22, 2007.

[37] Brookings Institution, November 2008.

[38] "Washington Watch," LatinNews Daily, August 14, 2008; and Randal C. Archibold, "2-Nation Border Conference Discusses Gun Trafficking," New York Times, August 16, 2008.

[39] "Mexico: Army Seizes Huge Weapons Cache," Los Angeles Times, November 8, 2008.

[40] U.S. Embassy, Mexico, "Border and Law Enforcement, Project Gunrunner,"ATF Factsheet, available at [http://www.usembassy-mexico.gov/eng/texts/et080116eTrace.html] Updated figures obtained from Bureau of Alcohol, Tobacco, Firearms, and Explosives official, November 28, 2008.

[41] U.S. Immigration and Customs Enforcement, "Fact Sheet: Armas Cruzadas," available at [http://www.ice.gov/pi/news/factsheet/armas_cruzadas.htm]

[42] Tom Diaz, Violence Policy Center, "Disrupting Arms Trafficking to Mexico," October 17, 2008.

43 NDIC, National Drug Threat Assessment 2009, November 2008.

[44] P. Rydell and S. Everingham, "Controlling Cocaine Supply Versus Demand Programs," RAND: Santa Monica, C.A., 1994; David Boyum and Peter Reuter, An Analytic Assessment of U.S. Drug Policy, Washington, D.C.: American Enterprise Institute, 2005.

[45] "FY02-FY09 Budget Emphasizes Least Effective Ingredients of Drug Policy," Carnevale Associates, February 2008.

[46] For more information on U.S. domestic drug policy, seeCRS Report RL32352, *War on Drugs: Reauthorization and Oversight of the Office of National Drug Control Policy*, by Mark Eddy.

[47] Testimony of John P. Walters, Director of the Office of National Drug Control Policy, before the House Oversight and Government Reform Subcommittee on Domestic Policy, March 12, 2008.

[48] For more information, see CRS Report RL32724, *Mexico-U.S. Relations: Issues for Congress*, by Mark P. Sullivan and June S. Beittel.

[49] U.S. Department of State, Bureau of International Narcotics and Law Enforcement Affairs, International Narcotics Control Strategy Report 2008, March 2008.

[50] NDIC, National Drug Threat Assessment 2009, November 2008.

[51] Laurence Iliff, "Calderón's 2nd Year Ends With Fresh Turmoil," Dallas Morning News, December 1, 2008.

[52] "Mexico Says Gang Killings More Than Double in 2008," Associated Press, December 8, 2008; Ken Ellingwood, "Mexico Under Siege: Attacks on Police Continue Amid Crackdown on Drugs," Los Angeles Times, November 4, 2008.

[53] U.S. Government Printing Office, "The Mérida Initiative: Guns, Drugs, and Friends," Minority Staff Report to Senate Committee on Foreign Relations, United States Senate, December 21, 2007.

[54] Tracy Wilkinson, "Mexico Under Siege: Elite Police Tainted by Drug Gang," Los Angeles Times, October 28, 2008.

[55] Sara Miller Llana, "Setbacks in Mexico's War on Corruption," Christian Science Monitor, December 29, 2008.

[56] Woodrow Wilson Center, Mexico Institute, "The United States and Mexico: Toward a Strategic Partnership," January 2009.

[57] David Shirk and Lourna M. Márquez-Carrasquillo, "Border Brief: State Level Judicial Reform Initiatives in Mexico," February 21, 2008.

[58] Alfredo Corchado, "U.S. Denies Involvement in Training Videos Showing Mexican Officers Using Torture," Dallas Morning News, July 3, 2008.

[59] Roderic al Camp, "Role of Military to Military Cooperation and the Implications and Potential Risks to Civil-Military Relations," Testimony before the Congressional Policy Forum, May 8, 2008.

[60] Woodrow Wilson Center, Mexico Institute, "The United States and Mexico: Toward a Strategic Partnership," January 2009.

[61] Manuel Roig-Franzia, "Central Americans See Peril in Bush's Anti-Drug Priorities," Washington Post, November 29. 2007.

[62] U.S. Department of State, International Narcotics Control Strategy Report, March 2008.

In: Politics and Economics of Latin America. Volume 6
Editor: Samantha R. Dawes
ISBN: 978-1-61668-014-5

Chapter 4

COLOMBIA: ISSUES FOR CONGRESS*

Clare Ribando Seelke and June S. Beittel

ABSTRACT

The 111th Congress will likely continue to review the progress of aid provided to Colombia through the Andean Counterdrug Program and continue oversight of human rights, alternative development, eradication efforts, the environmental consequences of aerial fumigation, and the paramilitary demobilization process.

SUMMARY

In the last decade, Colombia—a key U.S. ally in South America—has made significant progress in reasserting government control over much of its territory, combating drug trafficking and terrorist activities by illegally armed groups, and reducing poverty. Since the development of Plan Colombia in 1999, the Colombian government, with substantial U.S. support, has stepped up its counternarcotics and security efforts. Congress has provided more than $6 billion to support Colombia from FY2000 through FY2008. Proponents of the current U.S. policy towards Colombia point to the inroads that have been made in improving security conditions and in weakening the Revolutionary Armed Forces of Colombia (FARC) guerrillas. Critics argue that, despite these security improvements, U.S. policy has not rigorously promoted human rights, provided for sustainable economic alternatives for drug crop farmers, or reduced the amount of drugs available in the United States.

President Alvaro Uribe, re-elected in May 2006, has made headway in addressing Colombia's 40- year plus conflict with the country's leftist guerrillas, as well as the rightist paramilitary groups that have been active since the 1980s. Uribe enjoys wide popular support, which has not been significantly affected by an ongoing scandal concerning past government

* This is an edited, reformatted and augmented version of a CRS Report for Congress publication dated February 2009.

ties to illegal paramilitary groups. Uribe's popularity soared after Colombia's March 2008 raid of a FARC camp in Ecuador resulted in the killing of a top guerrilla commander and the seizure of his computer files. It spiked again following the Colombian military's successful July 2, 2008 rescue of 15 hostages long held by the FARC. Those hostages included three U.S. defense contractors and a former Colombian presidential candidate. While some Colombians are calling for President Uribe to seek a third presidential term, others have been disillusioned by his handling of a series of illegal investment schemes or have concerns about his attempt to remain in power.

Concerns in the 110th Congress regarding Colombia focused on funding levels and U.S. policy regarding Plan Colombia, U.S. hostages, trade, and human rights. The FY2008 Consolidated Appropriations Act (P.L. 110-161) raised the level of U.S. funding provided for economic and social aid closer to that provided for security-related programs. In July 2008, both the House and Senate passed resolutions expressing gratitude to the Colombian government for successfully rescuing the three U.S. hostages being held by the FARC (H.Con.Res. 389/S.Res. 627). The House also passed an amendment (H.Amdt. 112 to H.R. 5959) expressing the importance of continuing to provide U.S. assistance to Colombia. An enacted continuing resolution (P.L. 110- 329) will provide funding at FY2008 levels through March 6, 2009. While acknowledging the progress that the Uribe government has made in improving security conditions in Colombia, some Members of Congress have expressed concerns about labor activist killings and the parapolitical scandal. These issues received increased attention as the Bush Administration called for Congress to approve implementing legislation for the Colombia Free Trade Agreement (CFTA). For more information, see CRS Report RL34470, *A U.S.-Colombia Free Trade Agreement: Economic and Political Implications* and CRS Report RL34759, *Proposed Colombia Free Trade Agreement: Labor Issues*. The future of the CFTA in the 111th Congress remains uncertain.

The 111th Congress will likely continue to review the progress of aid provided to Colombia through the Andean Counterdrug Program and continue oversight of human rights, alternative development, eradication efforts, the environmental consequences of aerial fumigation, and the paramilitary demobilization process.

Recent Developments

On December 12, 2008, Colombian drug trafficker Diego Montoya who authorities claim was responsible for some 70% of cocaine brought into the United States and Europe when he directed the Valle del Norte cartel was extradited to the United States to stand trial on drug charges.

On December 11, 2008, the U.S. Drug Enforcement Administration released a report that indicated an 89% increase in the price of cocaine in the United States between January 2007 to September 2008 and a marked decline in average drug purity during the same period.

On December 11, 2008, Colombia became "compact-eligible" with the Millennium Challenge Account. Colombia successfully met competitive selection criteria designed to demonstrate a strong commitment to political, economic and social reforms. Because the Millennium Challenge program is recipient-driven, Colombia must now formulate a proposed assistance program for a 5-year award (i.e. compact) from the U.S. aid agency, the Millennium Challenge Corporation.

On November 17, 2008, President Uribe declared a state of emergency in response to riots over the collapse of a series of pyramid investment schemes that had victimized hundreds of thousands of Colombians, particularly from the four poorer southern departments. In the aftermath of the crisis, polling indicated a downturn in support for the President reducing the likelihood of his reelection to a third term, the possibility of which would require a constitutional amendment.

In October 2008, President Uribe fired 27 Colombian soldiers and army officers, including three generals, who were implicated in the murder of 11 civilians whose bodies had been dressed as guerillas allegedly to inflate the military's body count. On November 4, 2008, the head of Colombia's military, Army Commander Mario Montoya, resigned over the scandal.

On October 6, 2008, the U.S. Government Accountability Office (GAO) released a report that found that while Plan Colombia had made significant security gains, it had not succeeded in reducing the amount of drugs flowing to the United States. The report also found that coca cultivation had risen by 15% and the production of pure cocaine by 4% in Colombia since 2000 when the Plan Colombia was launched. (U.S. GAO, *Plan Colombia: Drug Reduction Goals Were Not Fully Met, but Security Has Improved; U.S. Agencies Need More Detailed Plans for Reducing Assistance*, GAO-09-7 1, October 2008).

On September 10, 2008, the U.S. Office of National Drug Control Policy (ONDCP) reported that while the area under coca cultivation in Colombia increased slightly in 2007, the productivity of that area fell sharply due to aerial spraying and manual eradication efforts.

On August 19, 2008, the Colombian Prosecutor General's office ordered the release of Mario Uribe, a second cousin and ally of President Alvaro Uribe, stating that the evidence against him did not merit his imprisonment while he awaits his trial. Mario Uribe, a former Senator, was arrested on charges of suspected collusion with paramilitary groups. Approximately one-fifth of Colombian legislators, many from pro-Uribe parties, are under investigation for possible paramilitary ties.

On July 28, 2008, Secretary of State Condoleezza Rice certified to Congress that the Colombian government and armed forces are meeting the U.S. statutory requirements with regard to human rights.

On July 2, 2008, the Colombian military successfully rescued 15 hostages long held by the Revolutionary Armed Forces of Colombia (FARC) guerrillas. Those hostages included three U.S. citizens—Marc Gonsalves, Thomas Howes, and Keith Stansell—held since February 2003 and former Colombian presidential candidate Ingrid Betancourt held since February 2002.

On May 25, 2008, the FARC confirmed that its leader, Manuel Marulanda, died of a heart attack in March.

In mid-May 2008, President Uribe extradited 15 top paramilitary leaders, including Salvador Mancuso and Carlos Mario Jiménez, to the United States to stand trial on drug trafficking charges.

On May 15, 2008, Interpol released a report confirming that Colombian officials did not tamper with computer files seized during a raid of a FARC camp in Ecuador.

On April 10, 2008, the House voted 224-195 in favor of changing the rules that had allowed the President to "fast-track" trade agreements through Congress, effectively putting congressional consideration of the U.S.-Colombia Free Trade Agreement (CFTA) on hold.

On March 18, 2008, after extended debate, the OAS adopted a resolution rejecting, but not condemning, Colombia's bombing raid of a FARC camp in Ecuador and calling for the restoration of diplomatic ties between Ecuador and Colombia. Those ties still have not been fully restored.

On March 11, 2008, the State Department released its annual human rights report, which stated that "although serious problems remained, the [Colombian] government's respect for human rights continued to improve, which was particularly evident by progress in implementing the Justice and Peace Law." (See the full report at http://www.state.gov/g/drl/rls/hrrpt/2007/.)

On March 5, 2008, a second member of the FARC's secretariat, Ivan Rios, was murdered by his own security agent.

On March 1, 2008, the Colombian military bombed a FARC camp in Ecuador, killing at least 25 people, among them, Raúl Reyes, the terrorist groups' second highest commander. Colombia alleged that computer files found on laptops seized during the raid indicated that the government of Hugo Chávez of Venezuela was planning to provide millions of dollars in assistance to the FARC for weapons purchases.

INTRODUCTION

Colombia is a South American nation of roughly 44 million people, the third most populous country in Latin America. It is an ethnically diverse nation—58% of the population is mestizo, 20% white, 18% black, 3% black-Amerindian, and 1% Amerindian.[1] Colombia has one of the oldest democracies in Latin America, yet it has been plagued by violence and a conflict that has been ongoing for over 40 years. The country's rugged terrain historically made it difficult to establish state control over large swaths of the nation's territory. High rates of poverty have also contributed to social upheaval in the country. In 2006, 45% of Colombians lived in poverty, down from close to 60% in 2000.[2] Colombia's ability to reduce poverty in recent years is at least partly due to increases in the country's economic growth rates, which reached 7.5% in 2007.[3] Security improvements and a more stable economy have likely led to the recent increase in foreign direct investment (FDI). FDI grew from roughly $6.5 billion in 2006 to some $9 billion in 2007, with the bulk of new investments occurring in the oil, manufacturing, and mining sectors. Despite the Colombian government's success in reducing poverty levels, income inequality and land concentration are still significant problems.[4]

Drug trafficking has helped to perpetuate Colombia's conflict by providing earnings to both left- and right-wing armed groups. The two main leftist guerrilla groups are the FARC and the National Liberation Army (ELN), both of which have kidnapped individuals for ransoms, committed serious human rights violations, and carried out terrorist activities. Most of the rightist paramilitary groups were coordinated by the United Self-Defense Forces of Colombia (AUC), which disbanded in 2006 after more than 30,000 of its members demobilized. Members of the AUC have been accused of gross human rights abuses and collusion with the Colombian Armed Forces in their fight against the FARC and ELN.

Colombia is a democratic nation with a bicameral legislature. The Liberal and Conservative parties, which dominated Colombian politics from the 19th century through much of the 20th century, have been weakened by their perceived inability to resolve the roots of violence in Colombia. In 2002, Colombians elected an independent, Alvaro Uribe, as President, largely because of his aggressive plan to reduce violence in Colombia. The major political parties currently represented in the Colombian Congress include the Liberal, Conservative, Alternative Democratic Pole, National Unity, and Radical Change parties, as well as several smaller political movements. To some observers, the legitimacy of the Colombian Congress has been seriously called into question because more than 70 of its 268 members, many from pro-Uribe parties, have either been jailed or placed under investigation for alleged ties to illegal paramilitary groups.[5]

POLITICAL SITUATION

The First Uribe Administration

During his first term (2002-2006), President Uribe took steps to fulfill his campaign promises to address the paramilitary problem, defeat leftist guerrilla insurgents, and combat narcotics trafficking.[6] President Uribe took a hard-line approach to negotiations with illegally armed groups, declaring that the government would only negotiate with those groups who are willing to give up terrorism and agree to a cease-fire, including paramilitary groups with which former President Pastrana had refused to negotiate. Negotiations with the AUC paramilitaries resulted in a July 15, 2003 agreement in which the AUC agreed to demobilize its members by the end of 2005. President Uribe endorsed a controversial Justice and Peace Law that was designed to provide a framework for those demobilizations. At the same time, Uribe sought to build up the size and strength of the Colombian military and police, whose forces stepped up their counternarcotics operations and activities against the FARC. High public approval ratings, likely due to reductions in violence that had occurred largely as a result of his security policies, prompted Colombia to amend its constitution in 2005 to permit Uribe to run for re-election.

The Second Uribe Administration

On August 7, 2006, Alvaro Uribe was sworn into his second term as president. Pro-Uribe parties won a majority of both houses of congress in elections held in March 2006, giving President Uribe a strong mandate as he started his second term. The domination of pro-Uribe parties, most of them new, appears to have further weakened the traditionally dominant Liberal and Conservative parties. Nevertheless, there is not a high level of unity among the pro-Uribe parties.

Entering the third year of his second presidential term, President Uribe retains widespread support in Colombia. His popularity derives from the progress his government has made in improving security situation in Colombia, demobilizing the AUC, and defeating the FARC and ELN. According to U.S. State Department figures, kidnappings in Colombia have declined by 83%, homicides by 40%, and terrorist attacks by 76% since Uribe first took office in 2002. Police are now present in all of Colombia's 1,099 municipalities, including areas from which they had been previously ousted by guerrilla groups.[7] President Uribe has also overseen the demobilization and disarmament of more than 31,000 AUC paramilitaries, although the demobilization process has been criticized for failing to provide adequate punishments for perpetrators and reparations to victims of paramilitary violence.[8] On March 1, 2008, the Colombian military successfully carried out a raid of a FARC camp in Ecuador that resulted in the killing of a top FARC leader and the capture of his computer files. This was followed by a successful operation on July 2 that resulted in the rescue of 15 hostages long held by the FARC, including three U.S. defense contractors and a former Colombian presidential candidate.

Despite this progress, Colombia continues to face serious challenges. While its numbers have been dramatically reduced in the last year or so, the FARC still has thousands of fighters capable of carrying out terrorist attacks, kidnappings, and other illicit activities.[9] Not all paramilitaries demobilized, and still others have returned to paramilitary activities since demobilizing. One of the weaknesses of the demobilization program has been reintegration of demobilized forces into law-abiding civilian life.[10] Moreover, there are credible reports that a new generation of paramilitaries is forming that is much more criminal than political in nature.[11] An estimated 9,000 new fighters have formed and as many as 15% to 20% of the new paramilitary groups may consist of former combatants.[12] Although President Uribe has not been personally implicated, the Colombian Supreme Court is pursuing ongoing investigations into possible links between Colombian politicians, many from pro-Uribe parties, and paramilitary groups. Ongoing peace talks with the ELN have yet to yield any tangible results. Since the 2006 elections, there have several scandals involving some Colombian military officials and lingering concerns exist about extrajudicial killings committed by Colombian security forces.[13] The latest scandal occurred in October when 27 soldiers and military officers (including three generals) were fired over the discovery of eleven murdered civilians who had been dressed as guerilla fighters to increase military body counts. As a result, General Mario Montoya, the commander of the Colombian army, stepped down on November 4, 2008.

Drug production and trafficking continue to generate millions of dollars annually for illicit groups. While ONDCP recently reported large declines in Colombia's coca production potential, a June 2008 U.N. Office on Drugs and Crime (UNODC) report found that, although yields were down, the coca acreage planted in Colombia increased by 27% in 2007.[14] Additionally, as a result of the ongoing conflict and drug-related violence, Colombia now has one of the largest populations of internally displaced persons in the world, with more than 250,000 people displaced in 2007.

Uribe Re-Election Debate Moves Ahead

President Uribe's high approval ratings have led many of his supporters to urge him to seek a third presidential term. In order for Uribe to be re-elected, the Colombian constitution would have to be amended again (as it was in 2005) to allow him to seek a third term. Uribe's supporters have delivered a petition with five million signatures to Colombian election authorities urging them to convoke a referendum to reform the constitution to allow a third Uribe term. The petition must now be debated in the Colombian legislature and reviewed by the country's Constitutional Court. On December 17, in a special session of Congress, the lower house of the Congress passed an ambiguously worded bill authorizing President Uribe to run in either 2010 or 2014. Some analysts view this as a defeat of his re-election bid in 2010, but others project that the interpretation of the bill may allow for a go-ahead with a consecutive third term. The legislation still requires action in Colombia's Senate when the legislature recovenes in March 2009.

President Uribe has yet to publicly comment on whether or not he wishes to run again. His popularity has dipped as a result of the declining economy and the collapse of a massive illegal pyramid scheme in November that ensnared many of his working class supporters, although his approval rating still hovers around 70%.[15] Many Colombian and international observers have urged Uribe not to seek another term out of respect for the integrity of Colombian democracy. Some have expressed concerns about his past conflicts with Colombian democratic institutions and his attempt to remain in power.[16]

Progress in Addressing Colombia's Internal Conflict

Roots of the Conflict

Colombia has a long tradition of civilian, democratic rule, yet has been plagued by violence throughout its history. This violence has its roots in a lack of state control over much of Colombian territory, and a long history of poverty and inequality. Conflicts between the Conservative and Liberal parties led to two bloody civil wars—The War of a Thousand Days (1899-1903) and The Violence (1946 to 1957)—that killed hundreds of thousands of Colombians. While a power sharing agreement (the so-called National Front pact) between the Liberal and Conservative parties ended the civil war in 1957, it did not address the root causes of the violence. Numerous leftist guerrilla groups inspired by the Cuban Revolution formed in the 1960s as a response to state neglect and poverty. Right-wing paramilitaries were formed in the 1980s when wealthy landowners organized armed groups to protect themselves from the leftist guerrillas. The shift of cocaine production from Peru and Bolivia to Colombia in the 1980s increased drug violence, and provided a new source of revenue for both guerrillas and paramilitaries. The main paramilitary organization, the AUC, began demobilization in 2003 and disbanded in 2006. Major armed groups today are the FARC, the National Liberation Army (ELN), and the new generation of paramilitary groups.

Revolutionary Armed Forces of Colombia (FARC)

The FARC can trace its roots to armed peasant self-defense groups that had emerged during "the Violence" of the 1940-50s. By the 1960s, those groups, located in the remote, mountainous regions between Bogotá and Cali, had developed into a regional guerrilla movement. In 1966, the guerrillas announced the formation of the FARC.[17] The FARC is the oldest, largest, and best- equipped and financed guerrilla organization in Latin America. It mainly operates in rural areas, but has shown its ability to strike in urban areas, including

Bogotá. It conducts bombings, murders, mortar attacks, kidnappings, extortion, and hijackings mainly against Colombian targets. The FARC is fully engaged in the drug trade, including cultivation, taxation of drug crops, and distribution, from which it reaps significant profits. In recent years, the FARC has increased it activities along Colombia's borders with Ecuador and Venezuela.

During the Pastrana Administration, the FARC entered into peace negotiations under which it was granted control of a Switzerland-size territorial refuge while the peace process was underway. With continued FARC military activity, including the kidnapping of a Colombian senator, President Pastrana halted the negotiations and ordered the military to retake control of the designated territory. During the inauguration of President Uribe on August 7, 2002, the FARC launched a mortar attack on the Presidential Palace that killed 21 residents of a nearby neighborhood.

In mid-2003, the Colombian military's *Plan Patriota*, a campaign to recapture FARC-held territory, began operations in what was largely seen as a successful effort to secure the capital and environs of Bogotá. In 2004, military operations, conducted by up to 17,000 troops, turned to regaining FARC territory in the southern and eastern regions of the country. The FARC initially responded with a tactical withdrawal of forces, but launched a new counter-offensive in February 2005. The conflict with the FARC has, however, largely remained in the countryside and the FARC was unable to disrupt President Uribe's August 7, 2006, inauguration. In 2006 the FARC controlled an estimated 30% of Colombian territory.[18] The Colombian government maintains that *Plan Patriota* enabled it to reduce FARC ranks, recapture land held by the FARC, and confiscate large amounts of materials used to process cocaine. Despite these advances, critics pointed out that large numbers of civilians were displaced during the campaign.

Colombia's Raid of a FARC Camp in Ecuador

On March 1, 2008, the Colombian military bombed a FARC camp in Ecuador, killing at least 25 people, among them, Raúl Reyes, the terrorist groups' second highest commander whose real name is reportedly Luis Edgar Devia Silva, four Mexican students visiting the camp, and one Ecuadorian citizen reportedly tied to the FARC.[19] This mission marked the first time in the Colombian military's 44-year struggle against the leftist FARC insurgency that it has been able to kill a member of the FARC's seven-member ruling secretariat. A few days later, Ivan Rios, another member of the FARC's secretariat, was murdered by his own security agent. Many assert that these high-level killings dealt a significant blow to the FARC, particularly following a FARC announcement in May 2008 that its top commander, Manuel Marulanda, had died in March of a heart attack.

During the raid, the Colombian military captured three laptop computers that allegedly belonged to Reyes. Computer files on those laptops allege that the government of Hugo Chávez of Venezuela was planning to provide millions of dollars in assistance to the FARC for weapons purchases. As a result, some Members of Congress called for the Bush Administration to include Venezuela on the U.S. state sponsors of terrorism list; the Administration began an inquiry into the matter in March. The files also allege that President Raphael Correa of Ecuador received campaign donations from the FARC in 2006. Both Chávez and Correa vigorously reject these claims. Venezuelan officials have dismissed the data as having been fabricated even though Interpol verified in May 2008 that the files had not been tampered with since they were seized. In a welcome turn of events on June 8, 2008,

President Chávez called for the FARC to release all hostages unconditionally and to cease military operations, maintaining that guerrilla warfare "has passed into history," signaling a major change in his public stance.[20] Tensions persist between Colombia and Ecuador following the Colombian incursion into Ecuadorian territory in March. Colombian-Venezuelan relations also remain strained despite a subsequent rapprochement with President Chavez.[21]

Hostage Releases, Escapes, and the July 2008 Hostage Rescue

Since 2007, prisoner escapes, hostage deaths, and later hostage releases have focused international attention on the plight of hundreds of hostages held by the FARC. In April 2007, Colombian police office Jhon Frank Pinchao escaped after eight years in FARC custody. In June 2007, eleven departmental deputies who had held since 2002 were reportedly executed by the FARC.[22] In August 2007, President Uribe authorized leftist Senator Piedad Córdoba and Venezuelan President Hugo Chávez to conduct dialogue with the FARC to secure the release of some 45 high-profile hostages, including the three American contractors held since 2003. Negotiations stalled in November due to the FARC's failure to provide proof of life of the hostages and allegations that President Chávez inappropriately contacted the head of the Colombian Army. However, the Colombian government did find over a dozen proof of life videos, including videos of the three American contractors, in a November 2007 raid on the FARC. In December 2007, Fernando Araujo, a former Minister of Development, escaped from the FARC after being held as a hostage for more than six years. From February through July 2008, Araujo served as Colombia's Foreign Minister.

Six hostage releases occurred during early 2008. In January 2008, two hostages were released to a delegation led by President Chávez and the Colombian government was able to successfully reunite one of the hostages with a son born to her in captivity that the FARC had turned over to the Colombian foster care system more than two years ago. A day after the two hostages' release, Chávez's called for the international community to no longer label the FARC and the ELN as terrorist groups prompted widespread condemnation. Nevertheless, his role in the release of hostages continued. On February 27, 2008, the FARC released four former members of the Colombian Congress to Venezuelan officials in Colombian territory.

On July 2, 2008, after months of planning and tracking the FARC, the Colombian military successfully tricked the FARC into releasing 15 of their prized hostages. Those hostages included three U.S. defense contractors—Marc Gonsalves, Thomas Howes, and Keith Stansell—held since February 2003 and former Colombian presidential candidate Ingrid Betancourt held since February 2002. The success of the bloodless hostage rescue has been widely cited as an example of the Colombian military's increasing professionalism and intelligence capabilities, which has occurred largely as a result of years of the U.S. training and security assistance programs provided through Plan Colombia.[23] Some press reports indicate that the United States provided millions of dollars to help Colombia find and rescue the hostages, including tactical support and training provided by the U.S. military and technical assistance supplied by a unit of planners, intelligence analysts, and hostage negotiators based in Bogotá.[24]

Many analysts have hailed the recent hostage rescue as evidence that the FARC is disintegrating, but others think it may be too premature to draw that conclusion. This year the FARC has lost three of its top commanders and suffered a series of humiliating defeats at the hands of the Colombian military. Their communications systems have been infiltrated, their leadership is in disarray, and reports indicate that many guerrilla units are running short on supplies.[25] By mid-June 2008, more than 1,506 FARC guerrillas had voluntarily demobilized. Many rebels reportedly hoped to take advantage of the Colombian government's offer to allow the Justice and Peace Law's provisions to apply to those who surrender.[26] Although the FARC, now led by Alfonso Cano, is still unwilling to negotiate with the Uribe government, their position is much weaker than it was a short time ago. In late December 2008, the FARC announced plans to release six hostages unconditionally including two captive politicians and four members of the Colombian armed forces who had been held for years in jungle camps.[27]

National Liberation Army (ELN)

The smaller ELN was formed in 1965, inspired by the ideas of Fidel Castro and Che Guevara. With a membership of about 3,000, it is less active than the FARC, but has still been able to carry out a number of high profile kidnappings and bombings. In addition to the rural civilian population, the ELN has also targeted the country's infrastructure, especially its oil and electricity sectors. Its operations are mainly located in the rural areas of the north, northeast, the Middle Magdalena Valley, and along the Venezuelan border. The ELN earns funds from the taxation of illegal crops, extortion, attacks on the Caño-Limón pipeline, and kidnapping for ransom. Its size and military strength have been dramatically reduced since the late 1990s.[28]

In recent years, the ELN has shown more of a willingness to attempt peace negotiations with the government. In December 2003, President Uribe revealed that he had met with an ELN leader to discuss possible peace initiatives, but a subsequent ELN statement ruled out any possibility of demobilization. However, in 2004, the ELN and the Colombian government accepted an offer from Mexican President Vicente Fox to facilitate peace negotiations. In June 2004, Mexico named Andres Valencia, a former Mexican ambassador to Israel, as its facilitator. Meetings with Valencia and the ELN occurred, but the rebel group rejected Uribe's offer of a cease-fire.[29] In April 2005, the ELN rejected further Mexican facilitation after Mexico voted to condemn Cuba at the U.N. Human Rights Commission. The Colombian government and the ELN held several rounds of exploratory talks in Havana, Cuba between December 2005 and August 2007, but those talks resulted in no concrete agreements. In June 2008, the ELN announced that it would not continue negotiating with the Uribe government for the time being. President Uribe responded by ordering the Colombian military to step up its operations against the ELN.[30]

Paramilitaries

Paramilitary groups trace their origins to the 1980s when wealthy ranchers and farmers, including drug traffickers, organized armed groups to protect them from kidnappings and extortion plots by the FARC and ELN. The largest paramilitary organization, the AUC, was formed in 1997 as an umbrella organization for a number of local and regional paramilitary groups operating in the country. As discussed in more detail below, the AUC disbanded in 2006. Not all paramilitary groups joined the AUC umbrella. The AUC conducted massacres and assassinations of suspected insurgent supporters and directly engaged the FARC and ELN in military battles. The Armed Forces of Colombia have long been accused of turning a blind eye to these activities. The AUC, like the FARC, earned most of its funding from drug trafficking. *Jane's World Insurgency and Terrorism* estimated that in 2006 paramilitaries handled 40% of Colombian cocaine exports.[31]

On July 15, 2003, the AUC reached an agreement with the Colombian government to demobilize its troops by the end of 2005. At that time, the State Department estimated that there were between 8,000 and 11,000 members of the AUC, although press reports used numbers ranging up to 20,000. The demobilization process begun in 2004 officially ended in April 2006. As of that time, over 30,000 AUC members had demobilized and turned in over 17,000 weapons.[32] AUC leaders remained at large, however, until August 2006 when President Uribe ordered them to surrender to the government to benefit from the provisions of the Peace and Justice Law.[33] It remains to be seen how Uribe's May 2008 decision to extradite 15 paramilitary leaders to the United States to stand trial for drug trafficking charges will affect ongoing investigations into the "parapolitical" scandal, as well as efforts to ensure that victims of paramilitary violence receive compensation for their suffering.

Not all paramilitaries demobilized, and still others have returned to paramilitary activities since demobilizing. Moreover, there are credible reports that a new generation of paramilitaries has formed and may be recruiting demobilized paramilitaries. Membership in the new paramilitary organizations is estimated at 3,000 to 9,000. Some former AUC members continue to be active in the drug trade.[34] There are reports that the AUC continues to take part in drug trafficking, in spite of the demobilization process. *Jane's World Insurgency and Terrorism* reports that since demobilization the AUC's purpose has shifted from combating the FARC and ELN to protecting drug trafficking networks and preventing the extradition of leaders wanted on drug trafficking charges in the United States. The State Department and U.N. both note that the new illegal groups do not share the political ideology of the AUC, which sought to defeat leftist guerrillas. Despite their ad-hoc nature, the new illegal groups pose a threat to Colombian civilians and the Uribe government is taking steps to combat them.[35]

Remaining Political Challenges

Parapolitical Scandal

A scandal involving alleged paramilitary ties to politicians, including current members of the Colombian Congress, erupted in November 2006. On November 9, 2006, the Colombian Supreme Court ordered the arrest of three congressmen for their alleged role in establishing paramilitary groups in the Caribbean state of Sucre. Since the scandal broke, several Colombian politicians, including several past and current members of the Colombian Congress, have been charged with ties to paramilitary groups. Former Foreign Minister Maria Consuelo Araujo was forced to resign due to the investigation into her brother's and father's connections to the paramilitaries and their involvement in the kidnapping of Alvaro Araujo's opponent in a Senate election. In December 2007, Congressman Erik Morris was sentenced to six years in prison for his ties to the paramilitaries, making him the first Member of Congress to be sentenced in the ongoing scandal. In February 2008, the former head of Colombia's Department of Administrative Security (DAS), Jorge Noguera, was formally charged with collaborating with paramilitaries, including giving paramilitaries the names of union activists, some of whom were subsequently murdered by the paramilitaries. In April 2008, Mario

Uribe, a former senator, second cousin, and close ally of President Alvaro Uribe, was arrested for colluding with the paramilitaries. As of early August 2008, some 70 legislators were under investigation for possible ties with the paramilitaries.[36] As of November 2008, more than 30 congressmen from pro-Uribe parties had been indicted for past links to the paramilitaries.[37]

The parapolitical scandal has increased tensions between President Uribe and the Supreme Court, which is charged with investigating the politicians accused of having paramilitary ties, many of whom are from pro-Uribe parties. In July 2008, representatives from the two branches met in a series of meetings to discuss President Uribe's concern that the paramilitary investigations were advancing too quickly. Despite those meetings, the Supreme Court ordered the arrest of Senator Carlos Garcia, head of Uribe's main coalition party, in late July. Tensions escalated again in August when press reports announced that two of President Uribe's advisers had met with representatives of Don Berna, the top paramilitary leader, at the presidential palace in April.[38] Government critics have questioned whether President Uribe's decision in May 2008 to extradite key paramilitary figures to the United States may have been done, at least partially, in order to thwart ongoing investigations into government-paramilitary ties. They have also questioned the motives behind a judicial reform package submitted by Uribe to the Congress that would remove the Supreme Court's power to investigate legislators.[39] The judicial reform bill was ultimately withdrawn by the government after it received strong criticism from the courts and from members of Colombia's Congress.[40] In October 2008, Human Rights Watch released a report that examined the government's efforts to investigate and prosecute paramilitaries and those who collaborated with them. It warns that the Uribe administration has harassed the Supreme Court as it has carried out prosecutions of politicians, security forces and others with alleged paramilitary ties.[41]

The Justice and Peace Law and Demobilization

As part of the paramilitary demobilization process, President Uribe introduced a Justice and Peace Law granting conditional amnesties to illegal combatants, which would mean that the law could also apply to FARC and ELN fighters if they decide to enter into negotiations with the government. Colombia's Congress approved the legislation in 2005. The Justice and Peace Law called on demobilized fighters to provide a voluntary account of their crime and to forfeit illegally acquired assets in exchange for an alternative penalty of up to eight years' imprisonment. If the accused was subsequently found to have intentionally failed to admit to a crime, the alternative penalty could be revoked and the full sentence imposed. Critics contended that the penalties provided for in the law were too lenient and amount to impunity. The Uribe Administration argued that without the inducement of the new law, paramilitary leaders and fighters would be unwilling to demobilize and a spiral of violence would continue in Colombia.

In July 2006, Colombia's Constitutional Court upheld the constitutionality of the law. In the same ruling, however, the Constitutional Court limited the scope under which demobilizing paramilitaries can benefit from the reduced sentences. Paramilitaries who commit crimes or fail to fully comply with the law will have to serve full sentences. The ruling also stipulates that paramilitaries must confess all crimes and make reparations to victims using both their legally and illegally obtained assets. Paramilitary leaders reacted by stating that they would not comply with the law. In response, President Uribe ordered paramilitary leaders to turn themselves in. By October 2006 all but 11 paramilitary leaders had complied with this order.[42]

The merits of the Justice and Peace Law have been fiercely debated both in Colombia and the United States. Supporters believe it is an effective means to end paramilitary activities. The Bush Administration has expressed support for the law, noting that it has facilitated the demobilization of more than 31,000 paramilitary members. Supporters of the law maintain that paramilitaries must act in good faith and avoid further participation in illegal activities in order to benefit from the peace process. The Uribe Administration has removed some demobilized paramilitaries, including Carlos Mario "Macaco" Jiménez, from the Justice and Peace process due to their continued participation in illegal activities. In May 2008, Uribe extradited Jiménez, Salvatore Mancuso, and 13 other paramilitary leaders who had violated the terms of the law to the United States where to stand trial on drug trafficking charges.

Despite these results, the OAS Mission to Support the Peace Process in Colombia and other observers have expressed concern about the institutional frailty of the Justice and Peace process. Although more than 155,000 victims have registered in the three years since the law's passage, the International Crisis Group describes implementation as "lagging." Their report cites lack of interest in victim's rights from the Uribe government, inadequate support for the implementing institutions, and the persistence of armed conflict and threatening presence of new illegal armed groups.[43] Human rights organizations are also concerned that the paramilitaries have not been held accountable for their illegal activities and, that by under reporting illegally obtained assets, have failed to provide adequate reparation to their victims.[44] Other observers have expressed concerns that many paramilitaries have elected not to participate in the Justice and Peace process. Of the more than 31,000 paramilitary members that had demobilized as of June 2008, just 3,297 had been found eligible to receive benefits under the Justice and Peace Law's framework. In response to concerns that the Justice and Peace Unit tasked with investigating and prosecuting the paramilitaries was severely understaffed, the Uribe government issued a decree in spring 2008 to authorize tripling the size of its staff.[45] The International Criminal Court is monitoring the investigations and prosecutions of former paramilitaries to ensure that those who guilty of human rights abuses are held accountable for their crimes.[46]

Human Rights Violations by Colombian Security Forces

In its 2008 State of the World's Human Rights report, Amnesty International asserted that, between June 2006 and June 2007, at least 280 civilians were extrajudicially killed by Colombian security forces and that many of them were subsequently presented by those forces as guerrillas killed in conflict. The State Department's *Country Reports on Human Rights Practices* for Colombia covering 2007 stated that "while the government's overall respect for human rights continued to improve...there were periodic reports that members of the security forces committed extrajudicial killings." In a February 2008 report, the U.N. High Commissioner for Human Rights acknowledged that, although it continued to receive complaints of extrajudicial killings by security officers, Colombian military and civilian officials have developed new directives to deal with allegations of abuses by security officials. However, this year human rights groups have continued to document extrajudicial killings by some Colombian military forces.[47] In October 2008, armed forces were linked to the murder of 11 poor civilians from Soacha whose bodies had been disguised as guerillas in order to inflate military body counts. As a result, the government fired 27 soldiers and officers (including three generals) and the commander of the Colombian army, General Mario Montoya, resigned on November 4, 2008.[48]

Internally Displaced Persons (IDPs)

Colombia has one of the largest internally-displaced populations in the world—more than 3 million IDPS—with indigenous and Afro-Colombians disproportionately represented among those displaced. There is some discrepancy over the current rate of displacement. The Colombian government registered over 250,000 IDPs in 2007, a decline of about 8,000 from 2006. Some IDPs do not register with the Colombian government out of fear and procedural barriers. As such, estimates of new displacements put forth by NGOs tend to be higher than government figures. For example, the Consultancy for Human Rights and Displacement (CODHES), a Colombian NGO, estimated that some 305,000 people were displaced in 2007, about 27% higher than the number CODHES recorded in 2006. Although still concerned by the overall numbers of individuals displaced, international NGOs found that the rate of mass displacements decreased in 2007. Colombian government assistance to IDPs increased by 10% in 2007, with total assistance provided estimated at $500 million.[49] In 2008, the U.N. High Commissioner for Refugees (UNHCR) expressed particular concern about new displacements occurring along southern Colombia's Pacific Coast.[50] CODHES recently reported more than 270,000 people were displaced in the first six months of 2008 and that was "a record high level in the last twenty years."[51] In contrast, the government's index on displaced populations found a decline in the number of IDPs in 2008 totaling 137,699 from January through September.[52]

Landmines

Landmines are an ongoing problem in Colombia. The International Committee to Ban Landmines reports that Colombia had the highest number of landmine casualties in the world in 2006, with 1,106 casualties.[53] Although Afghanistan and Cambodia continue to have higher rates of landmine casualties (per capita) than Colombia, Colombian casualties are high. Both Human Rights Watch and the International Committee to Ban Landmines report that the vast majority of landmines are laid by the FARC and ELN.[54] Landmine Monitor cites a decline in landmine casualties to 895 in 2007, the first decline since 2002. The change was attributed to setbacks suffered by the FARC.[55]

Colombia and Global Drug Trends

Colombia's prominence in the production of cocaine and heroin is cited as justification for the U.S. focus on anti-narcotics efforts in the Andean region. According to various sources, Colombia produces 60% of the world's cocaine.[56] It is the source of over 90% of cocaine consumed in the United States. Even though Colombia produces only a small fraction of global heroin production, it is the leading supplier of heroin in the eastern United States, according to the State Department's 2008 *International Narcotics Control Strategy Report.*

The world's supply of cocaine is produced by just three countries: Peru, Bolivia, and Colombia. Until the mid-1990s, Peru and Bolivia were the two major producers. Colombia eclipsed Bolivia in 1995 and Peru in 1997, the result of increased eradication programs in those two countries and the displacement of coca cultivation to Colombia. Cocaine production in Colombia increased fivefold between 1993 and 1999. UNODC recently reported a 27% increase in coca cultivation in Colombia in 2007, with smaller increases of 5% and 4% reported in Bolivia and Peru respectively.[57]

Global production of the opium poppy, from which heroin is produced, increased 17% in 2007, largely due to production increases in Afghanistan and Burma (Myanmar). Its principal source countries are Afghanistan (82%) and Burma (Myanmar) (11%). Most heroin consumed in the United States, however, comes from Mexico and Colombia. In 2007, the U.N. found that opium poppy cultivation in Colombia fell to about 714 hectares, whereas cultivation in Mexico increased to 19,147 hectares.[58] In its October 2008 report, the U.S. Government Accountability Office reported that opium poppy cultivation and heroin production had declined by about 50% between 2000-2006 in Colombia.[59]

In recent years, the Colombian government, with significant U.S. assistance, has stepped up its eradication efforts, with manual eradication accounting for an increasing percentage of total eradication efforts. In 2007, the Colombian government eradicated over 219, 529 hectares of elicit coca crops, up from 215,421 hectares eradicated the previous year. Aerial eradication accounted for 70% of the coca crops destroyed in 2007.[60] ONDCP has credited ongoing aerial spraying and manual eradication programs with recent declines in the cocaine productivity of the coca currently cultivated in Colombia.[61] The Colombian Ministry of Defense has asserted that, due to recent declines in U.S. security assistance, its forces will probably only be able to spray about 100,000 hectares in 2008 (as compared to the roughly 153,000 hectares they eradicated through aerial spraying in 2007).[62]

After a long period of stable prices, purity, and availability of illegal drugs in the United States, evidence indicated that the price of cocaine rose dramatically from January 2007 to September 2008 according to a report from the U.S. Drug Enforcement Administration (DEA). On December 11, 2008, the DEA announced that the average price of a gram of cocaine rose 89%—from $96.61 to $182.73—over the 21-month period ending in September. Over the same time frame, the agency reported a decline in cocaine average purity from 67% to 46% drawing data from 24,000 drug seizures reported in the DEA's System to Retrieve Information from Drug Evidence (STRIDE) database. The supply of drugs is often judged by changes in price, with higher prices signifying decreased supply. Declining purity is also used as a measure indicating decreased availability. DEA's Acting Administrator Michele Leonhart credited the changes in price and purity to regional counternarcotics efforts, including U.S. funded programs in Colombia.[63] The *National Drug Threat Assessment 2009,* published in December 2008, found a decline in cocaine availability in the United States that may have been responsible for price increases and purity declines. While the report states "the leading cause of the decrease in domestic availability is unclear," the likely factors include the exceptionally large drug seizures made while the drugs are in transit to the United States, the crackdown in enforcement by the Mexican government, intercartel violence in Mexico, U.S. law enforcement efforts along the Southwest border, and expanding markets in Europe and South America.[64]

Some observers have expressed caution in interpreting government figures on price, purity, and availability. They maintain that short-term fluctuations are not uncommon and may not be sustainable.[65] Still others express caution because cocaine production levels have not fallen. Another possible explanation for the declining cocaine supply in the United States is that cocaine is being diverted to Europe where drug traffickers can earn more money, presumably because of the strong euro.[66]

Colombia and Regional Security

Another justification of current U.S. policy in the Andean region is that drug trafficking and armed insurgencies in Colombia have a destabilizing effect on regional security. With porous borders amid rugged territory and an inconsistent state presence, border regions are seen as particularly problematic. Colombia shares a 1,367 mile border with Venezuela, approximately 1,000 miles each with Peru and Brazil, and much smaller borders with Ecuador and Panama. The conflict in Colombia and its associated drug trafficking have led to spillover effects in Colombia's neighboring countries.

Cross-Border Incursions and Safe Havens

Colombia's relations with its neighbors have been strained by the spillover from Colombia's civil war, including cross-border military activity. Colombia has asked both Venezuela and Ecuador for assistance in patrolling border areas where the FARC is strong. Press accounts in 2006 and 2007 reported numerous FARC attacks in Colombia along its border with Venezuela. The State Department's *2007 Country Reports on Terrorism* report states that Venezuelan President Hugo Chávez's "ideological sympathy for the FARC and ELN limited Venezuelan cooperation with Colombia in combating terrorism." The FARC and ELN use Venezuelan territory as safehavens, and to transship arms and drugs, secure logistical supplies, and commit kidnappings and extortion. Splinter groups of the FARC also operate in Venezuela where they participate in drug trafficking.

Opponents of President Chávez regularly accuse him of harboring FARC guerrillas. While the FARC uses Venezuelan territory as a safe haven, the State Department notes, "it remained unclear to what extent the Venezuelan Government provided material support to Colombian terrorist organizations. However, limited amounts of weapons and ammunition, some from official Venezuelan stocks and facilities, have turned up in the hands of Colombian terrorist organizations"[67] The same report noted that Venezuela does not systematically police its nearly 1,400 mile border with Colombia to interdict arms or the flow of narcotics. President Chávez's comments that the FARC and ELN should be considered belligerent groups, not terrorist organizations, following the January 2008 release of two hostages held by the FARC increased tension between Colombia and Venezuela. Tensions grew following the March 2008 raid of the FARC camp in Ecuador because of captured computer files describing material support of the FARC by the Venezuelan government. In June, two Venezuelan nationals (one a national guard sergeant) and two Colombians were arrested in Eastern Colombia for gun running with ammunition allegedly destined for the FARC. On September 12, 2008, the U.S. Treasury Department froze the assets of two senior intelligence officers and the former Venezuelan interior minister for alleging helping the FARC with weapons and drug trafficking.[68]

Tensions with Ecuador have also increased, with accusations of incursions by Colombian troops chasing FARC units across the border. Colombia is concerned that the FARC are using Ecuadorean territory to launch attacks. Leftist Ecuadorean President Rafael Correa opposes

U.S. involvement in Colombia and has indicated that he will not renew the United States' lease on the Manta air base when it is up for renewal in 2009. Ecuador is also concerned that aerial spraying of coca crops in southern Colombia is reaching into Ecuador potentially damaging licit Ecuadorean crops. Other concerns between the countries relate to refugees from Colombia's conflict.[69]

Crisis in the Andes and Efforts at Resolution

In March 2008, Colombia's unauthorized raid on a FARC camp in Ecuador prompted one of the most serious diplomatic crises that the Andean region has faced in recent years. President Correa responded to the raid by breaking diplomatic ties with Colombia and sending additional troops to the Ecuador-Colombia border. In a show of solidarity with Ecuador, President Chávez broke diplomatic and trade ties with Colombia and sent 10 battalions of troops to Venezuela's border with Colombia.

While some feared that the diplomatic crisis might escalate into a military conflict, those concerns were allayed after a Rio Group summit held in the Dominican Republic on March 7. At the Rio summit, Uribe, Chávez, and Correa each had a chance to voice his concerns, which resulted in heated exchanges that lasted some six hours. President Uribe publicly apologized for the incursion and vowed that it would never happen again. President Chávez appeared to accept the apology and called for an end to the crisis, but President Correa remained angered by the affair. The Rio Group issued a resolution that rejected Colombia's incursion of Ecuadorian territory, but acknowledged Uribe's apology.[70]

The Rio Group summit was followed by a March 17-18, 2008, OAS Meeting of Consultation of Ministers of Foreign Affairs held at the organization's headquarters in Washington D.C. On March 18, after extended debate, the OAS adopted a resolution rejecting, but not condemning, the bombing raid and calling for the restoration of diplomatic ties between Ecuador and Colombia.[71] While Colombia and the United States reportedly view the raid as justified within the context of Colombia's longstanding battle against terrorist groups, most countries reject it as a violation of Ecuador's national sovereignty per Article 21 of the OAS Charter.[72]

Tensions between Colombia and its two neighbors—Ecuador and Venezuela—continued throughout the spring of 2008, particularly after Interpol published a report in May confirming that Colombian officials did not tamper with computer files seized at the FARC camp in Ecuador. Those files allege that the government of Hugo Chávez of Venezuela was planning to provide millions of dollars in assistance to the FARC for weapons purchases and that the Correa government received campaign contributions from the FARC. Venezuelan and Ecuadorian officials have dismissed the data as having been fabricated. Whereas Venezuela has restored diplomatic relations with Colombia, Ecuador has yet to do so.

ISSUES FOR CONGRESS

Recent debate on U.S. policy toward Colombia has taken place in a context of concern over the sheer volume of illegal drugs available in the United States and elsewhere in the world. The United States approved increased assistance to Colombia as part of a six-year plan called Plan Colombia in June 2000, and has provided over $6 billion in assistance from

FY2000 to FY2008. The United States now provides assistance to Colombia on an annual basis through the Andean Counterdrug Program (ACP) account, formerly known as the Andean Counterdrug Initiative (ACI), and other aid accounts.

In addition to the larger debate over what role the United States should play in supporting Colombia's ongoing struggle against drug trafficking and illegally armed groups, Congress has repeatedly expressed concern with a number of specific policy issues. These include continuing allegations of human rights abuses; the health and environmental consequences of aerial eradication for drug control; the progress of alternative development to replace drug crops with non-drug crops; judicial reform and rule of law programs; and the level of risk to U.S. personnel working in Colombia. Prior to the release of the three U.S. hostages held by the FARC in early July 2008, securing the release of those hostages was also a key issue of congressional concern.

In October 2008, the GAO released a report stating that Plan Colombia had only partially fulfilled its drug reduction goals. In the years 2000-2006 coca cultivation and production of cocaine had actually increased by about 15% and 4%, respectively. The report concludes that while significant security gains were achieved by the Colombian government with U.S. assistance, coca farmers had undermined eradication goals by taking effective countermeasures and alternative development programs had not been implemented in the areas where the majority of coca is grown.[73] Moreover, the report criticized the "nationalization" of Plan Colombia programs—the transfer of U.S.-administered programs to the Colombians—as too slow and lacking coordination.[74]

Proponents of the current U.S. policy towards Colombia point to the progress that has been made in improving security conditions in Colombia and in weakening the FARC guerrillas. They favor maintaining the current level of security assistance to Colombia in order to help Colombian security forces continue to combat the FARC and ELN, solidify their control throughout rural areas, and eradicate illicit narcotics. They also believe that guerrilla forces regularly cross borders using neighboring countries' territory for refuge and supplies, and that this has a potentially destabilizing effect in the region.

Opponents of current U.S. policy in Colombia respond that the counterdrug program uses a repressive approach to curbing drug production which could provoke a negative popular reaction in rural areas. They argue for halting aerial fumigation of drug crops, limiting aid to the Colombian military, and stressing interdiction rather than eradication so that the direct costs to peasant producers is less. Some critics of U.S. policy support a policy that focuses largely on economic and social aid to combat what they consider to be the conflict's root causes, curbs human rights abuses by paramilitary groups and security forces, provides vigorous support for a negotiated end to the fighting, and emphasizes illicit drug demand reduction in the United States.[75]

Plan Colombia and the Andean Counterdrug Program (ACP)

Plan Colombia was developed by former President Pastrana (1998-2002) as a plan to end the country's 40-year old armed conflict, eliminate drug trafficking, and promote development. The initial plan was a $7.5 billion three-year plan, with Colombia providing $4 billion of the funding and requesting $3.5 billion from the international community. The U.S.

Congress approved legislation in support of Plan Colombia in 2000, as part of the Military Construction Appropriations Act of 2001 (P.L. 106-246) providing $1.3 billion for counternarcotics and related efforts in Colombia and neighboring countries. Plan Colombia was never authorized by Congress and subsequent funding has been approved annually. President Bush has continued support for the plan under the ACP aid account. The ACP account also funds counternarcotics programs in Bolivia, Brazil, Ecuador, Panama, Peru, and, until recently, Venezuela. Because narcotics trafficking and the guerrilla insurgency have become intertwined problems, in 2002 Congress granted the Administration flexibility to use U.S. counterdrug funds for a unified campaign to fight drug trafficking and terrorist organizations.[76]

Through the ACP and Foreign Military Financing (FMF) accounts, the United States supports the eradication of coca and opium poppy crops, the interdiction of narcotics shipments, and the protection of infrastructure through training and material support for Colombia's security forces. U.S. assistance also supports alternative crop development and infrastructure development to give coca and opium poppy farmers alternative sources of income, and institution building programs to strengthen democracy. Alternative development (AD) programs were shifted from the ACP account to the Economic Support Fund (ESF) account in FY2008. U.S. assistance includes human rights training programs for security personnel in response to Congressional concerns about human rights abuses committed by Colombian security forces. Congress has prohibited U.S. personnel from directly participating in combat missions and has capped the number of U.S. military and civilian contractor personnel that can be stationed in Colombia in support of Plan Colombia at 800 and 600 respectively.[77]

The United States also supports the interdiction of drug shipments through the Air Bridge Denial (ABD) Program. The Air Bridge Denial program began as a joint interdiction effort between the United States, Peru, and Colombia that sought to identify possible drug flights and to interdict them by forcing them to land, and if necessary to shoot down the aircraft. The program was suspended in 2001 after a flight carrying American missionaries was shot down over Peru. Following the establishment of new safeguards against accidental shootdowns, the program was renewed in Colombia in 2003. The State Department credits the ABD program with reducing the number of illegal flights over Colombia by some 73% since 2003.[78] In 2008, the U.S. government began to transfer control of the ABD program to the Colombian government.

Aerial Eradication and Alternative Development[79]

Upon taking office, President Uribe announced that aerial eradication, along with alternative crop development, would form a significant basis of the government's efforts. The Plan Colombia eradication spraying program began in December 2000 with operations by the U.S.-funded counternarcotics brigade in Putumayo. It should be noted, however, that spraying does not prevent, although it may discourage, the replanting of illicit crops. During 2007, the Colombian government sprayed 153,000 hectares of coca and poppy and manually eradicated 66,000 hectares of coca and poppy.[80]

The United Nations and United States use different methodologies to estimate annual coca cultivation levels in Colombia. The different methodologies yield results that not only show different levels of cultivation, but different trends as well. **Table 1** and **Table 2** include United Nations and United States data on coca cultivation in Colombia since 2000. The area of cultivation is measured in hectares. For 2007, the United Nations reported a 27% increase in coca cultivation to 99,000 hectares.[81] U.S. data from the ONDCP showed a 6.2% increase in coca cultivation in 2007. Some of the 9% increase in cultivation that ONDCP reported for 2006 may be attributed to the fact that the area surveyed increased significantly from the previous year.

Aerial eradication has been controversial both in Colombia and the United States. Critics charge that it has unknown environmental and health effects, and that it deprives farmers of their livelihood, particularly in light of a lack of coordination with alternative development programs.[82] With regard to environmental and health consequences, the Secretary of State, as required by Congress, has reported that the herbicide, glyphosate, does not pose unreasonable health or safety risks to humans or the environment. In consultation for the certification, the U.S. Environmental Protection Agency confirmed that application rates of the aerial spray program in Colombia are within the parameters listed on U.S. glyphosate labels. However, press reports indicate that many Colombians believe the health consequences of aerial fumigation are grave, and many international non-governmental organizations criticize the certification for being analytically inadequate.

The U.S. Agency for International Development (USAID) funds alternative development programs to assist illicit crop farmers in the switch from illicit to licit crops, and provides assistance with infrastructure and marketing. Through 2007, the United States has completed 1,179 social and productive infrastructure projects. These programs have benefitted more than 135,000 families in 17 departments.[83] The USAID Mission in Colombia reports significant progress since funding started flowing for alternative development through Plan Colombia. In an October 2008 fact sheet, USAID states that to date there have been 238,263 hectares of licit crops supported in areas that illicit crops once predominated, and more than 280,000 jobs have been created.[84]

The success of alternative development in Colombia has been limited both by security concerns and the limited scope of the program. Various reports, including the recent GAO report that examined the progress of Plan Colombia, have identified weaknesses in the program including that a majority of the USAID alternative development projects were not located in areas where the majority of coca is grown in Colombia and they have not been evaluated with regard to drug reduction goals or sustainability. Security concerns were blamed for the planned withdrawal of USAID assistance to five departments where coca production was increasing, according to a USAID memo leaked to the press in October 2006. UNODC reported in June 2006 that alternative development programs have been successful, but only reach 9% of Colombian coca growers and called for a tenfold increase in international donor support for alternative development programs. In 2007, UNODC reported a disparity in spending on alternative development programs. The departments of Norte de Santander, Antioquia, and Santander received 65% of ongoing alternative development project funding, yet coca cultivation in these three departments is about 10% of the national total. In contrast, 40% of current coca cultivation is in the departments of Meta, Caqueta, Guaviare, and Vichada, which receive just 10% of ongoing alternative development project funding. Proponents of U.S. policy argue that both eradication and alternative development programs need time to work. USAID has argued that alternative development programs do not achieve drug crop reduction on their own, and that the Colombia program was designed to support the aerial eradication program and to build "the political support needed for aerial eradication efforts to take place."[85]

Table 1. UNODC Coca Cultivation in Colombia

Year	2000	2001	2002	2003	2004	2005	2006	2007
Area	163,000	145,000	102,000	86,000	80,000	86,000	78,000	99,0000
% change	-	11%	-30%	-16%	-7%	8%	-9%	27%

Table 2. U.S. ONDCP Coca Cultivation in Colombia

Year	2000	2001	2002	2003	2004	2005	2006	2007
Area %	136,200	169,800	144,450	113,850	114,100	144,000	157,200	167,00
% change	—	25%	-15%	-21%	0.2%	26%	9%	6.2%

Table 3. U.S. Assistance to Colombia: FY2007-FY2009

Program	FY2007	FY2008 Estimate	FY2008 Est. Compared to FY2007	FY2009 Request
Andean Counterdrug Program (ACP)-Interdiction/Eradication	325.10	244.62	-80.40	329.56
ACP-Alternative Development	139.90	0.00	—	—
Economic Support Fund	0.00	194.41	54.51	142.37
International Narcotics and Law Enforcement	0.00	41.91	41.91	0.00
Non-Proliferation, Antiterrorism, Demining, and Related Programs	4.09	3.72	-0.37	3.15
Foreign Military Financing	85.50	55.05	-30.0	66.39
International Military Education and Training	1.65	1.43	-0.22	1.40
P.L. 480 (Food Aid)	4.86	0.00	4.86	0.00
Total DOS	**561.10**	**541.14**	**-19.96**	**542.87**
Defense Department Counternarcotics Aid (Section 1004/1003)		na		na

Source: U.S. Department of State *Foreign Operations Congressional Budget Justifications*, FY2008-FY2009; DOD "Counterdrug Activity" Reports to Congress for FY2005-FY2007.

a. In FY2008, the Andean Counterdrug Initiative (ACI) was renamed the Andean Counterdrug Program (ACP). Until FY2008, ACI funds were divided between programs that supported drug eradication and interdiction efforts and those focused on alternative development and democratic institution building. In FY2008 funding for alternative development programs and institution building were requested from the Economic Support Fund (ESF) rather than the ACP account.

b. This column compares Alternative Development figures from FY2008 and FY2007.

Funding for Plan Colombia

From FY2000 through FY2008, U.S. funding for Plan Colombia and its follow-on, the Strategy for Strengthening Democracy and Promoting Social Development, totaled over $6 billion in State Department and Defense Department programs. Most U.S. assistance is provided through the ACP account. In FY2008 Congress funded eradication and interdiction programs through the ACP account, and funded alternative development and institution building programs through the Economic Support Fund (ESF) account. In previous years, alternative development and institution building were funded through the ACP account. In addition, support for aerial eradication programs is provided from the State Department's Air Wing account. The Defense Department requests a lump sum for all counternarcotics programs worldwide under Sections 1004 and 1033, and under Section 124, of the National Defense Authorization Act. DOD can reallocate these funds throughout the year in accordance with changing needs. While not considered a formal component of the ACP Program, the Defense Department has provided Colombia with additional funding for training and equipment for a number of years, as well as the deployment of personnel in support of Plan Colombia.

Table 4. U.S. Assistance For Plan Colombia, FY2000-FY2009 (in millions $)

	ACI	ESF	FMF	IMET	INCLE	NADR	Air Wing	DOD	Total
FY2000	60.1	—	—	—	—	—	38.0	128.5	226.6
P.L. 106-246	832.0	—	—	—	—	—	—	100.7	932.7
FY2001	48.0	—	—	—	—	—	38.0	190.2	276.2
ACI ESF FMF IMET INCLE NADR Air Wing DOD Total									
FY2002	379 . 9[a]	—	—	—	—	25.0	38.2	119.1	562.2
FY2003	580.2[b]	—	17.1	1.2	—	3.3	41.5	165.0	808.3
FY2004	473.9	—	98.5	1.7	—	.2	45.0	122.0	741.3
FY2005	462.8	—	99.2	1.7	—	5.1	45.0	200.0	813.8
FY2006	464.8	—	89.1	1.7	—	—	45.0	112.0	712.6
FY2007	465. 0	—	85.5	1.6	—	4.1	na	na	556.2
FY2008 (est)	244.6	194.4	55.1	1.4	41.9	3.7	na	na	541.1
FY2009 (req)	329. 6	142.4	66.4	1.4	—	3.2	na	na	543.0
Total	4,340.9	336.8	510.9	10.7	41.9	44.6	290.7	1,137.5	6,714.0

Sources: Figures are drawn from the annual State Department Foreign Operations Congressional Budget Justifications for fiscal years 2002 through 2009; the State Department's Washingto n File, "U.S. Support for Plan Colombia, FY2000 Emergency Supplemental Appropriations," July 5, 2000; the FY2006 Foreign Operations Appropriations Act, P.L. 109-102, and conference report, H.Rept. 109-265; and the FY2008 Consolidated Appropriations Act (P.L. 110-161) and Division J Joint Explanatory Statement.

Notes: For FY2000 and thereafter, Plan Colombia funds are assigned to the State Department's International Narcotics and Law Enforcement Bureau (INL) or the Andean Counterdrug Initiative (ACI). The State Department transfers funds to other agencies carrying out programs in Colombia, of which USAID has received the largest portion. Defense Department funding is from is Counter Narcotics account. DOD requests one sum for programs around the world and adjusts its regional allocations as needed.

a. Includes $6 million appropriated to FMF but transferred to the ACI account.

b. Includes $93 million in FMF regular appropriations and $20 million in FMF supplemental funds that were transferred to the ACI account.

Recently there has been significant debate in Congress over the proper level and components of U.S. assistance to Colombia. While some Members support the Bush Administration's emphasis on security-related assistance to Colombia, others have expressed concerns that the Administration has put too much of an emphasis on so-called "hard-side" security assistance, rather than traditional development and rule of law programs. Many Members have expressed a desire to see a more rapid transfer of responsibility for the military operations associated with Plan Colombia from the United States to Colombia. The FY2008 Consolidated Appropriations Act (P.L. 110-161) reduced interdiction, eradication, and military aid to Colombia by roughly $104 million to about $305 million and increased funds for alternative development, human rights, and institution building programs by some $84 million to $236 million. **Table 3** details how U.S. aid to Colombia shifted from FY2007 through the FY2009 request. **Table 4** at the conclusion of this chapter provides a more detailed breakdown of U.S. assistance to Colombia from FY2000 through the FY2009 request. The FY2008 changes reflected an attempt to raise the level of U.S. funding provided for economic and social aid closer to that provided for security- related programs. These changes were criticized by Bush Administration officials.

The Colombian Ministry of Defense has asked Congress to consider restoring a higher level of security assistance in the FY2009 budget at levels that are similar to the Bush Administration's FY2009 request. Although Congress has yet to complete action on the FY2009 foreign operations legislation, the Senate Appropriations Committee report (S. 3288, S.Rept. 110-425) would, as in FY2008, cut security-related assistance to Colombia from the levels requested by the Administration. An enacted continuing resolution (H.R. 2638/P.L. 110-329) will provide funding at FY2008 levels through March 6, 2009.

Paramilitary Demobilization

The 111th Congress will likely remain concerned over the developing scandal involving paramilitary ties to Colombian politicians. Some Members of Congress have expressed concern about both the AUC demobilization process and the overall demobilization framework under the Justice and Peace Law approved by the Colombian Congress in 2005. The FY2006 Foreign Operations Act (P.L. 109-102) provided $20 million to assist in the demobilization of former members of foreign terrorist organizations, provided that the Secretary of State certified that the assistance only went to individuals who had verifiably renounced and terminated membership in the FTO; that the Colombian government was cooperating with the United States on extradition; that the Colombian government was working to dismantle FTO structures; and that the funds would not be used to make cash payments to individuals. A foreign operations appropriations measure was not enacted for FY2007 and funding remained at FY2006 levels under a continuing resolution (P.L. 110-5). The FY2008 Consolidated Appropriations Act (P.L. 110-161) provided just over $11 million to assist the demobilization of former members of foreign terrorist organizations (FTOs), pending a certification from the Secretary of State that was issued on August 28, 2008. In that certification, Secretary of State Rice certified the following to Congress:

- that assistance will be provided only for individuals who have verifiably renounced and terminated any affiliation or involvement with FTOs, and are meeting all the requirements of the Colombia Demobilization program, including disclosure of past crimes; the location of kidnapped victims and bodies of the disappeared; and, knowledge of FTO structure, financing, and assets.

- that the Colombian government is fully cooperating with the United States in extraditing FTO leaders and members who have been indicted in the United States for murder, kidnapping, narcotics trafficking, and other violations of U.S. law; and is extraditing former paramilitary leaders who have been indicted in the United States and have breached the terms of the demobilization process;
- that the Colombian government is not knowingly taking steps to legalize titles of land or other assets illegally obtained by FTOs, their associates, or their successors; and that the Colombian government has established effective procedures to identify such land and assets;
- that the Colombian government is implementing a concrete and workable framework for dismantling the organizational structures of FTOs; and
- that funds will not be used to make cash payments to individuals, and funds will only be available for any of the following activities: verification, reintegration (including training and education), vetting, recovery of assets for reparations for victims, and investigations and prosecutions.

Human Rights

Debate in Congress has continued to focus on allegations of human rights abuses by the FARC and ELN, paramilitary groups, and the Colombian Armed Forces. In its 2008 State of the World's Human Rights report, Amnesty International asserted that, between June 2006 and June 2007, at least 280 civilians were extrajudicially killed by Colombian security forces and that many of them were subsequently presented by those forces as guerrillas killed in conflict. The State Department's *Country Reports on Human Rights Practices* for Colombia covering 2007 stated that "while the government's overall respect for human rights continued to improve.. .there were periodic reports that members of the security forces committed extrajudicial killings." In a February 2008 report, the U.N. High Commissioner for Human Rights acknowledged that, although it continued to receive complaints of extrajudicial killings by security officers, Colombian military and civilian officials have developed new directives to deal with allegations of abuses by security officials. However, this year human rights groups have continued to document extrajudicial killings by some Colombian military forces.[86] In February 2008, Senators Dodd and Feingold reportedly sent a letter to Secretary of State Condoleezza Rice expressing their concern over reports that civilian killings by Colombian army forces appear to have increased in recent years.

Congress has annually required that the Secretary of State certify to Congress that the Colombian military and police forces are severing their links to the paramilitaries, investigating complaints of abuses, and prosecuting those who have had credible charges made against them. Congress has made funding to the Colombian military contingent on these certifications. In the latest certification, issued on July 28, 2008, the Secretary of State asserted that the Colombian government and armed forces are meeting the statutory requirements with regard to human rights. The Secretary noted that "while the Government of Colombia needs to do more to address serious human rights problems that persist, we see encouraging signs, including concrete examples of progress: the suspension, arrest, or conviction of military violators of human rights, including several general officers; greater civilian access and handling of human rights cases involving the military; and credible investigations of dozens of politicians who allegedly collaborated with the paramilitaries."[87]

Congress has also regularly included the so-called Leahy amendment in foreign operations appropriations legislation that denies funds to any security force unit for which the Secretary of State has credible evidence of gross human rights violations. The Secretary may continue funding if she determines and reports to Congress that the foreign government is taking effective measures to bring the responsible members of these security forces to justice. According to a State Department official, Congress released its last hold on FY2006 funds in mid-August 2008, but approximately $72 million of FY2007 and FY2008 funds for the Colombian military remain on hold.[88] Despite these actions, human rights organizations claim that the U.S. government often turns a blind eye to questionable activities of Colombian security forces.

U.S.-Colombia Free Trade Agreement[89]

In 2003, the Bush Administration announced its intentions to begin negotiating an Andean region free trade agreement (FTA) with Colombia, Peru, Ecuador, and Bolivia. In its announcement, the Administration asserted that an FTA would reduce and eliminate barriers to trade and investment, support democracy, and fight drug activity. After regional talks broke down, the United States pursued bilateral trade agreements with Colombia and Peru. The United States and Colombia signed the U.S.-Colombia Trade Promotion Agreement on November 22, 2006, now called the U.S.-Colombia Free Trade Agreement (CFTA); the agreement must now be ratified by both nations' congresses. Colombia, Bolivia, Ecuador, and Peru currently benefit from the Andean Trade Preference Act (ATPA).[90] On October 16, 2008, the 110th Congress enacted legislation to extend ATPA trade preferences until December 31, 2009 for Colombia and Peru, and until June 30, 2009 for Bolivia and Ecuador (P.L. 110-436).[91] The ATPA authorizes the President to grant duty-free treatment to certain products, with more than half of all U.S. imports in 2004 from the Andean countries entering under these preferences.

Critics of the free trade agreement are concerned about the status of labor rights in Colombia and the ongoing parapolitical scandal. Critics argue that violence against labor activists in Colombia is excessive and inadequately addressed by the Uribe government. Labor activist killings declined under President Uribe, but increased in 2006. Data on the number of labor leaders murdered in any given year vary widely by source. In 2002, the Colombian government estimated that 99 labor activists were killed, while the National Labor School (ENS, a Colombian NGO) estimated that 178 labor activists were killed. In 2006, the Colombian government estimated that 60 labor activists were killed, while ENS estimated that 72 labor activists were killed. In 2007, both groups reported a drop, with the Colombian government reporting 26 labor activists killed and ENS estimating 39 labor activists according to the U.S. State Department.[92] One reason for the discrepancy is that the Colombian government counts deaths of unionized teachers separately from other labor union deaths.

Source: Map Resources. Adapted by CRS. (K. Yancey 2/6/04)

Figure 1. Map of Colombia

Another area of concern is whether labor activists were killed because of their union activity. Very few investigations have been completed. More than 2,000 killings between 1991 and 2006 remain unsolved. Of the 470 union murders that have occurred since President Uribe first took office in 2002, 97% remain unsolved. In January 2007, the Colombian Attorney General's office set up a unit of 13 prosecutors and 78 investigators to investigate 200 priority cases. In 2007, 36 people were convicted on charges related to the murder of union members, more convictions than in 2004 through 2006 combined.[93] As of October 20, 2008, a total of 147 convictions were made in cases involving violence against trade union members between 2001 and 2008, with 97 (65%) of them handed down in 2007 and 2008.[94]

On April 8, 2008, President Bush submitted implementing legislation to Congress for the CFTA. The 2002 Trade Promotion Authority procedures stipulated that Congress must vote on that implementing legislation within 90 legislative days of its introduction. But on April

10, 2008, the House voted 224-195 in favor of changing those procedures, effectively putting congressional consideration of the U.S.-Colombia Free Trade Agreement on hold. It is unclear whether and how the 111th Congress will consider implementing legislation for the pending CFTA in the future. It could be considered pursuant to the usual rules or the House could restore TPA-like "fast track" procedures.[95]

The likelihood of reintroduction and passage of the CFTA under the new Obama Administration is also unclear. During his campaign, President-elect Obama favored delaying consideration of the trade agreement in order to pressure the Colombian government to further reduce labor violence.[96] Given these misgivings, some predict the Obama Administration will not support moving the legislation any time soon.[97] Other analysts believe that President Obama may push for approval of the trade agreement with stronger human rights provisions.[98]

End Notes

[1] U.S. Department of State, "Background Note: Colombia," March 2008.

[2] These statistics are taken from the Colombia National Planning Department as cited by the U.S. Department of State. See U.S. Department of State, "Charting Colombia's Progress," March 2008. The United Nations Economic Commission for Latin America and the Caribbean's (ECLAC) *Social Panorama 2006* data also showed a decline in both poverty and indigence rates since 1999. ECLAC reported that 55% of Colombians lived in poverty in 1999, with 27% living in indigence. By 2005 those poverty and indigence rates fell to 47% and 20%, respectively. No new data on poverty rates in Colombia were included in ECLAC's *Social Panorama 2007*.

[3] "Country Report - Colombia," *Economist Intelligence Unit*, August 2008.

[4] ECLAC reports that Colombia is now the fourth most unequal society in Latin America and the Caribbean, after Bolivia, Brazil, and Honduras. Colombia also has one of the most unequal land tenure patterns in Latin America, with 0.4% of land holders owning 61% of registered rural property. See ECLAC, *Social Panorama 2006*; J.D. Jaramillo, *El Recurso Suelo y la Competividad del Sector Agrario Colombiano*, 2004.

[5] Frank Bajak, "Head of Colombian Governing Party Arrested for Alleged Paramilitary Ties," *Associated Press*, July 25, 2008. For the most recent data, see "Parapolitics: Power and Democracy Seized by Mafias," presentation at the Inter-American Dialogue, December 9, 2008, by Claudia López.

[6] See CRS Report RS21242, *Colombia: The Uribe Administration and Congressional Concerns*, by Nina M. Serafino.

[7] U.S. Department of State, "Charting Colombia's Progress," March 2008.

[8] Latin American Working Group, "The Other Half of the Truth," June 2008.

[9] The FARC is believed responsible for more than half of the cocaine entering the United States according to the November 2008 "Background Note on Colombia," by the U.S. Department of State.

[10] Jonathan Morgenstein, *Consolidating Disarmament: Lessons from Colombia's Reintegration Program for Demobilized Paramilitaries*, United States Institute of Peace, Special Report 217, Washington, DC, November 2008.

[11] Those concerns are cited in the U.S. Department of State, *Country Reports on Human Rights Practices 2007*, March 2008. See also: International Crisis Group (ICG), "Colombia's New Armed Groups," May 2007; Chris Kraul, "In Colombia, Paramilitary Gangs Control Much of Guajira State," *Los Angeles Times*, August 31, 2008.

[12] Chris Kraul, "New gangs run Colombians off their land; The government says paramilitary groups no longer exist. But more and more people are being displaced," *Los Angeles Times*, December 3, 2008.

[13] "Amnesty Says all Sides in Colombia Have Bloody Hands," *EFE*, May 28, 2008; Chris Kraul, "Colombia Military Atrocities Alleged," *Los Angeles Times*, August 20, 2008.

[14] United Nations Office on Drugs and Crime (UNODC), *Coca Cultivation in the Andean Region*, June 2008.

[15] "Ex Minister Aims for Colombian Presidency," *LatinNews Daily*, January 6, 2009. Several sources quote the 70% figure which reflects the results of a December Invamer-Gallup poll. *The Economist* reports "According to InvamerGallup, a pollster, Mr. Uribe's popularity rating remains above 70%. But only 54% of those asked supported his reelection, down by 20 points since July." "Politics in Colombia: Third Term Temptation," *The Economist*, January 10, 2009.

[16] Patricia Markey, "Colombia's Uribe Mulls Re-election, but Will he run?" *Reuters*, August 22, 2008; "Editorial: Mr Uribe's Choice," *New York Times*, August 22, 2008.

[17] See Mark Chernick, "FARC-EP: From Liberal to Marxist to Post-Cold War Guerrillas," in *Terror, Insurgency, and the State*, edited by Marianne Heiberg, et al., Philadelphia: University of Pennsylvania Press, 2007.

[18] "Colombia: Executive Summary," *Jane's Sentinel Security Assessment*, August 24, 2006.

[19] Simon Romero, "Files Released by Colombia Point to Venezuelan Bid to Arm Rebels," *New York Times*, March 30, 2008.

[20] "Analysis: Chávez Reverses FARC Stance, Domestic Moves Ahead of Elections," *Open Source Center*, June 19, 2008.

[21] Economist Intelligence Unit, *Country Report: Colombia*, December 2008.

[22] U.S. Department of State, *Country Report on Human Rights Practices 2007*, March 11, 2008.

[23] "Colombian Officials Recount Rescue Plan; Commandos Took Acting Classes to Prepare," *Washington Post*, July 6, 2008.

[24] "U.S. aid was a key to the Hostage Rescue," *New York Times*, July 13, 2008.

[25] Patrick McDonnell and Chris Kraul, "Colombian Rebels Splintering," *Los Angeles Times*, July 5, 2008; "After the War in Colombia," *El Pais*, July 10, 2008.

[26] "Closing the net on the FARC, Striking at the ELN," *Latin American Security and Strategy Review*, July 2008.

[27] Patrick Markey, "Colombian Rebels Say to Free Six More Hostages," *Reuters*, December 22, 2008.

[28] International Crisis Group, "Colombia: Moving Forward with the ELN?" October 11, 2007.

[29] Kate Joynes, "ELN Rebels Rebut Colombian Government's Peace Pledge," *WMRC Daily Analysis*, July 12, 2004.

[30] "Closing the net on the FARC, Striking at the ELN," *Latin American Security and Strategy Review*, July 2008.

[31] U.S. Department of State, *Country Reports on Terrorism 2005*, and, "Autodefensas Unidas de Colombia," *Jane's World Insurgency and Terrorism*, August 10, 2006.

[32] "Only 2% of 30,150 Demobilized Paramilitaries to Stand Trial," *Associated Press*, April 18, 2006.

[33] Vicente Castaño, brother of AUC founder Carlos Castaño, remains at large. Vicente Castaño is under investigation by Colombian authorities for ordering the 2004 murder of his brother who reportedly planned to turn paramilitary leaders over for extradition to the United States as part of peace negotiations.

[34] International Crisis Group, *Colombia's New Armed Groups*, May 10, 2007; WOLA, *Captive States: Organized Crime and Human Rights in Latin America*, October 2007.

[35] United Nations General Assembly - Human Rights Council, "Report of the United Nations High Commissioner for Human Rights on the Situation of Human Rights in Colombia," February 29, 2008; U.S. Department of State, "Memorandum of Understanding Concerning Human Rights Conditions with Respect to Assistance for the Colombian Armed Forces," July 28, 2008, available at http://justf.org/files/primarydocs/080728cert.pdf.

[36] "Saving Congress at a Cost to the Courts," *Latin American Andean Group Report*, August 7, 2008.

[37] Economist Intelligence Unit, *Colombia risk: Government effectiveness risk*, November 14, 2008.

[38] "Uribe Squares up to Supreme Court and Liberals as Parapolitical Scandal Deepens," *Latin American Weekly Report*, August 28, 2008.

[39] Juan Forero, "U.S. Extraditions Raise Concerns in Colombia," *Washington Post*, August 19, 2008; Human Rights Watch, "Colombia: Proposal Threatens 'Parapolitical' Investigations," August 4, 2008.

[40] Sibylla Brodzinsky, "Rights group rips government; Colombia hinders paramilitary prosecutions, a human rights group said," *The Miami Herald*, September 17, 2008.

[41] Human Rights Watch, *Breaking the Grip?: Obstacles to Justice for Paramilitary Mafias in Colombia*, October 2008.

[42] "Country Report - Colombia," *Economist Intelligence Unit*, October 2006; Human Rights Watch, "Colombia: Court's Demobilization Ruling Thwarts Future Abuses," July 19, 2006; "Gobierno colombiano abrirá debate público sobre decretos reglamentarios de ley de Justicia y Paz," *El Tiempo*, August 29, 2006.

[43] International Crisis Group, *Correcting Course: Victims and the Justice and Peace Law in Colombia*, Latin America Report 29, October 30, 2008.

[44] Latin America Working Group Education Fund, *The Other Half of the Truth*, June 2008.

[45] U.S. Department of State, "Memorandum of Understanding Concerning Human Rights Conditions with Respect to Assistance for the Colombian Armed Forces," July 28, 2008.

[46] "International Criminal Court not to Allow Colombian Paramilitary Members Impunity," *Noticias Financieras*, August 31, 2008.

[47] "Amnesty Says all Sides in Colombia Have Bloody Hands," *EFE*, May 28, 2008; "Activists say Army Killing Civilians to Gain Points," *Irish Times*, March 25, 2008.

[48] Simon Romero, "Colombian Army Commander Resigns in Scandal Over Killing of Civilians," *New York Times*, November 5, 2008.

[49] U.S. Department of State, *Country Reports on Human Rights Practices 2007*, March 2008

[50] U.N. High Commissioner for Refugees (UNHCR), "Thousands Displaced in Southern Colombia," August 22, 2008.

[51] Latin America Working Group, et al., *A Compass for Colombia Policy*, October 2008.

[52] The U.S. Department of State reports the figures of the Colombian Government's Acción Social General Index on Displaced Populations (2008 data through September) in "Charting Colombia's Progress," November 5, 2008.

[53] Landmine casualties increased nearly 25% in 2005.

[54] International Committee to Ban Landmines, *Landmine Monitor 2007* and Human Rights Watch, *Maiming the People*, July 2007.

[55] International Committee to Ban Landmines, *Landmine Monitor 2008.*

[56] United Nations Office on Drugs and Crime (UNODC), *Coca Cultivation in the Andean Region*, June 2008.

[57] United Nations Office on Drugs and Crime (UNODC), *Coca Cultivation in the Andean Region*, June 2008

[58] UNODC, *World Drug Report 2008.*

[59] U.S. Government Accountability Office, *Plan Colombia:Drug Reduction Goals Were Not Fully Met, but Security Has Improved; U.S. Agencies Need More Detailed Plans for Reducing Assistance*, October 2008.

[60] U.S. Department of State, *International Narcotics Control and Strategy Report (INCSR) 2008.*

[61] U.S. Office of National Drug Control Policy, "Official U.S. Colombia Survey Reveals Sharp Decline in Cocaine Production," September 10, 2008.

[62] Republic of Colombia, Ministry of National Defense (MOD), "Colombian MOD Observations to U.S. Security Assistance for 2009," July 2008.

[63] U.S. Drug Enforcement Administration, DEA News: U.S. Cocaine Market Disrupted, Prices Continue 21-month Surge, December 12, 2008.

[64] U.S. Department of Justice, National Drug Intelligence Center, *National Drug Threat Assessment 2009*, December 2008.

[65] "U.S. Drug Czar Claims Cocaine Prices Fall," Associated Press, November 8, 2007.

[66] Ibid and Chris Kraul, "U.S. Says War on Narcotics is Working," *Los Angeles Times*, November 9, 2007; "Editorial: Not Winning the War on Drugs," *New York Times*, July 2, 2008.

[67] Department of State, Office of the Coordinator for Counterterrorism, *Country Reports on Terrorism 2006.*

[68] For further information on these developments, see CRS Report RL32488, *Venezuela: Political Conditions and U.S. Policy*, by Mark P. Sullivan.

[69] "Ecuador Moves Colombians from Border," *LatinNews Daily*, August 28, 2007; "Some 50,000 Colombians in Ecuador to be Registered Under Un-backed Scheme," *States News Service*, December 12, 2008.

[70] "How Diplomacy Silenced the Drums of War in Less Than a Week," *Latin American Security and Strategic Review*, March 2008; Francis Robles, "Ecuador Rages, Colombia and Venezuela Make Up," *LatinNews Daily*, March 14, 2008; "Leaders Defuse South American Crisis," *Miami Herald*, March 8, 2008.

[71] Report of the Organization of American States (OAS) Commission That Visited Ecuador and Colombia, Washington D.C., March 17, 2008; Resolution of the Twenty-Fifth Meeting of Consultation of Ministers of Foreign Affairs, Washington D.C., March 17, 2008.

[72] "OAS Resolution Stops Short of Condemning Colombia," *Latin America Weekly Report*, March 19, 2008; "Latin America: Insecurity Raises Sovereignty Fears," *Oxford Analytica*, March 25, 2008.

[73] According to the report: "...alternative development is not provided in most areas where coca is cultivated and USAID does not assess how such programs relate to strategic goals of reducing the production of illicit drugs or achieving sustainable results."

[74] U.S. Government Accountability Office, *Plan Colombia: Drug Reduction Goals Were Not Fully Met, but Security Has Improved; U.S. Agencies Need More Detailed Plans for Reducing Assistance*, October 2008.

[75] Julia E. Sweig, *Andes 2020: A New Strategy for the Challenges of Colombia and the Region*, Council on Foreign Relations Center for Preventive Action, January 2004.

[76] The State Department and the Department of Defense explain expanded authority as providing them with flexibility in situations where there is no clear line between drug and terrorist activity.

[77] The FY2005 National Defense Authorization Act (H.R. 4200; P.L. 108-375) raised the military cap from 400 to 800 and the civilian cap from 400 to 600. The cap does not apply to personnel conducting search and rescue operations, or to U.S. personnel assigned as part of their regular duties to the U.S. embassy. According to the State Department, military personnel levels in 2007 varied from 194 to 563, while civilian personnel levels varied between 257 and 440.

[78] U.S. Department of State, *INCSR 2008.*

[79] Also see CRS Report RL33163, *Drug Crop Eradication and Alternative Development in the Andes*, by Connie Veillette and Carolina Navarrete-Frias.

[80] U.S. Department of State, *INCSR 2008.*

[81] U.N. Office on Drugs and Crime (UNODC), *World Drug Report* 2008; and "Coca Cultivation in the Andean Region," June 2008.

[82] "Chemical Reactions: Spreading Coca and Threatening Colombia's Ecological and Cultural Diversity," *Washington Office on Latin America*, February 2008.

[83] U.S. Department of State, *INCSR 2008.*

[84] USAID/Colombia, "Program Overview: Alternative Development," Fact Sheet, October 2008.

[85] Joshua Goodman, "U.S. Pulling Economic Aid from Colombia's Coca Infested South," Associated Press, October 12, 2006; United Nations Office on Drugs and Crime (UNODC), "Coca Cultivation in Andes Stabilizes in 2005," June 20, 2006; UNODC, *Coca Cultivation in the Andean Region*, June 2006; and, UNODC, *Colombia Coca Cultivation Survey*, June 2007.

[86] "Amnesty Says all Sides in Colombia Have Bloody Hands," *EFE*, May 28, 2008; "Activists say Army Killing Civilians to Gain Points," *Irish Times*, March 25, 2008.

[87] U.S. Department of State, "Memorandum of Understanding Concerning Human Rights Conditions with Respect to Assistance for the Colombian Armed Forces," July 28, 2008, available at http://justf.org/files/primarydocs/080728cert.pdf.

[88] Information provided by State Department official, December 23, 2008.

[89] See CRS Report RL34470, *A U.S.-Colombia Free Trade Agreement: Economic and Political Implications*, by M. Angeles Villarreal.

[90] See CRS Report RS22548, *ATPA Renewal: Background and Issues*, by M. Angeles Villarreal.

[91] Ibid.

[92] U.S. Department of State, "Charting Colombia's Progress," November 5, 2008. Another possible reason for the decline in murders is the overall decline in labor union membership in Colombia. Unions have dwindled from 13% of the formal labor force in 1965 to 4% currently. For further information on labor violence and trends, see CRS Report RL34759, *Proposed Colombia Free Trade Agreement: Labor Issues*, by Mary Jane Bolle.

[93] Frank Bajak, "U.S. Unionists Alarmed by Colombia Woes," *Miami Herald*, February 13, 2008; and "Trade, Death and Drugs," *The Economist*, May 19, 2007.

[94] Embassy of Colombia. From the Colombian Embassy letter to the Honorable George Miller, November 5, 2008, attachment 5, p. 4.

[95] For more information on procedures, see CRS Report RL34470, *A U.S.-Colombia Free Trade Agreement: Economic and Political Implications*, by M. Angeles Villarreal. The author notes: "The CFTA implementing legislation... could still be re-introduced in the next Congress under the general rules of both houses, and could be considered in the House under a TPA-like procedure pursuant to a special rule reported by the Committee on Rules and approved by the House."

[96] Obama for America, "A New Partnership for the Americas," press release. May 2008, available at: http://obama.3cdn.net/f579b3802a3d35c8d5_9aymvyqpo.pdf.

[97] Adam B. Kushner, "The Truth About Plan Colombia," *Newsweek*, January 5, 2009.

[98] For example, Peter Hakim, president of the Washington-based think tank the Inter-American Dialogue, has stated this view. See: Jack Chang, "Obama Win Brings High Hopes to the Hemisphere," from The Miami Herald web edition posted on November 6, 2008 at http://www.miamiherald.com/news/politics/campaign-2008/story/758999.html.

In: Politics and Economics of Latin America. Volume 6 ISBN: 978-1-61668-014-5
Editor: Samantha R. Dawes

Chapter 5

CHILE: POLITICAL AND ECONOMIC CONDITIONS AND U.S. RELATIONS*

Peter J. Meyer

SUMMARY

Following a violent coup against democratically elected Marxist President Salvador Allende in 1973, Chile experienced 17 years of military rule under General Augusto Pinochet before reestablishing its elected civilian democracy in 1990. A center-left coalition of parties known as the Concertación has governed Chile for the nearly two decades since the end of the dictatorship. The coalition has enacted a number of constitutional changes to strengthen civilian control of the military and to undertake the prosecution of those alleged to be responsible for human rights violations during the Pinochet-era. Chile has made significant economic progress under the Concertación's free market economic policies and moderate social programs, which have produced notable economic growth and considerable reductions in poverty.

Current President Michele Bachelet has faced a number of challenges since her 2006 election. Widespread demonstrations over education, increased militancy by indigenous groups, and opposition control of the legislature have hindered President Bachelet's ability to govern. The international financial crisis is President Bachelet's latest challenge, though the government's timely decision to save recent fiscal surpluses will allow Chile to pursue counter-cyclical policies and minimize the effects of the economic downturn.

Chile has enjoyed close relations with the United States since its transition back to democracy. Both countries have emphasized similar priorities in the region, designed to strengthen democracy, improve human rights, and advance free trade. Chile and the United States have maintained strong commercial ties, which have become more extensive since the bilateral free trade agreement between them entered into force in 2004. U.S. officials have

* This is an edited, reformatted and augmented version of a CRS Report for Congress publication dated January 2009.

also expressed appreciation for Chile's leadership and moderating influence in a region increasingly characterized by political unrest and anti-American populism.

This chapter provides a brief historical background of Chile, summarizes recent political and economic developments, and addresses issues in U.S.- Chilean relations.

POLITICAL AND ECONOMIC BACKGROUND

Allende Era

Chile declared independence from Spain in 1810, but did not achieve full independence until 1818. By 1932, Chile had established an electoral democracy, which endured until 1973. During much of this period, Chile was governed by reform-minded presidents who pursued import- substitution industrialization (ISI), the expansion of the welfare state, and other statist economic policies. The pace of change quickened following the election of Eduardo Frei of the Christian Democratic Party (PDC) in 1964. Frei's government took majority ownership of the copper mines, redistributed land, and improved access to education. Despite these actions, some Chileans felt more radical change was needed. In 1970, Salvador Allende, a Socialist and the leader of the Popular Unity coalition, was elected president. Allende accelerated and furthered the changes of the previous administration by fully nationalizing firms, expanding land reform, and generally socializing the economy. While Allende's supporters pushed him to move more quickly, the political center, represented by the PDC, joined with the parties of the right to block Popular Unity initiatives in the legislature. This ideological difference prevented the Chilean government from addressing the faltering economy and served to further radicalize supporters on both ends of Chile's already polarized society. When the situation continued to deteriorate following the indecisive 1973 Legislative elections, the military intervened.[1]

Pinochet Era

On September 11, 1973, the Chilean military, under the control of General Augusto Pinochet, deposed the Allende government in a violent coup and quickly consolidated control of the country. The military junta closed Congress, censored the media, declared political parties in recess, and regarded the organized left as an internal enemy of the state. Within the first few months of military rule, at least 1,261 people in Chile were killed or disappeared for political reasons, nearly 20,000 were imprisoned, and many of them were tortured. By the end of the dictatorship in 1990, the number of killed or disappeared had risen to at least 2,279 and the number of imprisoned and tortured is said to have exceeded 30,000.[2] General Pinochet emerged as the figurehead of the junta soon after the coup and won a tightly controlled referendum to institutionalize his regime in 1978. Pinochet reversed decades of statist economic policies by rapidly implementing a series of changes that liberalized trade and investment, privatized firms, and dismantled the welfare state. Pinochet won another tightly controlled referendum in 1980, which approved the Constitution that continues to govern Chile today. The new constitution called for a plebiscite to take place in 1988 in which

Chileans would have the opportunity to reelect Pinochet to another 8-year term or reject him in favor of contested elections. Although the Chilean economy enjoyed a period of rapid economic growth between 1976 and 1981, it collapsed in 1982, sparking widespread protests. Following these initial demonstrations, Chilean civil society groups became more active in criticizing the policies of the Pinochet regime. At the same time, political parties began to reemerge to challenge the government. In 1988, several civil society groups and political parties formed a coalition in opposition to Pinochet's reelection. In the plebiscite, 55% of the Chilean people voted against another 8-year term for Pinochet, triggering the election campaign of 1989.[3]

Return to Democracy

The 1989 elections created the political dynamics that prevail in Chile today. Two major coalitions of parties were formed to contest the elections. The center-left Coalition of Parties for Democracy, or Concertación, united 17 groups that were opposed to the Pinochet dictatorship. The major parties in the coalition were the centrist PDC and the center-left Radical Party (PR), Social Democratic Party (PSD) and Party for Democracy (PPD), which was created by Socialists in 1987 to circumvent the Pinochet regime's ban on Marxist parties. The center-right Democracy and Progress coalition included the center-right National Renovation (RN) and the rightist Independent Democratic Union (UDI). A third coalition, the Broad Party of the Socialist Left (PAIS), was composed of leftist parties unwilling to participate in the Concertación, including the Communist Party (PC). Patricio Alwyn, a Christian Democrat and the candidate of the Concertación, won the presidency with 55% of the vote and the Concertación won majorities in the Chamber of Deputies and among the elected members of the Senate.[4]

The Concertación coalition has governed Chile continuously since the transition to democracy and has undergone few changes. The coalition is now composed of the PDC, the PPD, the Socialist Party (PS), which officially began contesting elections as a part of the Concertación in 1993, and the Radical Social Democratic Party (PRSD), which was created through a merger of the PR and PSD in 1994. The center-right coalition has consistently held a minority of elected seats in both legislative houses and has never won the presidency. It has undergone a number of name changes, most recently becoming the Alliance for Chile, or Alianza. The leftist coalition that includes the PC is now called "Together We Can Do More" (JPM), and has never elected a Member of Congress. Eduardo Frei Ruiz-Tagle of the PDC was elected president in 1993, followed by Ricardo Lagos of the PPD in 1999, and Michelle Bachelet of the PS in 2005. Concertación governments have pushed through a number of constitutional reforms that strengthened civilian control over the military, eliminated the institution of unelected Senators, and reduced presidential terms from 6 years to 4. They have been unable to eliminate the binomial election system, which has historically inflated conservative representation as a result of two-member districts that require a coalition to win by 2-1 margins in order to secure both seats.[5]

All of the Concertación administrations have generally maintained the open economic policies of the Pinochet regime and promoted export-led development through their pursuit of free trade agreements and encouragement of new export sectors such as forestry products, salmon, fresh fruit, wine, and methanol. Chile now has 57 bilateral or regional trade agreements, more than any other country, and has established a diverse economy much less reliant on its traditional copper exports.[6] Concertación administrations have also implemented some redistribution policies to address poverty and inequality in Chile. Although income distribution remains virtually unchanged since the dictatorship, economic growth and the social programs of the Concertación have been successful in reducing poverty. The percentage of Chileans living in poverty fell from 39% in 1990 to 13.7% in 2006. The World Bank classifies Chile as an upper middle income developing country based on its 2006 per capita income of $6,980.[7] Chile is also the only country in Latin America and the Caribbean on pace to meet all eight of the United Nations (UN) Millennium Development Objectives by 2015.[8] The objectives work toward the goals of eradicating extreme hunger and poverty, achieving universal primary education, promoting gender equality, reducing child mortality, improving maternal health, combating disease, ensuring environmental stability, and developing a global partnership for development.

Recent Political and Economic Developments

2005 Presidential and Legislative Elections

The most recent presidential and legislative elections were held in December 2005. Michelle Bachelet, the Concertación candidate for president and a member of the PS, won 45.9% of the first round vote. The Alianza split its vote, with the RN's Sebastián Piñera taking 25.2% and Joaquín Lavín of the UDI winning 23.2%. Since no candidate won a majority, a run-off election was held in January of 2006 in which Bachelet defeated Piñera 53.5% to 46.5%. Bachelet is the first female president in Chile's history. The Concertación also won majorities in both legislative houses, with 65 of the 120 seats in the Chamber of Deputies and 20 of the 38 seats in the Senate.[9] As a result of the 2005 constitutional reform that eliminated the institution of unelected Senators, the Concertación established true majorities in both legislative houses for the first time. Presidents and Deputies are elected to 4-year terms, with Presidents ineligible to serve consecutive terms. Senators are elected to 8-year terms, with half of the Senate up for election every 4 years.

Loss of Concertaci on Control over Legislature

The Concertación has struggled in the legislature since the 2005 election. A number of corruption scandals involving missing public funds and falsified election campaign financial reports hit the Concertación in late 2006. These scandals led to the Concertación losing two Deputies to corruption charges, one from the PPD and one from the PS. Soon after, the PPD expelled one of the party's founders, Deputy Jorge Schaulsohn, for accusing the Concertación of having a culture of corruption. This expulsion led to two other high profile members of the party, Deputy Javier Etcheberry and Senator Fernando Flores, leaving the party and the Concertación. Senator Flores and Deputy Schaulsohn have since created a new party, Chile Primero.[10]

In November 2007, President Bachelet requested a new public subsidy for the failing Transantiago transportation system. Senator Adolfo Zaldívar of the PDC joined with Senator Flores of Chile Primero, an Independent Senator, and the Senators of the Alianza to defeat the proposal. The PDC expelled Senator Zaldívar from the party for his lack of party discipline on an issue of importance to the ruling coalition, leading 5 Deputies from Zaldivar's faction of the PDC to leave the party and the Concertacíon.[11]

After all of the corruption charges, expulsions, and resignations, the Concertación was left with only 56 of the 120 seats of the Chamber of Deputies and 18 of the 38 seats in the Senate.[12] The Alianza reached an agreement with the unaffiliated members of the Senate to make Senator Zaldívar the Senate President in 2008 in exchange for making a member of the Alianza the Senate President in 2009. In the Chamber of Deputies, the Concertación remained in control of the Presidency in 2008 but handed control to the Alianza at the beginning of 2009.[13] This is the first time that the Alianza has had control of both houses since the transition to democracy.

2008 Municipal and 2009 Presidential and Legislative Elections

In the municipal elections held on October 26, 2008, Chileans overwhelmingly voted for a change of direction, with more than half of the country's 345 mayors losing their seats. For the first time, the Concertación split into two smaller coalitions to contest council seats, the Democratic Concertación, composed of the PDC and PS, and the Progressive Concertación, consisting of the PPD and the PRSD. The four parties contested mayoral races as a single coalition. A new coalition, "For a Clean Chile," which includes Chile First, the Regional Party of Independents, and the Ecological Party, contested elections for the first time. The Alianza and JPM coalitions also took part in the elections.

Although the Concertación won more council and mayoral seats than the Alianza, the Alianza won a larger share of the national vote than the Concertación for the first time. With 95% of the vote counted, the Alianza won 40.49% of the vote with 38.4% going to the Concertación, 6.4% to JPM, 4% to For a Clean Chile, and 10% to Independents. When considering only votes for council seats, the Democratic Concertación took 27.9% of the national vote and the Progressive Concertación took 17.3%.[14]

These election results will figure prominently as parties broker their positions within the coalitions and as the coalitions consider their candidates going into the December 2009 presidential and legislative elections. They also suggest the Alianza and its likely presidential candidate, Sebastián Piñera, are in a strong position while the Concertación appears weaker than it has at any point since the return to democracy. The Concertación will choose its presidential candidate in an April 2009 primary. Now that former president Ricardo Lagos and current Secretary General of the Organization of American States, José Miguel Insulza, have withdrawn from the race, potential candidates include former President Eduardo Frei Ruiz-Tagle of the PDC and Senator José Antonio Gómez of the PRSD.[15] A poll taken in December 2008 showed Piñera maintaining double digit leads over each of his potential Concertación opponents.[16]

Education Demonstrations

Since the transition to democracy, many Chileans have called on the government to address the inequality in the education system that activists contend is a result of Pinochet-era privatization reforms. Despite successive Concertación governments' lack of action, students had high hopes following Bachelet's election since she had based her campaign around themes of social justice. When President Bachelet neglected to even mention education during a state of the nation speech in May 2006, Chilean students organized the largest social demonstrations in the country since the return to democracy. With nearly 75% of the public backing them, students filled the streets, took over schools, and organized rallies that drew as many as 800,000 people.[17] The resulting street violence and near complete shut down of Chile's education system forced President Bachelet to shuffle her cabinet, replacing the education, economy, and interior ministers. President Bachelet also increased education spending and created a commission to consider education reform. The administration put forward the General Education Law (LGE), which was designed to better regulate the current system. Student groups and teachers unions have protested the new law, saying it fails to address the privatization of education, which they contend is the root problem.[18]

Mapuche Activism

Confrontation with the Mapuche population has been a persistent problem for the Bachelet Administration. The Mapuche are Chile's largest indigenous group and comprise approximately 4% of the population or 660,000 of Chile's 16.5 million citizens.[19] They are mainly located in the central and southern regions of Bíobío, Araucanía, Los Ríos, and Los Lagos (See Figure 1 for a map of Chile). The Mapuche have long sought official recognition as a people, protection of indigenous rights, and restoration of full ownership of their ancestral lands. Mapuche groups have pursued these ends through a variety of means. Some, like the Council of all the Lands, have pushed for the ratification of convention 169 of the International Labour Organization (ILO) on indigenous rights. Others, such as the Coordinating Committee of Mapuche Communities in Conflict Arauco-Malleco (CAM), have pursued more militant actions, occupying ancestral Mapuche lands and burning vehicles, machinery, and buildings on them, frequently targeting logging companies. Most recently, a number of Mapuche intellectuals formed their own political party, Wallmapuwen. Despite promises from successive Concertación governments to rectify Chile's relationship with its indigenous groups, Mapuche groups maintain that action has been slow, both in terms of the transfer of lands to Mapuche communities and land titling.

CAM has increased its militant actions in recent years, because of its dissatisfaction with the government's efforts on indigenous issues. As a result, the Bachelet Administration has captured and imprisoned many of CAM's leaders. Nonetheless, conservative politicians and media have accused the government of inaction and alleged connections between the Mapuche and foreign terrorist organizations like the Revolutionary Armed Forces of Colombia (FARC) and Basque Homeland and Freedom (ETA) in Spain. The government insists that there is no credible evidence of operational links between these groups, and CAM denies having any foreign ties. Human rights groups have also criticized the Bachelet

Administration, accusing Chile's *carabineros* (police force) of arbitrary arrests, torture, and beatings of Mapuche people and criticizing the government's use of Pinochet-era anti-terrorism laws to prosecute Mapuche activists. In addition to the arrests, Bachelet has replaced the governors of several regions with substantial Mapuche populations, appointed a new interior minister, and created a special commission to reformulate government policy towards the Mapuche.[20] In September 2007, Chile approved the United Nations (UN) Declaration on the Rights of Indigenous Peoples and in September 2008, President Bachelet promulgated ILO convention 169 on indigenous rights.[21]

Human Rights

In recent years, Chile has continued to address human rights violations from the Pinochet era. In September 2005, the Chilean Supreme Court upheld a court of appeals ruling that stripped Pinochet of immunity and allowed him to stand trial for his role in the killing of 119 political dissidents who were found dead in Argentina in 1975. In January 2006, an appeals court again stripped Pinochet of his immunity from prosecution for his role in the killing of two of Allende's bodyguards in 1973. Pinochet was stripped of immunity a third time in September 2006 by Chile's Supreme Court so that he could stand trial for the abuses at the Villa Grimaldi detention center, an infamous center for torture whose victims included President Bachelet. In December 2006, after having several charges dropped because of his failing health (but still under indictment in two human rights cases and on tax evasion), Pinochet died of complications from a heart attack.[22]

Other dictatorship-era officials have also been prosecuted for human rights violations. Former intelligence chief, retired General Manuel Contreras, was sentenced to two life prison terms in July 2008 for organizing the 1974 double assassination of General Carlos Prats and his wife in Buenos Aires, Argentina. Contreras was already imprisoned as a result of convictions stemming from other dictatorship-era crimes, including the 1976 assassination of former Ambassador to the United States, Orlando Letelier and his American associate, Ronni Moffitt, in Washington, D.C.[23] In October 2008, Sergio Arellano Stark, the commander of the so-called "Caravan of Death" that executed 80 political prisoners of the dictatorship shortly after the coup in 1973, was sentenced to 6 years in prison.[24] In all, over 100 former members of the Chilean military have been convicted for their dictatorship-era crimes.[25] Family members of the disappeared and other human rights advocates continue to push for greater transparency concerning the actions of the dictatorship and for those responsible to be brought to justice.

Energy Challenges

As a result of limited domestic energy resources and increasing demand due to its strong economic growth, Chile has become heavily dependent upon foreign energy imports. Between 1990 and 2006, primary energy imports increased from 45% to 67% of the total supply. Chile now imports about 99% of its crude oil, 72% of its natural gas, and 92% of its coal.[26] While Chile has tried to secure sufficient energy resources through its open economic policies, its supply has been threatened by a number of regional developments, including the use of resource nationalism in Bolivia. In 2004, Argentina cut its natural gas exports to Chile as a result of a domestic energy crisis. Since then, Argentine natural gas exports to Chile have fluctuated between 50% and 80% of their contracted volumes and have occasionally completely stopped flowing.[27]

These export cutbacks have adversely impacted Chilean economic activity and have forced Chile to reconsider its energy options. Chile is now focusing on diversifying both its energy suppliers and supplies. In 2005, Suez Energy International began a feasibility study to link Peru's Camisea natural gas project to northern Chile. This pipeline is part of a proposed natural gas ring to connect Peru, Chile, Argentina, Uruguay and Brazil. The ring would allow greater South American energy integration and would reduce several countries dependence on Bolivia, which re-nationalized its gas industry in 2006. The Chilean government and private firms began developing liquefied natural gas (LNG) terminals in 2006. Chile has also increasingly focused on domestic renewable sources of energy, beginning construction on a number of new hydroelectric plants, studying geothermal energy potential, and developing wind power plants.[28]

Economic Challenges

The international financial crisis and economic slowdown has weakened Chile's economy. Real gross domestic product (GDP) growth slowed from 5.1% in 2007 to an estimated 3.9% in 2008. Likewise, the Santiago Stock Exchange (IPSA), like those in many emerging markets, suffered considerable losses in the months following the international recognition of the financial crisis in September 2008. Additionally, the price of copper—which provides 40% of the government's revenues—fell below $2 per pound for the first time in three years in October 2008.[29]

Despite these trends, Chile's economy remains stable. Foreign direct investment (FDI) for the first seven months of 2008 reached $6.62 billion and Chile registered a $7.65 billion fiscal surplus through the first half of the year.[30] Inflation, which had risen from 3.7% in 2005 to 9% in 2008, is expected to slow to 3.7% in 2009. The Chilean government has also taken a number of proactive steps to prepare for and confront the crisis. It invested $22 billion in fiscal surpluses generated by high copper prices in recent years in 2 sovereign wealth funds. These funds will allow the government to pursue counter-cyclical policies and inject liquidity in the financial sector as needs arise.[31] In October and November 2008, President Bachelet pledged $2.7 billion to support small businesses, inject liquidity in local banks, and provide subsidies to working and middle class sectors to purchase homes.[32] In January 2009, President Bachelet announced a new $4.7 billion economic recovery package that will fund infrastructure projects to generate jobs, provide subsidies to low income families, cut taxes, and provide capital to the state-owned copper producer, Codelco.[33]

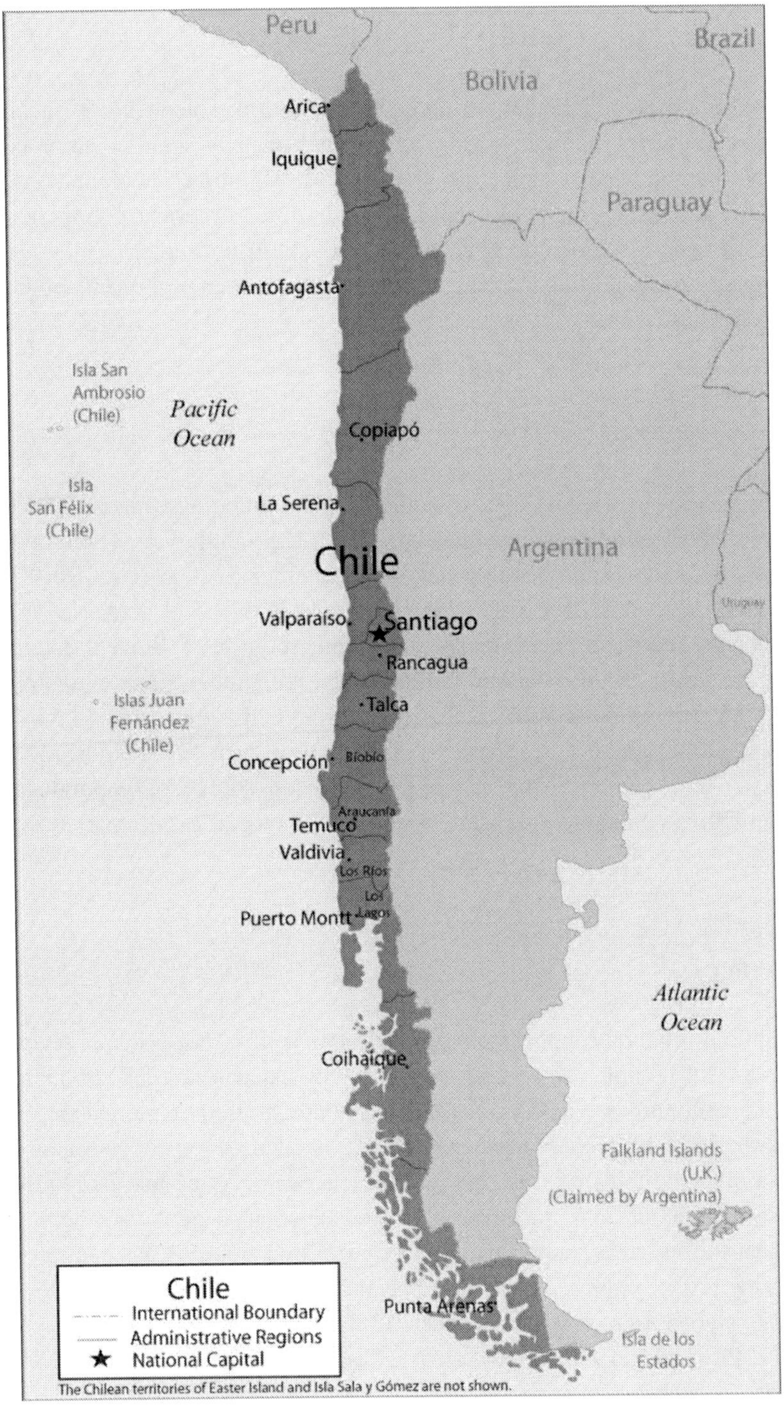

Source: Map Resources. Adapted by CRS.

Figure 1. Map of Chile

CHILE-U.S. RELATIONS

The United States and Chile have enjoyed close relations since Chile's transition back to democracy. The countries maintain strong commercial ties and share common commitments to democracy, human rights, and free trade. Both countries have demonstrated these commitments by supporting the implementation of the Inter-American Democratic Charter as an instrument to ensure democratic governance throughout the region. Chile and the United States also signed a bilateral free trade agreement and have been proponents of the Free Trade Area of the Americas (FTAA).[34]

Free Trade Agreement

The United States and Chile signed a bilateral free trade agreement (FTA) on June 6, 2003. Following the House and Senate passage of the U.S.-Chile Free Trade Implementation Act, President Bush signed the bill into law on September 3, 2003 (P.L. 108-77). The FTA established immediate duty-free treatment for 85% of bilateral trade in consumer and industrial products, increasing market access for both countries.[35] Since the agreement went into force on January 1, 2004, bilateral trade between the United States and Chile has nearly tripled, totaling $17.3 billion in 2007. U.S. imports from Chile grew from $3.7 billion in 2003 to $9 billion in 2007 while U.S. exports to Chile grew from $2.7 billion in 2003 to $8.3 billion in 2007. The United States is now Chile's top source of imports and the main destination for Chile's exports while Chile was the 28th largest export market for U.S. goods in 2007.[36]

U.S. Assistance

Given Chile's relatively high level of development, it is not a major recipient of U.S. assistance. In FY2007, Chile received $1.4 million in assistance and in FY2008, it received an estimated $1.5 million. In FY2009, the Bush Administration requested $1.6 million for Chile.[37] The majority of U.S. assistance to Chile is focused on modernizing the Chilean military by improving its capacity to act as a peacekeeping force and its ability to conduct joint operations with the U.S. military. U.S. assistance also goes to programs that deter weapons of mass destruction, improve civilian control over the military, and upgrade military equipment. The 110th Congress passed the Naval Vessel Transfer Act of 2008 (H.R. 7177, P.L. 110-429, signed into law on October 15, 2008.), which contains a provision that authorizes the President to transfer by grant a Kaiser class oiler, Andrew J. Higgins (AO-190), to the government of Chile.

Regional Leadership

Chile has been an active participant and frequent leader in multilateral engagement at both the regional and global levels. Chile has joined with the United States as part of the multinational peacekeeping force in Haiti since 2004, first as a part of the Multinational Interim Force-Haiti (MIFH) and subsequently as a part of the UN Stabilization Mission in Haiti (MINUSTAH). Chile has committed more human and material resources to MINUSTAH than it has to any previous peacekeeping mission and the country's early presence in the MIFH encouraged a number of other countries in the region to play a role in MINUSTAH.[38] The United States and Chile also worked together as members of the so-called "Group of Friends of Venezuela," to foster discussion between President Hugo Chávez and the political opposition.[39]

Chile has taken on the role of regional leader in fora that do not involve the United States as well. In September 2008, President Bachelet called an emergency summit of the Union of South American Nations (UNASUR) to resolve the domestic turmoil in Bolivia. Following the summit, UNASUR released a statement of support for the constitutional government of President Evo Morales, condemned the political violence, and sent commissions to investigate a massacre of farm workers and facilitate dialogue between President Morales and the political opposition.[40] These actions led to an end to the violence and identification of those responsible as well as a resumption of talks among President Morales and the Bolivian opposition.

Table 1. Chilean Political Acronyms

Acronym	Political Organization	Description
CAM	Coordinating Committee of Mapuche Communities in Conflict Arauco-Malleco	Militant Mapuche organization
JPM	Together We Can Do More	Leftist coalition of parties
PAIS	Broad Party of the Socialist Left	Leftist coalition of parties at retu democracy
PC	Communist Party	Leftist member party of JPM
PDC	Christian Democratic Party	Centrist member party of the a
PPD	Party for Democracy	Concertación Center-left member party of the Concertación
PR	Radical Party	Center-left member party of the Concertación at return to democracy
PRSD	Radical Social Democratic Party	Center-left member party of the Concertación, merger of PR and PSD
PS	Socialist Party	Center-left member party of the Concertación
PSD	Social Democratic Party	Center-left member party of the Concertación at return to democracy
RN	National Renovation	Center-right member party of the b
UDI	ndent Democratic Union	Alianza he Alianza

Source: Compiled by CRS

Notes:

a. The Concertación is a center-left coalition of parties.

b. The Alianza is a center-right coalition of parties.

Narcotics and Human Trafficking

Chile has worked with the Drug Enforcement Administration (DEA) to address the increased narcotics trafficking taking place within its borders that has resulted from interdiction efforts in the Andean region. Although Chile is not a drug producing country, it is increasingly used as a transshipment point for cocaine and heroine destined for the United States and Europe and is a source for chemicals used in the processing of cocaine. The United States provides support for training prosecutors, police, judges, and public defenders in the administration of justice as well as enhanced investigation and intelligence capabilities in Chile.[41]

Chile is also a source, transit, and destination country for trafficking in persons for commercial sexual and labor exploitation. The U.S. Department of State's 2008 Trafficking in Persons (TIP) Report states that Chile does not fully comply with the minimum standards for the elimination of trafficking because it's statutory framework does not specifically prohibit labor trafficking. However, Chile made significant efforts to fully comply with the U.S. standards during the 2007- 2008 reporting period, introducing anti-trafficking legislation, opening a significant number of trafficking investigations, and improving assistance for trafficking victims. As a result, the U.S. Department of State designated Chile a "Tier 2" country.[42]

End Notes

[1] *Chile: A Country Study*, ed. Rex A. Hudson, (Washington, D.C.: Library of Congress, 1994).

[2] Report of the National Commission for Truth and Reconciliation, February 1991; Report of the National Commission on Political Imprisonment and Torture, November 2004.

[3] Alan Angell & Benny Pollack, "The Chilean elections of 1989 and the Politics of the Transition to Democracy," *Bulletin of Latin American Research*, Volume 9 (1), 1990.

[4] Ibid.

[5] Peter M. Siavelis, "Electoral System, Coalitional Disintegration, and the Future of Chile's Concertación," *Latin American Research Review*, Volume 40 (1), 2005.

[6] Central Intelligence Agency, "World Factbook," September 2008.

[7] World Bank, "World Bank Development Report," 2008.

[8] "Chile: Leading the Millennium Objectives League," *Latin News Latin American Regional Report: Brazil & Southern Cone*, September 2008.

[9] "Chile: Country Report," *Economist Intelligence Unit*, January 2006; February 2006.

[10] "Chile: Concertación Faces Schism," *Latin News Weekly Report*, May 10, 2007.

[11] "Chile: DC Crisis Sets Scene for 2009 Contest," *Latin News Latin American Regional Report: Brazil & Southern Cone*, December 2007.

[12] "Defections Leave Chile's Ruling Coalition in Precarious Situation," *Latin News Latin American Regional Report: Brazil & Southern Cone*, January 2008.

[13] "Chile: Zaldívar Assumes Presidency of Senate," *Latin News Weekly Report*, March 19, 2008.

[14] "Chileans Vote for Change," *Latin News Daily*, October 27, 2008.

[15] "Descarta Insulza Candidatura a la Presidencia de Chile," *Agencia Mexicana de Noticias*, January 5, 2009; For more information on the Organization of American States, see: CRS Report RS22095, *Organization of American States: A Primer*, by Clare Ribando Seelke.

[16] "Mantiene Piñera Liderazgo en Pronósticos Electorales Chilenos," *Agencia Mexicana de Noticias*, December 30, 2008.

[17] Monte Reel, "Chile's Student Activists: A Course in Democracy," *Washington Post*, November 25, 2006.

[18] Andrea Arango, "The Failings of Chile's Education System: Institutionalized Inequality and a Preference for the Affluent," *Council on Hemispheric Affairs*, July 30, 2008.

[19] Central Intelligence Agency, "World Factbook," September 2008.

[20] "Chile: Mapuche Party Born as Legislative Battle Rages," *Latin News Special Report*, July 2007; "Chile: Bachelet reacts to Challenge by Radical Activists," *Latin News Security & Strategic Review*, January 2008.

[21] "Bachelet Makes Gesture to Chile's Indigenous Groups," *Latin News Weekly Report*, September 25, 2008.

[22] Jack Epstein, "Augusto Pinochet: 1915-2006/Chilean Leader's Regime Left Thousands of 'Disappeared'," *San Francisco Chronicle*, December 11, 2006.

[23] Helen Hughes & Jack Chang, "Ex-Chilean Intelligence Chief Gets 2 Life Sentences," *Miami Herald*, July 1, 2008.

[24] "Condenan a General Chileno por Crímenes de 'Caravana de la Muerte'," *Agencia Mexicana de Noticias*, October 15, 2008.

[25] "Familiares de Víctimas de Pinochet Mantienen Viva Demanda de Justicicia," *Agencia Mexicana de Noticias*, September 5, 2008.

[26] Oscar Landerretche, "Chile's Choices: Maintaining Growth and Securing Supply," in *Energy and Development in South America: Conflict and Cooperation*, eds. Cynthia J. Arnson et al., 27-34, (Washington, D.C.: Woodrow Wilson International Center for Scholars, 2008).

[27] Energy Information Administration, "Country Analysis Briefs: Chile," September 2006.

[28] Ibid.

[29] "Ministro Chileno: Presupuesto Fiscal Sólido Pese a Baja Cobre," *Dow Jones Newswires*, October 22, 2008; "Chile: Country Report," *Economist Intelligence Unit*, December 2008.

[30] "Chile: Inflation Could Cost Concertación Elections," *Latin News Weekly Report*, August 7, 2008.

[31] "Chile: Country Report," *Economist Intelligence Unit*, December 2008.

[32] Eva Vergara, "Bachelet Crea Comisión para Enfrenter Desempleo por Crisis," *Associated Press*, December 15, 2008.

[33] "Chile Unveils Anti-Crisis Package," *Latin News Daily*, January 7, 2009.

[34] For more information on the FTAA, see: CRS Report RS20864, *A Free Trade Area of the Americas: Major Policy Issues and Status of Negotiations*, by J. F. Hornbeck.

[35] For more information on the U.S.-Chile Free Trade Agreement, see: CRS Report RL31144, *The U.S.-Chile Free Trade Agreement: Economic and Trade Policy Issues*, by J. F. Hornbeck.

[36] U.S. Department of Commerce statistics, as presented by *World Trade Atlas*; Office of the United States Trade Representative, "Chile FTA Policy Brief," September 2007.

[37] U.S. Department of State "FY2009 International Affairs Budget,"2008.

[38] Enzo Di Nocera García & Ricardo Benavente Cresta, "Chile: Responding to a Regional Crisis," in *Capacity Building for Peacekeeping: The Case of Haiti*, eds. John T. Fishel & Andrés Sáenz, 66-90 (Dulles, VA: Potomac Books, 2007).

[39] Juan Forero, "Friends of Venezuela Are There to Help," *New York Times*, January 31, 2003.

[40] Patrick J. McDonnell, "Regional Summit Calls on Bolivians to Avoid Strife," *Los Angeles Times*, September 16, 2008; "Bolivia's Morales Receives UNASUR backing," *Latin News Daily*, September 16, 2008.

[41] Bureau for International Narcotics and Law Enforcement Affairs, "Counternarcotics and Law Enforcement Country Program: Chile," July 14, 2005.

[42] U.S. Department of State Office to Monitor and Combat Trafficking in Persons, "Trafficking in Persons Report," June 2008.

INDEX

D

G

H

I

J

K

L

M

N

O

S

T